White River Johnboats from the hey-day of float fishing.

Rivers to Run

Swift water, sycamores and smallmouth bass

By Larry Dablemont

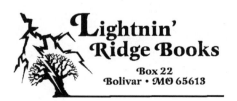

Lightnin' Ridge Books
Box 22
Bolivar • MO 65613

First Edition
First Printing

Rivers to Run

Swift Water, Sycamores
and Smallmouth Bass

Copyright 2004 by Larry Dablemont

Published by:
Lightnin' Ridge Books
Box 22
Bolivar, Missouri 65613
USA

Cover design • Barbara Young
Layout • Dorothy R. Loges

All rights reserved no portion of this book may be repro-
duced in any form, stored in a retrieval system or trans-
mitted in any form or by any means - electronic,
mechanical, photocopy, recording, or any other - except
brief quotations in printed reviews, without the prior
written permission from the author.

ISBN - 0-9673975-4-5
Library of Congress Catalog Number - 2002094021

Acknowledgement

This is the first printing of 'Rivers to Run'. We may someday expand this book to include more material about river guides and river stories I have not yet been able to collect and organize or I may do a second book. There are so many people to talk to, so much good information from those who built boats and guided float-fishermen, I couldn't get to everyone. And I couldn't include in this edition all the information which was gathered. This first edition includes a substantial amount of information, and I hope it includes some enjoyable reading as well.

I want to thank many people for the help they gave. Thanks to David Barnes, the grandson of old-time boat builder and guide Charlie Barnes, for much information and many old photos. Thanks to National Park Service Naturalist Bryan Culpepper, who helped immensely with information on the Current and Jacks Fork, and supplied some old photos from the area. I also want to thank Mrs. Ted Sare, who, in mourning the loss of her husband just a few months before this book was published, granted us permission to use some of his writings, which were a great addition to this book.

And thanks to my dad, Farrel Dablemont, who built several johnboats while I watched and took photos, and made the step by step building process explainable.

Thanks also to Tom Goldsmith and Max Thompson for artwork at the beginning of the chapters.

This book is dedicated to my grandfather, Fred Dablemont and all the old rivermen and johnboat builders like him who ran the rivers when they were clean and clear and filled with fish.

Table of Contents

Author's Note viii

Chapter 1 - Growing up With Johnboats....................1

Chapter 2 - Early Days of the Float- Boat 11

Chapter 3 - The History of Float Fishing....................27

Chapter 4 - Charlie Barnes & Robert Page Lincoln 49

Chapter 5 - Recollections of Ted Sare....................63

Chapter 6 - "In Quest of the Red-eyes"- 1912.........81

Chapter 7 - Current River Country 95

Chapter 8 - Giggers and Tie Rafters 113

Chapter 9 - Buffalo River Country 129

Chapter 10 - A Big Smallmouth 143

Chapter 11 - Overnight on a Gravel Bar 167

Chapter 12 - Sycamores 183

Chapter 13 - River Birds..193

Chapter 14 - Furbearers 207

Chapter 15 - Underwater Creatures.........................221

Chapter 16 - River People 243

Chapter 17 - All About the Rivers 257

Chapter 18 - Diverse Waters 275

Chapter 19 - Swift Waters 287

Chapter 20 - Techniques of Building Johnboats 299

Chapter 21 - Building Your Own Johnboat 311

Chapter 22 - The Last of the Ozark River Guides 349

Chapter 23 - The Dying Rivers 359

Author's Note

Back in the late '70's I wrote a book entitled, "The Authentic American Johnboat". It was published by David McKay Publishing Company in New York, and I think they printed about 60,000 copies or so. They had ideas of publishing outdoor books, with an editor in charge who had been with Outdoor Life magazine for awhile, and he knew me from articles I had sold to that magazine.

That editor didn't stay long, and when he left the publishing company, they decided to drop their outdoor books and not reprint any more of them. They returned all rights for the book to me. Actually, "The Authentic American Johnboat" did alright. They sold most of those 60,000 books without making much of an attempt to do so.

For years afterward, I got calls and letters from people here and there wanting to know how to find the book, and I always told them in a year or two I would republish it somewhere, somehow. So basically, here's that book and then some. This one has about twice as much in it as the first one, and a different name. It includes much, much more, but still it doesn't scratch the surface. Pick any one of these chapters and I could have done enough research to come up with a complete book, I think. Well, at least most of the chapters.

But I need to explain what this book is not. It is not an attempt to tell anyone where the best floating is, or where the best float-fishing is. Years ago, I thought that the job of an outdoor writer was to find the fishing and tell everyone else where it was. Find the lures that worked best and tell everyone about how to use them. I don't think that way any more.

Sure, I know where there's some great fishing on rivers in the Midwest. If I found it, you can find it if you are worth your salt. Why send a horde of undeserving canoe bangers to the best waters I know of.

No, this book will tell you what it's like to be there, and what the rivers were once, what they are today. It will tell you how to build a wooden johnboat, how to paddle, how to float safely and how to take a one-day or several-day float trip. It will tell you a little about the wildlife and the plantlife and the old-time people who first lived along the rivers and how they lived. It will be a book about the rivers I've seen and experienced and loved. It will be enough, for someone whose heart and soul is in flowing waters and majestic bluffs and a distant gravel bar where you can get away from everything for just awhile.

An old wooden johnboat, and the author, at the age of 18, with a flathead catfish from the Big Piney river.

1
GROWING UP WITH JOHNBOATS

As far back as I can remember, we always had johnboats in our back yard. They sat on sawhorses beneath the big elm tree, two or three at a time. Dad would rent them on weekends during the spring and summer and occasionally the folks who floated the rivers of the Ozarks, and those who had small resorts here and there, would ask him to build one, or two or a half dozen.

That was in the 1950's and early 1960's. In those days it seemed that most rivers had two or three wooden johnboats chained and locked to trees at every access point. These wooden boats played a big part in the lives of river families across the nation for several decades, but I don't suppose they meant more to anyone than they meant to the Dablemonts. It all began with my grandfather, Fred Dablemont, just after the turn of the century.

He was five years old when he first saw the Ozarks of south-central Missouri. The Big Piney river flowed into the Gasconade just a few miles from the farm his father bought in 1901. My grandfather was a born outdoorsman, and as a youngster he was quick to acquaint himself with the flocks of

Growing up With Johnboats

wild turkey that roosted along the river and with the flocks of waterfowl that dropped in to feed along the Big Piney in the fall.

He and his older brother Perry worked hard on the farm, but still they found time to hunt. They got a coonhound from a widow who lived in nearby Edgar Springs, Missouri and slowly accumulated coon pelts during the winter. They also found a buyer nearby, an old-timer who trapped the river and had an old wooden johnboat.

They made his acquaintance eventually and during spring and summer the two boys used his boat to fish from. It wasn't much of a boat, something like a feed trough, with straight sides and a flat bottom. It didn't maneuver well and it didn't hold course. But it floated and that was the most important thing.

As Grandpa began to save money by selling coon hides and groundhog hides, (the latter brought five cents apiece for leather boot laces) he began to think of making his own boat. But with six brothers and sisters in the family, other things were needed more than a boat. Getting the boat-building materials from a local sawmill would cost several dollars, a real investment in that day.

When the old trapper made a new boat, Fred and Perry Dablemont got the old one. It leaked but it was usable. That was when they began getting really interested in the river and the things it had to offer.

About that time, they found another old johnboat in a drift along the river. It was built differently and Grandpa told me the contrast in the two gave him ideas about how to make his own someday, fashioned mostly after the boat he had been given by that old riverman but with changes instigated by what he saw in the one they had found.

"The sides were straight but flared out at the top," Grandpa said of the boat they found in the drift. "The front and back were the same width but there was some rake at both ends. The old man told my brother Perry and me how he had made his, but

Growing up With Johnboats

we figured we could a do a better job by adding some things. After paddling that boat, I figured it would run better if the front and back were both narrowed and the sides were curved."

At a young age, they learned to trap, to gig redhorse suckers, and to set trotlines for the giant flathead catfish that could be sold in local settlements. They also learned to hunt the mallards and wood ducks along the river, discovering that boughs of oak, river maple, and willow arranged across the front of a wooden boat hid it fairly effectively and made it possible to float silently into the range of the largest flocks.

Grandpa turned fourteen years old in 1910 and by then he was an avid turkey hunter. He hunted gobblers by scattering the birds from their roosts just after dark and then waiting for them to return to that gathering place at dawn . Flocks of 60 to 70 turkeys were common in the Ozarks, and it wasn't a real task to get one. With his muzzle loader shotgun, Grandpa kept the family supplied with meat. His mother allowed him to kill another turkey only when the last one had been completely eaten.

In the fall of that year, a St. Louis surveyor passed through the Ozarks and made it known he was an avid hunter and very much interested in taking a wild gobbler. He had been hunting them in his spare time, with no luck. By that time, young Fred Dablemont was gaining something of a reputation. Everyone knew the boy from the Piney River who sold catfish and coon hides. And more than one farm wife in the vicinity of Edgar Springs had filled a Sunday table with wild

3

Growing up With Johnboats

turkey bought for five cents from the youthful hunter.

The surveyor was directed to the Dablemont farm where he met Victor Dablemont, a Frenchman who said assuredly in broken English, "Dat leettle boy, he halp you keel de turkee'."

The surveyor returned a week later with a breech-loading shotgun, fancy hunting clothes, and new confidence.

For my grandfather, it was a simple assignment. That evening he scattered the flock from a ridge that overlooked the river. The next day before dawn he situated the hunter in a makeshift blind right where the turkeys would regroup.

The first half dozen turkeys to return, young jakes with short beards, walked right up to the hidden hunter. He emptied both barrels, managing to kill what he swore was the biggest gobbler he'd ever laid eyes on. He was so happy he gave Grandpa the breech-loading Stevens as payment. Then the surveyor returned to the city with the story of a young hunter so gifted he could kill turkeys without calling. Of course he didn't know the turkeys were simply regrouping at the spot they had last seen their comrades.

The hunter returned with a friend. Fred Dablemont, perhaps the only 15-year-old hunting guide in the Ozarks, helped them each bag a young gobbler. He was paid well, about the best money a kid his age could ever hope to earn, and other hunters came to enlist his services. Later in the fall, he put two hunters in the front of his old boat, piled a blind on the front of it, and paddled them down the river into several flocks of ducks.

Because of his success, more and more hunters and fishermen from the city called on him. Though most of the money had to go to the family, Grandpa was able to save enough to buy materials for his own boat.

The first boat was surely quite an experiment. He and his brother, Perry, were blessed with efficient hands, though they were something short of efficient carpenters, and had few tools for the job. They knew somehow that the straight sides, which made a boat look like a feed trough, had to be improved. But

4

Growing up With Johnboats

was lighted by a pair of kerosene lanterns. He believed in getting to bed early anyway, always turning in an hour or so after dark and rising every day an hour before sunrise.

He never used a power tool. He had a good draw knife, a couple of planes, several types of handsaws, a brace and bit and an assortment of wood rasps. I spent many an hour watching him make johnboats and boat paddles, and then sitting in his little cabin listening to his stories, soaking up his knowledge of the river.

Throughout his life he took great care of all his belongings, from minnow seines and steel traps to the tools he used building his boats. In the corners of his home hung well-oiled traps, a pair of hip boots, a rolled-up seine. Trotline spools and boat paddles sat beneath them. Usually two or three guns hung in handmade gun racks. All of them were loaded, always. Grandpa came from a time when loaded guns were sometimes needed quickly, and he lived that way. His children were raised knowing that every gun was loaded and they never forgot it. Over the years, there was never a gun accident in the family.

The johnboat contributed indirectly to raising many a family in which trapping, fishing, and guiding were sources of income. Some rivermen earned a considerable amount of money from johnboats directly by building and selling them.

Grandpa never thought he would be making his boats for sale. But before his death at the age of 74, my grandfather estimated he had built nearly a thousand wooden johnboats and more than two thousand sassafras paddles. There's no way to know if those figures are accurate, because he never kept records, but he could build a 12- or 14-foot johnboat in two days and make a sassafras paddle from a blank in only a few hours. There were some years, when he was selling wooden johnboats to newly established resorts around the Ozarks on the various rivers where float-fishing was becoming a big thing, that he would make 50 boats and perhaps 150 paddles.

I remember going to his place when there would be four or

7

Growing up With Johnboats

five johnboats sitting on sawhorses in various stages of construction, and a dozen paddles being made with them. And he still had time to make me a sassafras bow, and make kites that

flew a mile high, it seemed, fed by line from his trotline spool.

In the 1950's, a man by the name of Appleby came to visit my grandfather. He was from over around Lebanon, and had started a small boat company he called Richline-Appleby. He said he was wanting to make an aluminum river johnboat and that folks had told him the Dablemont johnboats were the best for the Piney and Gasconade rivers. He asked if he could watch one being built and take some measurements.

My grandfather was cantankerous at times, and he'd be inclined to say 'no' to such a thing if he didn't like the person asking the favor. But he liked Mr. Appleby, and he gave him his opinion on how the whole damn world was giving away it's soul for the almighty dollar and he was proud that he built boats which ordinary people could afford and enjoy. He asked his visitor if he intended to build boats that common ordinary

Growing up With Johnboats

Ozark people like himself could afford. Mr. Appleby said he felt the same way and intended to do just that. And I guess he spent a day or so there watching and taking measurements as Grandpa told him what had to be done to make a good river boat.

Mr. Appleby talked to lots of boat builders, and came up with a design for one of the best aluminum boats I have ever seen. Years later, his daughter, Diana, and her husband Carl Lowe, established one of the Ozarks biggest and most successful boat companies, Lowe Boats.

They produced an aluminum river johnboat, which they always called a "paddle-jon" in lengths of 16 to 20 feet, with the majority of them 17- and 18-footers. They were very similar to Grandpa's boats, with the curved and slanted sides and a rake at both ends which allowed the boat to float higher and glide easily over the water rather than into it.

When the Lowe's eventually sold their boat company to O.M.C. their son Brent Lowe established another company which he named "Generation Three Boats" and he produced the river johnboat in limited quantities into the late '90's. Now the boat is out of production, and hard to find. But if you are serious about floating the rivers of the midwest and hunting and fishing or trapping, you can't find a better boat. No canoes of any kind will equal it. And it's almost as good as the wooden johnboats I floated in as a boy. Almost!

" At the time of this printing the Voyageur Boat Company of Camdenton, MO is producing the exact "paddle-jon" aluminum boats mentioned above in lengths from 16 to 20 feet. The company does not mass produce them. They make them upon request, and sell them through their dealers. For more information call 573-346-1904.

2
EARLY DAYS OF THE FLOAT BOAT

I came across the remains of an old wooden johnboat, filled with mud and leaves, decaying slowly, with only one end sticking up out of the water. It had become a playground for a mink, a shade-providing shelter for a green sunfish or a softshell turtle. But what had it been? The faithful means of transport for a river trapper? A trotline fisherman's dependable anchor against a lunging flathead in the glow of a carbide lamp?

Had there been a lunker smallmouth brought aboard, or had its greatest day been its contribution toward a string of rock bass for a small boy and his grandfather?

Wooden johnboats--once they were as much a part of the Ozark streams as the wood ducks and the acorns, the hog-mollies and muskrats and caves and springs and rope swings.

The old johnboat probably never caught the eye of the canoeists who shoot along the river so fast they don't know where they've been or what they've missed. But I just couldn't pass it by without stopping. What would my life have been without an old wooden johnboat? I was connected to my ancestry through an old johnboat or two like that one. My grandfather and my father and I all had similarities in our boyhood.

Early Days of the Float Boat

The foundation that connected us was the river and the johnboats we used.

About the time my grandfather's first johnboat was being built on the Big Piney River, others were being built on other waterways; the Meramec, the Gasconade, the James, the White, the Current, the Buffalo, the Kings. And they were being built for quite some time before that. I don't know when they first began calling them johnboats, or why. The first guides and boat-builders in the Ozarks apparently called johnboats by a host of names. The most commonly heard term in the early 1900's was 'float-boats' and 'flat-bottomed boats'. Grandpa Dablemont referred to early wooden boats with narrowed bow and stern as "sharpshooters".

Similar boats were in use in Louisiana by Cajun bayou people and in Canada by French trappers. The Cajuns used their boats to hunt from and apparently that went back many, many years. The flat bottomed boats were pushed through the marshes with poles to hunt rails and waterfowl. The Cajuns referred to them as 'jump-boats' and perhaps their French dialect pronunciation of 'jump-boat' eventually was interpreted as 'johnboat' by someone and carried on from there. There are many more and much better theories about how the boat got it's name.

Early Days of the Float Boat

Early giggers in the Ozarks, as far back as the 1880's and perhaps before, used a metal basket made from wagon wheel rims to hold the burning knots of jack pine, and those boats were called 'jack-light boats' or 'jackboats'. And some of them, used for gigging, were called 'redhorse runners' because they were used to chase big redhorse around the deep clear eddies with a gig. But we may never know where the name johnboat came from. Maybe they got that name because someone with the surname of John or Johns built the first one. I never saw anything in all the research I ever did that told me who invented them, or why they were named that way, or when.

But there was the story of John Murray, who lived all his adult life in a small cabin built atop a big twenty-foot by ten-foot boat on the Current river. To begin with, it was just a one room shanty sitting on a boat, and moved up the river by means of a home-made crank and winch. Murray and his wife had four children when he first built the "houseboat" and eventually he raised seven sons and two daughters, dividing the single-roomed building into three rooms. He made money by salvaging lost logs and railroad ties along the river, and surely sold some fish. He kept chickens in coops attached to the houseboat, and during the day, let them out on board walkways to the bank. They'd return to their coops at night. Murray had a trap door built in the floor of his cabin, and twice a day, someone would open it into the boat below which held it up, and would bail any water which had leaked in.

His nephew, Ed Murray, who was the son of John's brother said John had constructed a river boat which he kept tied alongside the houseboat, and used in his fishing and other river travel. He said that when people would pass and ask about the smaller boat, Murray would laugh and reply that it was his "John" boat. Who knows, maybe the name did originate there. About the time the name 'johnboat' first surfaced, John Murray was floating down the Current into the Black River and on down to Arkansas, where he lived for some time in the 1920's.

13

Early Days of the Float Boat

But no one has ever been able to say positively where the name 'johnboat' came from. Trying to learn more about the history of johnboats and float fishing, I looked everywhere for published information on the subject. I went back to my collection of Forest and Stream magazines from 1913 to 1922 and read all I could find about the Ozarks. I noticed that many times johnboats were shown in use accompanying stories about Florida, New England, even the northwest.

They were never referred to as johnboats of course, they were always called something else. Many types of wooden paddle boats were made and used in Michigan and Wisconsin and even into Canada. But the magazines seldom used pictures which matched the story. Photography by writers was rare; therefore the magazine used whatever pictures they could dig up. The story might be about Florida but the photo may have come from Louisiana.

Occasionally though, the story and photos were tied together. Perhaps the most interesting find was a story about fishing in Lake Long and Lake Seymour in Canada. The writer fished with Canadian Guide, Bebe Liret, who was shown standing in a wooden boat that was almost a duplicate to those I grew up with in the Ozarks. That was in September of 1923. Most of the time, magazine articles about wooden boats called them skiffs or fishing punts, or flat-bottomed boats.

What appeared to be another exact duplicate of an Ozark johnboat was pictured in the article, "Cooting on Cape Cod," in the October, 1923 edition of Forest and Stream. Another was shown in a November, 1923 article about the Great Watchet Lakes. A state was never mentioned. That boat, however, had oar-locks. Oar locks definitely do not fit in the Ozarks.

At the turn of the century in the Midwest and Midsouth, boats were being used for crossing the river to visit a neighbor or go to church. They were used for fishing, hunting, frogging, collecting mussels, trapping, trotlining and gigging. Most of the time rivermen used paddles. Sometimes they were pushed

14

Early Days of the Float Boat

upstream against a strong current with long push-poles. But when gigging, either by the light of pine knots or carbide lamps, the boats were often pushed along by long gigs with fifteen- to eighteen-foot handles.

And there was another way old-time rivermen collected fish from the rivers. They tricked them into jumping into the boat! People who haven't spent time on the river always laugh at tales of big fish jumping in the boat. But when the water is low in the summer and conditions are right, bass seem to go berserk when a boat and lights go past in the night. They jump out of the water several feet as if in blind panic and often they land in the boat. The more you bang on rocks with paddles, the more they jump.

I once had three or four bass from ten to fourteen inches in length land in my boat within a fifteen minute period under such circumstances and another glanced off the side of my head. One night I was jitterbug fishing for smallmouth on north Arkansas' Crooked Creek with two friends of mine who had never witnessed the phenomenon of flying bass.

We were in a 19-foot square-sterned canoe, and a smallmouth left the water beside the front seat and flew past me at the back of the boat a good three feet above the water. I had my headlamp on, and saw him coming. He passed my left ear about eighteen inches away, and I could hear his fins rattling as he passed me. I believe that fish thought he was still swimming.

The fish jump when the lights are on and boat paddles are banging against rocks. Sometimes they'll cover six or eight feet in a jump. Apparently the Ozark rivermen from that early day knew all about that. They may have been unable to gig the colored waters in the summer but they used gigs to beat against rocks and catch jumping bass in long johnboats. Usually, they attached a high 'sideboard' along one side of the boat, then slipped along the bank of the river with lights, banging the rocks with gigs or push-poles. In one of those old magazines, I

15

Early Days of the Float Boat

read an account of how nets were attached along the far side of the johnboat to catch jumping fish. And although it's hard to picture how it was done, it must have worked because according to the article I read, the night anglers brought back as many as 40 bass in a few hours. In a 1953 article by Townsend Godsey, who lived in the Forsyth-Branson area of Missouri he talked about the practice with old time guide Charlie Barnes who said, "We'd just rattle the rocks along the banks with our gigs, and the fool bass would come out of the water with their fins a'flappin' 'til it sounded like a bird a flyin' past. They'd fall in the boat or hit the boards on the other side and drop back in."

Barnes went on to say that one night in the middle of the summer he took two Kansas City sportsmen on a frogging trip and several bass jumped in the boat. So they decided to see how many jumpers they could boat if they made an effort. In three nights, they had more than 100 bass land in the boat, many of them from three to four pounds.

It sounds preposterous to some but those who have spent a lot of time on the river at night fishing or catching frogs, will tell you that the occurrence of flying smallmouth is not a fairy tale. It is one of the most amazing things I have ever seen.

River people made a large percentage of their income by selling fish. They gigged them in the fall and winter, and caught them on trotlines in the spring and summer. Big female flathead catfish up to 60 or 70 pounds were also caught by hand when they sought out hollow logs or underwater ledges and holes beneath the banks for spawning in mid-summer. This practice, which became known as "noodling" or "grannying," eventually would become outlawed but old time Ozarkers considered it something of an art.

The old timers who became proficient at noodling would get down in waist-deep to shoulder-deep water, reach back in one of those hollows and gently stroke a catfish which might feel as if it were nearly as big as they were. You'd think the

Early Days of the Float Boat

slightest touch would cause the fish to charge out of there and forget about spawning, but it doesn't.

The fisherman would then just get a firm grasp on the lower jaw of the catfish, pull it out of that log and all heck would break loose. Eventually, those "noodlers" learned they could sink a barrel in strategic spots, held in place with some large rocks, and create themselves a catfish sanctuary which would yield big mama flatheads every summer. Noodling became illegal because of the idea that such activity could nearly eliminate any successful spawn in miles and miles of stream.

Some hand-fishermen, or noodlers or whatever you want to call them, would get their hands all skinned up on the bigger flatheads because they have hundreds of tiny teeth inside their mouth which makes it sort of like sticking your hand inside a pair of really sharp wood-files. So the really technically advanced noodlers began to take big hooks on heavy nylon line with wooden handles, and when they'd find a hefty flathead, they would stick that hook inside the mouth and jerk it into a solid jaw, then pull out the catfish and begin the wrestling match that way.

A wooden handle attached to the other end of the line was a necessity, and I heard about one guy who came up with the idea of looping a cord around the handle which he could place over his wrist so the whole thing couldn't get away from him. They say he once got ahold of a 50 or 60 pound catfish which pulled him around one big eddy for a half hour and nearly drowned him, because he couldn't get the cord from around his wrist. His friends, who watched the event and chased up and down the bank yelling encouragement, say that if you could have painted him red and white he would have taken on the appearance of a great big blubbering bobber. The only thing that saved him was the availability of a wooden johnboat, which he finally got ahold of, and used to help him win the fight.

Rivermen also used johnboats to trap mink, muskrat, beaver and raccoon. With the johnboat, a trapper could set his traps

Early Days of the Float Boat

along two or three miles of river, run them each morning, reset them and prepare his furs. When he had spent several days on that stretch, he might pick up all his traps and move on downstream, setting them in a new stretch of water. Trappers of the early days in the Ozarks weren't exactly sportsmen because they weren't trapping for sport, they were rivermen trying to earn a living in a harsh world and though many of them didn't much enjoy the hardships of it, trapping fur was part of surviving in a difficult time.

Trappers might spend weeks covering the entire length of a river. My grandfather, in the late 20's, spent many nights sleeping in caves with only the supplies his johnboat would hold to sustain him. When fur prices were good, it gave him greater income than selling fish. While he was trapping he learned to put a blind of oak boughs on his boat and sneak up on ducks and other wildlife. This too was profitable because waterfowl and wild turkey sold quickly in area settlements.

As time went on, it became illegal to sell waterfowl, and fur prices declined substantially. It was inevitable that men who made johnboats to use for trapping and commercial fishing

Early Days of the Float Boat

would eventually become float fishing guides. As one door closed another one opened.

At first, float fishing was not something rivermen took part in because fishing gear was expensive and there was no casting gear in use at the turn of the century. Float-fishermen were fly fishermen, with silk line and artificially-made flies. Ozarkers looked upon such fishing as somewhat sissified. They could take a willow pole and some nightcrawlers, minnows, or crayfish and catch a tubful of bigger fish in half the time.

But usually a man with a fly-rod was somewhat more cultured and that meant he had money. A riverman with a good johnboat and some ability with a boat paddle was just what the fly fisherman was looking for.

And so it began, one man paddling and one man fishing, eventually one man paddling and two men fishing in a longer boat. Word got around that those boats they used in the hills were so stable you could stand in the front or even fall out without turning them over.

A letter to Forest and Stream in 1923 from a Kansas City angler said that he and several comrades had found outstanding trout fishing each year on the "Niagara" in southern Missouri. The fishing parties were guided by local natives and their handmade boats.

In that day, bass in southern waters were often known as trout and of course the river referred to may have been the Niangua. But it may well have been another small tributary of the White so named at that time. He made the comment in the article that the natives of this "Shepherd of the Hills country" were exceedingly poor and there was nothing in the region to give one much hope for anything except continuing poverty." If only he could see it now!

The thing that limited float fishing was transportation. Roads along the rivers were often muddy and impassable and bridges far apart.

Johnboats were best transported by horse-drawn wagons.

19

Early Days of the Float Boat

But the railway had an increasing part to play in all this. Fishermen from the city used the trains to get to the country, and in time, johnboats were transported by rail from take-out point to origin, especially on the James and the White and on the Jacks Fork of the Current River, where a railroad spur had been built for hauling logs. You have to assume some of the railroad transportation was used on other rivers as well, though there isn't much record of it. One old newspaper article told of fishermen in the 1930's floating down the Big Piney river from Cabool to Arlington, where a railroad crossed the river and catching a train back to Cabool. It doesn't say if the boats were left there or brought back by rail.

In his book, "Man and Wildlife in Missouri", Charles Callison points out that a fishing and hunting club was established on a Current River bluff in 1888 by a group of railroad builders. Members and guests recorded their catches. And in 1892 four members caught 452 fish in two-and-a half days of fishing. In 1896 two men caught 21 bass in one afternoon with the smallest weighing almost three pounds.

Fishing declined for many reasons on the Current but one guest's record in 1910 indicated what the greatest problems were: "Nearly all the old big spawning beds between Round Spring and the Junction have been abandoned by fish. The bluff holes have been bombed (by dynamite)," he wrote. "Fishing water is not so good. Turtles and gars have multiplied amazingly because of mud bottoms from soil washed in from plowed grounds."

In August of 1912, a Missouri game warden named J. B. Thompson wrote an article entitled, "In Quest of the Red Eyes." Thompson told of taking the train to Eminence, Missouri and traveling the Jacks Fork by johnboat, then walking cross country to Big Creek, a tributary of the Current, to fish for smallmouth. Said Thompson, "It is strange to hear an Ozarker call a smallmouth a trout. Usually they apply the misspellation of trout to the bigmouth bass; and the smallmouth is called 'yaller

Early Days of the Float Boat

bass'."

Thompson made friends with an Ozark family by applying first-aid treatment from an emergency medical pack to a small boy who had chopped off three fingers with his dad's tie-axe. He stayed with the family and fished Big Creek with fly tackle, landing a 21-inch smallmouth near the creek's junction with the Current River. He indicated in his article that natives were very suspicious of him and that he saw many indications of mountain dew being produced on a large scale.

He wrote the following as an addendum to the story. "In writing the article, I have purposely withheld the name of my host, Jessie, as he is a dangerous animal and the valley is full of lawless feudists. I would not care to have some of your readers run in there for a trip and meet with disaster. That district has been noted for its monthly killings of the most cold-blooded kind."

J.B. Thompson wrote most of the articles about the Ozarks in the early part of the century under the pseudonym of "Ozarks Ripley". In a following chapter, I have reprinted his article about Current River country in it's entirety.

By 1912, guided fishing trips on various waters were apparently very common. They probably began even before the 1890's especially on the Current, and perhaps on the White as well. In the magazine ads, however, there was no mention of the Ozarks or surrounding areas between 1912 and 1922. There were outfitters galore in Canada, Minnesota, and Wisconsin. But the main state was Maine, if you'll forgive the play on words. In 1912, an outfitter known as New England Lines advertised 1,000 registered guides available and countless excursions on waters teeming with fish. Their sales pitch stated:

"Come fishing with Pete! His camp's down on Moosehead Lake. He knows every fishing pool from Kineo to Canada. He will show you trout and salmon fishing that in three days will take 10 years off your life. Pete is some cook...broiled fish, fried

21

Early Days of the Float Boat

potatoes, griddle cakes, maple syrup, hot biscuits and coffee. He'll make you think campfire cooking is the finest in the world. Pete knows how to make a fellow comfortable on a bed of hemlock boughs under a tent beside a campfire."

Years later, Jim Owens would take note of that type of advertising, and make it draw fishermen to the Ozarks.

About that time, my grandfather was beginning to guide hunters and fishermen on the Big Piney as a mere teenager and over at Galena, Missouri several guides were preparing to go into float fishing in a big way because of the new White River Branch of the Missouri Pacific Railroad which enabled them to move johnboats back upriver after days of floating. The Ozark johnboat was approaching a stretch of fast water.

In the years just before World War I, when float fishing in the Ozarks was just getting underway, equipment was primitive. You can see it improve in the advertising published in the pages of Forest and Stream Magazine.

Canoes were advertised in the early issues. Several companies appeared, including Kennebec and Old Town, both from Maine, with the latter advertising sixteen- to nineteen-foot cedar canoes priced from $25 to $50.

In 1917, there were canoes by Racine Boat Company, Wisconsin; Morris Canoes, Maine; and Dean Canoe and Boat, Toronto, Canada. Most canoes were made of wood but a company in Michigan called the King Boat Company made a folding canvas canoe. The first metal boats were advertised in 1917, by Mullins Boat Company of Salem, Ohio. The Mullins boat shown in the ad was fourteen feet long, with a square stern and a sharp bow. The ad claimed there were 65,000 in use. I figure they meant 6,500, or they were exaggerating to the point of ignoring the truth. Another flat-bottomed, sharp-bowed steel boat was advertised by the F. H. Darrow Company from Michigan as a build-it-yourself kit.

By 1918, the johnboat made its first impact on metal boat builders when Mullins Boat Company advertised its "Isaac

22

Early Days of the Float Boat

Walton" model, a fifteen-foot metal boat built just like the more common wooden johnboats. It had a square stern and bow, rake on both ends, and curved-flared sides.

Little doubt exists that in that day there was a distinct style of boat that we today refer to as a johnboat. It was characterized by a flat bottom, curved sides, a squared bow and stern, and rake at both ends. When I talk about rake at both ends, I am speaking about the rise in the bottom of the boat, so that the bottom of the boat does not extend backward and forward at the same depth. The front and back ends rise above the water, and water does not pile up against the front of the boat as you go forward, or the back of the boat as you go backward. There were many types of johnboats, patterned as each particular boat builder made them. But each had that common feature, despite width or length.

But in the pages of Forest and Stream Magazine from 1912 to 1922, you never find the name "johnboat," even though they were pictured in use in almost all parts of the country. Searching through page after page, I was sure that I had conclusive evidence that the term "johnboat" evolved later in the century.

Then I came across something that surprised me. In the July, 1922 issue of Forest and Stream was an article entitled "Boat Building" by Dwight Simpson. The author gave details and drawings for building what he called a twelve-foot fishing punt. The boat was almost exactly identical to the johnboats built by my grandfather, though shorter. (*see next page*)

Most surprising was a drawing showing the boat bottom being put on. The sides were bent around a forming brace drawn together at the ends by ropes. I wondered when I found it if the author of that story, who was from New York, had seen firsthand my grandfather's boat and used it for a model. Then I realized how unlikely that was. But it shows that back in that time, a general idea had developed which most boat makers were learning to use. Still, Simpson called his boat a punt.

23

Early Days of the Float Boat

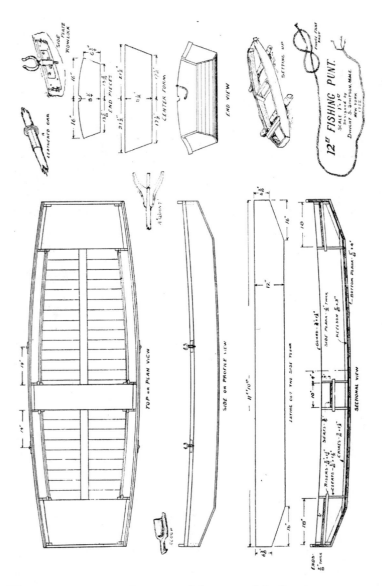

There was no mention yet of the term johnboat.

Then in the December, 1922 magazine, a writer named Raymond Spears, who wrote early articles on auto touring and camping, sent a letter congratulating Simpson on his boat-building article: "The boat would be practically ideal for trap-

Early Days of the Float Boat

ping the southern rivers," he said. "The model is very nearly that of the jon-boat." That is the first time I saw the word jon-boat or john-boat or johnboat, used.

So there went my theory that the johnboat had not yet been heard of. If Raymond Spears said he knew about jon-boats in 1922, someone must have been calling them that years before.

A well-known outdoor writer by the name of Robert Page Lincoln claimed credit in later years for coming up with the name 'johnboat'. He was irritated because J.B. Thompson, (Ozark Ripley) claimed he had invented the name. Thompson used the term in his writings in 1921. But so did Lincoln. To tell the truth, I doubt either of them came up with the name single-handed. And I don't know who did. I just know it wasn't me!

In the White River Valley Historical Quarterly, Winter 1998, writer Lynn Morrow put together a very precise account of johnboat and float-fishing history, and in doing so attempted to come up with a place and time that the term 'johnboat' was first used. He found the first use of the name in a 1919 federal report concerning the mussel industry on the White River in Arkansas. All I can say is, if those old time guides and float-fishermen only knew that their johnboats may have been named by a government man, they would surely be called something else today.

Who knows...I suspect that sometime in the late 1800's, when outdoor publications began to become popular, Ozark people began building and adapting their river boats according to boat-building plans they found in print here and there, like that set of plans I found in the 1922 magazine. And they were surely adapted and formulated according to the needs and whims of those who built them. There is little doubt that hundreds and hundreds of Ozark boat-builders made them between the mid 1800's and 1950. No two of them were alike and they didn't need to be. But a rose by any other name would smell as sweet and a johnboat by any other name would have done the same old reliable job... and smelled like fish.

25

3
THE HISTORY OF FLOAT FISHING

In 1921, Robert Page Lincoln wrote about fishing the rivers of Minnesota and Wisconsin. This famous writer said, "I located a boat builder in Lake Calhoun and he showed me a boat thirteen feet in length, forty inches at beam and fourteen inches deep that would cost me thirty dollars. I have always held that there is only one craft for fishing and that is the flat-bottomed boat and by that I do not mean a scow as heavy as a raft of deadheads, but a neatly built affair that will carry a fair load. In such a boat, one can stand up and move around without fear of tipping over or shipping water."

In several ads, wooden johnboats were shown in drawings and photos. The Rush Tango Minnow ad, for instance, showed a johnboat in use in Pennsylvania.

Still, the art of float-fishing was held back by a shortage of adequate casting equipment and lures. Between 1917 and 1922, the first efficient casting reels began to appear. New tackle companies started up, offering casting lures that would make float fishing enjoyable for those who weren't fly fishing enthusiasts.

The following is a list of tackle and equipment which sud-

The History of Float Fishing

denly came to be advertised in Forest and Stream during and after World War I:

"Complete Bait Casting Outfit--Complete with genuine Dowagiac Split Bamboo Rod--nickel plated wide spool reel, two enameled wood minnows, 50 yards finest silk line--$3.90--Boston, 1913.

Bristol Steel Casting Rods--Bristol, Connecticut--1913.
Sears & Roebuck Row Boat Engine--$49.95--1914
Worth Casting Reel--$7.50--Akron, Ohio--1914
Heddon Baby Crab lure--$.90, or 4 for $3.00--1917.
Rush Tango Minnow--$.75--New York--1917.
South Bend Casting Reel--Indiana--1917.
Evinrude Detachable Motors--Milwaukee--1917.
Pflueger Auto-Backlash reels--$20--1918.
Wilson's Wobbler lures--$1.00--Michigan--1921.
Johnson Outboard Motors--Indiana-1921.
Orvis Rods & Flies--Vermont-1922."

With that equipment beginning to appear, there was a great post-war interest in the outdoors and fishing. Then it became transportation that held things back.

In the Ozarks, the White River Branch of the Missouri Pacific Railway made the concept of commercial float fishing feasible. In 1914, a writer named Milt Bangs gave this account of his early trip:

"We floated down the James River and into the White traversing one-hundred-and-twenty-five miles of river and ending but twenty-one miles by rail from the starting point. At Galena, our party of four was equipped with two flat-bottomed skiffs, two guides, tent, cots, cooking gear, ice, and provisions.

Our party wanted bass fishing and got it. A hundred bass, none under ten inches long, most weighing from one to three pounds and one weighing four, were landed on the five-day trip. All smaller bass were returned uncounted. Frogs and young squirrels were plentiful and added to the variety of our menu. The days were warm but at night on the beautiful gravel beach-

The History of Float Fishing

es, heavy blankets were needed. Bass were eager to strike a red artificial minnow or a combination of Iris fly and pork-rind, with which we had the best success."

The writer went on to say that the state fish commissioners had just stocked 60,000 small bass, crappie and perch in the streams, so the water would not be fished out. When the floaters reached upper Taneycomo Lake, where the water backed up behind Powersite dam, they were met by motor boats which towed them back upstream to Branson; gear, guides, guests and boats were taken back to Galena by rail, the MOPAC railroad line.

It took five days and four nights to make that Galena to Branson trip, and it was said to be 125 river miles. I'm not sure the mileage is correct, but since Tablerock Lake was built, it is hard to estimate what the distance was. Back in that day, river mileage was never easy to figure. Most guides would just assume they had floated twice as far as they actually had. But five days of floating and camping was a considerable distance and time, and back in those days it amounted to seeing and traveling through a wilderness in the middle of the Ozarks.

On the Big Piney River about 1910, my grandfather, who was only fourteen, got into the float-fishing business accidentally with that group of surveyors from St. Louis who first hired him to help them find wild turkeys. In years to come when he started seriously guiding fishermen, Grandpa didn't outfit his float trips. He provided a boat and he paddled it and that was it. Usually he took only one-day trips. But when the day's fishing was over, he brought his boat back upriver alone after the floaters were picked up at a designated point, by whatever transportation they had previously arranged. So if he made a two-day trip, he was faced with another day of work bringing his boat back upstream. I never knew for sure how much he made, but knowing him as I did, I'm sure it was very little, maybe 50 cents a day.

Getting married just helped my grandfather's river business,

29

The History of Float Fishing

because he raised a family of a daughter and four sons, each of whom became float fishing guides as they grew up, helping him to expand and take on more customers. His oldest child was daughter Zodie, and even she was called upon to paddle boats down the river for fishermen. Zodie made her first guided float trip when she was about 15 years old, in 1934, and fishermen were pleasantly surprised to find a pretty girl who could handle a johnboat so well. She still remembers her first clients, Mr. Owens and Mr. Lynch, two fishermen from St. Louis, who floated and fished all day as she paddled, and had arranged for a truck to pick up them and the boat, miles down the river and return them to the place of origin.

Zodie said that my grandfather took many fishing parties to Lake of the Ozarks when it was first constructed and then to the new Ozark lake on the Arkansas border, Lake Norfork.

"Pop had some friends who owned trucks, and he would pay them to take several boats to the lakes." she told me. "We'd set up tents and a camp and spend several days there, with sometimes as many as six to ten fishermen. I would be busy paddling a johnboat for the ones who wanted to catch bass, and pop would set and bait trotlines for catfish."

A newspaper article about my grandfather and his life which appeared in the St. Louis Globe Democrat in 1927 no doubt helped his business. Eventually, about 1932 or 1933, he even set up a small campground at a place known as the Lone Star Mill, an old grist mill where a gravel road crossed the river on the way to Houston, Missouri, about five miles to the east. The crossing drew lots of people, and the campground and swimming hole caused them to stop.

Because of that location, my grandfather could rent boats, sell them, provide guides (his children and himself) and sell fish and garden produce. About then he began to sell his johnboats and sassafras paddles in considerable numbers to outfitters on other rivers and to the general public. Because many fishermen or picnickers or Sunday afternoon joy-riders wanted to rent

The History of Float Fishing

boats without guides, he kept plenty of boats at his access to the Big Piney River. He would sell them cheap, and replace them with new ones. In one year, he might build and sell as many as 50 or 60 boats, some of the resorts he sold to would order eight or ten at a time. If he got really ambitious, he could build three johnboats in a week.

My grandfather's operation was as large as he wanted it to be and became no bigger than he allowed it to be. He never let his work interfere with his enjoyment of the Big Piney. That's the way most of the float-fishing guides were. They kept to themselves and liked the solitude their outdoor life gave them.

Only one man involved in the Ozark float-fishing business was outgoing enough to make it a big-time business. He was Jim Owen, an entrepreneur without equal. And when you talk about guides and johnboats and Ozark float fishing, Jim Owen's name comes up more often than anyone else's. Yet Owen didn't grow up on an Ozark stream, didn't know how to build a boat, and didn't know how to paddle one. He was a big talker, overweight and unable to do much physical work. But he knew how to plan, administrate and publicize like no one else.

Jim Owen

The History of Float Fishing

Owen was an advertising manager for a Jefferson City, Missouri newspaper before he came to the Ozarks in 1933, visiting Branson. He never left.

Before his death in 1972, Owen had owned a drug store, a movie theater, and an auto dealership. He was the mayor of Branson for twelve years, president of the bank, and wrote a fishing column for the Arkansas Gazette. He owned champion fox hounds and bird dogs, produced his own brand of dog food and owned a large dairy. And on top of that he set up a business that was the largest and most successful Ozark float-fishing operation of that day.

The first floats took place in 1933, but things didn't really hit the big time until the spring of 1935. By then there were six boats, six guides, and a big truck.

Owen claimed 31 days of float fishing in his area without ever covering the same water twice. He didn't know all there was to know about the river, but he hired men who did, and he knew more about promotion and advertising than any other man in the hills.

He brought in as his guests the writers and editors who

The History of Float Fishing

could give him the publicity he needed. They were given free trips with steaks and wine and all the comforts one could get on an Ozark gravel bar. In no time at all, his float service was being plugged in the pages of Life, Look, Outdoor Life, and Sports Afield, plus dozens of large newspapers.

The History of Float Fishing

Writers Townsend Godsey and Dan Saults, both from Branson, knew Jim Owen and their writings relate much about Owen and his White River Float Service.

Key to his success were his boat-builder, Charles Barnes, and his trip guides, which included Barnes, Albert Cornett, Raymond Winch, Little Hoss Jennings, Tom Yocum, Deacon Hembree, Bill Brittain, Ted Sare and many others. Charlie Barnes was not new to the business, he had begun guiding with his brothers on the James and the White in 1906, and had built and sold his johnboats for 25 years before Owen came along. But Jim Owen made him famous.

Charlie Barnes with a model provided by LIFE Magazine which used this photo in a layout promoting Owen's Float Service in the 1930's

The History of Float Fishing

In the beginning his guides were paid two dollars per day, but during the heyday of the business they received about ten dollars per day, and that was exceptionally good pay for that time. Clients usually gave them generous tips as well, so a river guide who worked for Owen felt well-paid. Usually, Owen's float trips were several-day affairs, with a guide and two fishermen per boat. A large group required a commissary boat, a long, wide johnboat carrying the tents, sleeping and cooking gear and food, with no fishermen. The commissary boat went on ahead, with that guide selecting a campsite, setting up tents, and preparing for the evening meal.

Owen had a warehouse filled with gear. Barnes' johnboats had no middle seats; guests sat in comfortable folding camp chairs. At the peak of his business in the late 1940's, Owen had 40 boats and 35 guides at his disposal. During the 33 years his float service was in operation, Owen went through 300 wooden johnboats and attended to 10,000 fishermen from all over the country. Those fishermen included Charlton Heston and Gene Autry.

The History of Float Fishing

Very quickly, his services became something the average sportsman could not afford. It was float-fishing for the elite and a trip of several days was very expensive.

Owen ran his own tackle store and expected guests to buy their gear there. He also had a grocery list of more than 20 items from which fishermen could pick the food they would eat on a trip. And many of those trips involved large amounts of alcohol. Stories abound about things that happened when fishing guests became so intoxicated they could scarcely sit in the boat.

Townsend Godsey quoted one of Owen's top hands, "Jim was the best advertiser that ever lived. If he wasn't busy, he was the best of conversationalists, but if he was busy making a dollar he didn't have time to do anything else."

They say Owen worked his people uncommonly hard and many of his guides were not his strong supporters. You can imagine why, they were as opposite as night and day. Portrayed as the White River's champion, Jim Owen opposed the dams that buried the White and ended float-fishing on perhaps the greatest of Ozark rivers.

But it's been said that behind the scenes he was buying lakeshore real estate which would someday bring him ten times his investment when the dams were completed. He was a wheeler-dealer and he used the people who worked for him to further his businesses and make him fairly wealthy. But his guides never really shared in that wealth, and many were not prone to speak highly of him in private conversations. Still, they respected him for building the huge recreation fishing business which started the Branson area on the way to prosperity.

Jim Owen's last float was in 1958. A Cotter, Arkansas trout dock bought his equipment soon afterward. Owen had a stroke in 1966 and died in 1972.

There's no doubt that he played a great part in making the Branson area the tourist mecca that it is today. But it may be

36

The History of Float Fishing

that the old guides who worked for him, whose souls were a part of the White River, hated to see the change come. About those men, who were a part of the stream in the purest sense, not enough was ever written. And the shame of it is, Owen was only the organizer. His guides were the real thing, men who knew the river and how to find the fish and help mediocre fishermen catch them. Those men were doing what they loved, and I'm sure that to most of them, money wasn't the only reason they were White River fishing guides.

Ted Sare, who was one of them, in the late forties, wrote about many of them in his book, "Some Recollections of An Ozark River Guide." Some of what Sare experienced is included in a later chapter in this book, but if you want a first hand account of what many of those old time guides were like, you should acquire that book. The reading is fascinating, with great old photos from the historic White River Float-fishing era.

Some of those men might have said they saw the White River at its best. And perhaps they would say that we lost too much when that great river was buried beneath the dams and the progress that brought wealth to the Ozarks. But one thing for sure, none of those good, simple river people who lived in that day, would have believed what was to happen to the river and the land around it.

37

The History of Float Fishing

After World War II, float fishing enthusiasts found a recreational paradise in the Ozarks.

In 1950, the Missouri Department of Conservation published a list of outfitters on Ozark streams within the state's boundaries. There were more than 50 float services listed on a dozen rivers or so. My grandfather's name was there, along with Jim Owen, the Bales Boating Company, and the Galena Boating Company, some of the oldest in the state. Some rivers had as many as eight or ten outfitters and most outfitters and guides worked more than one river.

But I doubt if any float fishing guide ever worked as many rivers or floated as many miles as my grandfather's oldest son, Norten. Born in 1923, he made his first trip when he was only eleven years old. And he missed only those two years of the war when he was serving the country. As this book was being written, Norten was continuing to book float trips on the Niangua river, in his 68th year as a river guide.

He became well known when he was only a teenager because of his ability with a paddle. At the age of 14, he left the Piney and went to work full time for a float-fishing outfitter by the name of Alton Benson on the Meramec and Bourbeuse rivers near Sullivan, Missouri. Benson had a gas station, restaurant, tavern and dance hall there, and he bought boats from my grandfather. When he saw Norten's ability with a paddle, he made him an offer he couldn't refuse, and for three years Norten worked for him. At first he was in charge of the commissary boat, which he dearly loved because it gave him time to fish and learn about the river. But in time, most of the clients who came to fish wanted the youngest guide at Benson's place paddling the boat for them.

He found the best bass fishing was on the lesser known Bourbeuse.

"Meramec was good too," he recalls. "A St. Louis man named Herb Kempey fished with me on the Meramec in 1940 and caught a fourteen-pound walleye. He didn't want me guid-

38

The History of Float Fishing

ing for him at first because I was so young but I landed that fish and from that day on I was his personal guide. He sent lots of others my way."

Norten guided all over the for the remainder of his life missing only 1944 and 1945, when he was away from the Ozarks fighting in World II. I am confident in saying no man ever covered more river miles with more clients. Still today, people who float with him marvel at his strength and ability. He approaches his 81st birthday as the first edition of this book goes to press.

Norten Dablemont with a big smallmouth from the Niangua River 2003.

The History of Float Fishing

In Norten, you can see exactly what made float fishing with a guide so attractive to city fishermen...he was (and still is) colorful and talkative, and stories of the river and the old days and the things he had seen and the fish he had caught flowed from him like a fountain. He was in his element, and he liked people. Constantly laughing and happy, Norten made everyone who floated with him take on the same attitude.

"Sometimes you see someone trying so hard to catch a fish they are just working at it like it is a life or death thing," he told me once while we fished.

"And maybe they ain't catchin' a thing and they're really getting grumpy about it. So I start telling jokes, and man I know enough good jokes to last all week if necessary. I can't remember my own phone number or address, but I remember every joke I ever heard. Anyway, you get their mind off the fishing a little, get them laughing and telling their own jokes and next thing you know, they are catching fish. I don't know why it works like that so often, but it does. Happy people enjoying the river and the ride, catch fish."

Norten was made to be a river guide. No one I ever saw could match his ability with a paddle and a johnboat. He was as good as anyone could get. Later he became just as competent with a 19-foot square-sterned Grumman canoe, which he began using in 1968. He guided on more than twenty streams in Missouri and Arkansas and five Ozark lakes before he was 50 years old. His life story, from the first of his guiding experiences on the Big Piney until today, including the war years, when he survived the siege at Bastogne Belgium during the Battle of the Bulge as a member of the 101st Airborne, is detailed in the book, "Ridge-Runner".

He said he started so young because a local fisherman had rented one of Grandpa's boats and was having a hard time paddling it. He noticed that Norten, even at his young age, was capable with a boat paddle so he paid him 50 cents a day to paddle for him. Norten guided for his father on the Big Piney in

The History of Float Fishing

the late 1930's, eventually hauling in the grand sum of two dollars per day. He still remembers the name of that first client, a man named Albert Howell, in May of 1934. That trip was just a matter of fishing a few holes around the old Lone Star Mill eddy, but soon there were those wanting to go all the way down the river to the next crossing which was miles away.

"We didn't haul those boats back and forth," Norten recalls. "A driver would pick up the fishermen somewhere and then I'd bring the boat back up the river. But that was fine with me, I'd make more money that night on the way back by catching bullfrogs for Melito seafood company in St. Louis. I might get in at one or two o'clock in the morning and have another float-trip the next day."

Eventually his father (my grandfather) began hauling boats on old trailers made from pickup beds. But before the war, a leisurely float trip for clients meant a long, rough return upstream for Norten all alone.

On the Current River, it was almost impossible to get a boat back upstream against the flow, so one Shannon county company had a Cedar Grove boat builder make pine johnboats to float to Van Buren. This was a ten- to fifteen-day trip and the float fishing party paid for the boats that were used. At the end of the float trip, the boats were abandoned at Van Buren. The Shannon county outfitter learned that another outfitter in Van Buren was using the boats, so he contacted that man and tried to work out a deal in which the boats were sold to him after being floated to Van Buren.

The outfitter down river said no. Why pay for something that he was able to use free of charge? From then on, guides were instructed to knock holes in the boats or to burn them when they reached Van Buren. But I don't want to get into the Current river country much in this chapter. It will take a whole chapter to give that great river system the full attention it deserves, and that will follow.

In the late '20's and '30's it didn't take much money to

41

build a boat. Norten recalls that after the depression, Grandpa's johnboats were built out of rough sawn lumber.

"We didn't use planed lumber or paint a boat until just before the war," he says. "You just went to a sawmill and told them what you needed to build a few boats and they'd cut it for you. When I was fourteen or fifteen years old, (the mid '30's) dad was selling boats for seven or eight dollars each and materials cost about four dollars."

The History of Float Fishing

In the 1950's, a man named Kenzie at Flippin, Arkansas, began to make fiberglass johnboats for use on the White river. Aluminum boats were being used in small streams about that time but most were not designed properly for streams. Still and all, the introduction of these materials marked the beginning of the end for wooden johnboats.

Ninety-nine percent of the river floating done today takes place in a canoe. Many companies make them and they are designed for speed and easy handling.

Those of us who fish or hunt or trap the rivers seriously are not able to give the seventeen-foot double-end canoe a high recommendation. They are not a stable craft and won't hold much of a load. When it comes to hunting, trotlining, gigging or floating in extremely cold weather, a seventeen-foot canoe is inadequate to the point of being dangerous.

Longer and wider canoes are stable enough for serious fishing. For years I have used a nineteen-foot square-stern Grumman canoe and find it to be nearly as stable as the Lowe Paddle-John, mentioned in another chapter. The added length makes the square stern canoe a bit harder to handle. The length of the aluminum Paddle-John is nearly perfect for Ozark rivers but when floating in the wooden johnboats, I prefer a fifteen-foot boat. If you take away the weight factor, you could make a good case for wooden boats against aluminum craft on Ozark rivers...that is if you are serious about hunting or fishing, or river trips of several days.

Compare the three types of craft:

Weight: The seventeen-foot Paddle-John weighs approximately 140 pounds, the nineteen-foot square-stern canoe almost as much. A fifteen-foot wooden john-boat weighs from 180 to 200 pounds.

Stability: The wooden john-boat far exceeds the other two craft in stability and the Paddle-John has a slight edge over the 19-foot square-sterned canoe.

Maneuverability: The Paddle-John and the square-stern

43

The History of Float Fishing

will respond to lighter effort in handling. The 19-foot canoe, being longer, is more difficult to maneuver in swift water, more difficult to turn. The wooden boat, much shorter, is easier for an experienced floater to turn in swift water around obstacles. Inexperienced paddlers can handle the Paddle-John more easily than the other two.

Strength and Longevity: Obviously, the aluminum boats will outlast the wooden one under normal use because the wooden boat will deteriorate over the years. But the wooden boat will hold together very well under extreme pressure and abuse.

19-foot Grumman square-stern (left) 17-foot Lowe aluminum johnboat (center) and 16-foot wooden johnboat (right).

Any aluminum craft, if tipped in swift water against an obstacle, will bend and many are ruined this way. The wooden boat in the same circumstance can withstand much more force without breaking. The aluminum boats will need to have holes patched from time to time. When you hit a large rock in the

The History of Float Fishing

current, the aluminum boats will show damage--catching, grating, and occasionally rupturing. I've never knocked a hole in a wooden boat because the wood gives and bounces off. And the wood, of course, is so very much quieter.

Cargo: A seventeen- or eighteen-foot aluminum johnboat will hold more than the other two crafts and float as high. The fifteen-foot wooden boat, the seventeen-foot aluminum boat, and the nineteen-foot canoe hold about an equal amount of weight, which far exceeds the capacity of a seventeen foot double-end canoe.

Speed: Obviously, the nineteen-foot square stern wins out here but the Paddle-John isn't slow if you know what you are doing. Neither is the wooden boat. Two good paddlers can travel up to 20 miles per day in any of the three on a typical Ozark stream at normal level, when all shoals are high enough to be floated.

17-foot double-end canoe on left is cheaper, faster and less stable than the square stern 17-footer on the right. But the latter canoe is wider and easier to control if you are an experienced canoeist. The author wouldn't be seen in either if he had access to one of the three crafts on the opposite page.

The History of Float Fishing

Cost and Availability: Few wooden johnboats are being built today but there are still plans available for those who'd like to build their own. Cost of materials ranges from 200 to 300 dollars. The Paddle-John can't be found at dealers any more, but used ones often sell for about 500 dollars. A new one sold in that range in the early '90's when they were last being made. The cost today of similarly made aluminum river boats is over $1000. Several brands of eighteen- and nineteen-foot square stern canoes can be purchased through boat dealers. The cost will run from $900 to $1500. The Grumman will be the most expensive, but it will also be the strongest.

The one I use is 30 years old, the Grumman company gave it to me when I got out of college and began working for the Arkansas Democrat as a 21 year old outdoor editor. It was made from airplane aluminum and I have never seen anything tougher. You can't imagine where it has been and what it has done. A book could be written about the life and times of that one canoe that sits outside my home now, awaiting a further adventure.

19-foot Grumman square stern canoe.

The History of Float Fishing

I was fortunate to grow up on an Ozark river in a family that was part of the history of float-fishing. I have never been involved in anything I've enjoyed more than I did those trips as a boy and later as a young man, and even yet today when time allows, guiding float-fishermen. I've spent many hours on rivers in several states and Canada, and I have floated in every type of craft: the smallest and largest of canoes, ABS plastic, fiberglass, metal--even Styrofoam.

Still, I like the wooden johnboats which my dad and grandfather built. I've even thought at times that some day I would enjoy guiding a float trip again in a wooden johnboat, just like we did in the old days still using handmade sassafras paddles. But the river is easy for all to enjoy now. In caravans of canoes they come to ride the current and see the sights. Not many are good at it, most pass up wonders without seeing.....the sleeping owl in the hollow sycamore limb that leans across the river, the cave hidden by foliage where, in another time, men and women and children lived off the bounty of the river. Most will never see the mink, or hear the rain crow, or catch a lunker smallmouth, or drink from the bubbling spring "just up the holler."

Drawn by the rapids ahead, they'll pass the remains of the old johnboat without knowing of the people and the age it represents. But when the canoes have passed, when it's still and quiet and evening slips in, you can sit on the gravel bar and pretend nothing has changed. The bluff that towers above the water is the same. There are still wood ducks and bronzebacks and flathead catfish; caves and springs and rapids that won't stop for anyone or anything.

And if you sit quietly and close your eyes and listen, you can hear the slurping sound of a sassafras paddle dipping into the water as another old river guide heads out just before dark to bait his trotlines in a wooden johnboat he built with his own hands.

Charlie Barnes - White River Legend

4
CHARLIE BARNES AND ROBERT PAGE LINCOLN

When Jim Owen wrote an outdoor column for a Branson newspaper back in the 1950's, he once used this anecdote about Charlie Barnes....

"On the White River many years ago, we used extra large iron skillets and the guides, through many years of practice, knew just how to dip the batter with a big spoon to make three flapjacks fit this river skillet. Charlie was the commissary man and cook on one party, and as he was hunkered down over the open fire cooking pancakes, a woman member of the fishing party stepped up to watch. When she saw the size of the pancakes, she told Charlie, 'I just want two'. This stopped Charlie, and after giving it some thought he looked up and said, 'Lady, they come in three's.' He wasn't trying to be smart, he just didn't want her fouling up his many years of habits as a river cook."

Charlie Barnes was the king of float-fishing on the White River and the James. He began just after the turn of the century, working with two brothers, Herbert and John, and eventually he was the hub that made Jim Owen a big wheel. Charlie built the johnboats, knew the rivers and gave advice that Owen depended on. But he not only built great boats, he was a great guide. Fishermen found true Ozarkians in Barnes and his brothers.

Charlie Barnes far right and his brothers Jon and Herbert began their float service on the James River about 1904.

Charlie's grandson, David, who now lives in the Kansas City area, remembers that his grandparents were gentle, sweet natured and quiet people. Charlie Barnes wasn't a big talker, but he was written about by Robert Page Lincoln and Townsend Godsey, so we can get a little bit of a picture of him from their words.

Lincoln was a well-known outdoor writer who began doing hunting and fishing stories from all over the U.S. and Canada in an era before World War I. In the March 1948 issue of Fur, Fish and Game Magazine, for which he was the Travel Editor, Lincoln did an article entitled, "Floating Down the River."

Much of that article was devoted to blistering condemna-

Charlie Barnes and Robert Page Lincoln

tions of reservoirs that had been built in the Ozarks and were in the planning stages. As you read the following account, you need to remember that J.B. Thompson, who wrote under the pen name, Ozark Ripley, was a competitor of Lincoln's. They had something of a feud going, both of them taking credit for naming the wooden river boat a johnboat.

Here is some of what Robert Page Lincoln wrote in that magazine article......

"Fishing in the state of Missouri is confined almost entirely to stream operations since streams compose the greater part of all of the waters of the state. There are few if any natural lakes in the state. Those that are called lakes are reservoirs created by the installing of dams across the rivers, and these can be dismissed from consideration inasmuch as most of them are well silted in or are on their way to oblivion. The Lake of the Ozarks is a case in point. It was originally given a most dramatic real estate build-up, the assertion being made that the lake would provide the best fishing on the continent and that it would last for all time. It is true that for some years after the dam was created the lake produced fish in abundance and people believed, without question, that the impossible had been achieved.

"Today Lake of the Ozarks is a mudhole as we had predicted it eventually would be and while there is a fair amount of fishing in it, this is largely confined to the mouths of streams coming in, places where the fish have their only recourse to fresh or clear water and an unsilted bottom. What is true of the above reservoir is true of the other lakes of this nature in the state, including Wapappello, Taneycomo and Norfork Lake, although the latter is created by a dam on the North Fork, but in Arkansas, which pushes the water north into the State of Missouri. Bull Shoals Dam, on the White River in Arkansas, also pushes the water up into Missouri and will serve definitely to ruin this scenic part of the stream. An even greater dam proposal, Table Rock Dam, near Branson, Mo, will wipe out the

51

Charlie Barnes and Robert Page Lincoln

last vestiges of this beautiful stream and will succeed in doing no more than add another disgusting mud-hole to a large list of them already on their way out."

Later in the article, Lincoln got around to his conversations with Charlie Barnes. He wrote:

"Last fall I saw Charlie Barnes, the inventor of the so-called float-trip boat, also known as the "john-boat", in Branson, Mo., after a lapse of several years. Charlie is no longer active on the river of the Ozarks although he makes occasional trips with the boys just to keep a-breast of the times and see what's doing. But dragging these boats over riffles and prying them off of ledges is work that he admits he cannot take. All that, so far as he is concerned, is over and done with."

"It is odd that a great deal of the interest attached to float trips in the Ozarks is connected inseparably - with this boat invention of Charlie's. Without the boat, something of the charm and originality of this manner of fishing would be lost."

"I got some facts regarding Barnes and his invention this year that are worthy of putting down. Charlie Barnes was born on a farm thirty mile's from Galena, at Mt. Vernon, Mo., in Lawrence county, in 1878. When he was eight years old his family moved to a farm three miles from Galena, Mo. Having access to the James River, he, in common with his brothers, spent much time fishing this historic river and their catches were such that Barnes conceived of the idea of making boats and taking out fishing parties. At the age of 26, in 1904, Barnes started taking out his first parties."

"The so-called "johnboats" were made practically as they are made today in shape, length and other characteristics. They were not the result of much experiment. The main objective sought in these boats was that they should be able to carry a fairly large load; and at the same time, draw as little water as possible. The boats ranged 18 to 20 feet in length, were not much over 34 inches wide, with 14-inch sloped board sides. These boats, according to Barnes, would weigh 200 to 300

pounds."

"Barnes and his brothers, John and Herbert, guided parties from Kansas City, St. Louis and many other cities throughout the Middle West. Most of the fishing trips or floats were confined to the James River entirely but later on these trips were extended to Branson and in many instances to Cotter. When the trips went to the latter points the boats were shipped back to Galena by train. At about the time Barnes started his boat trips the railroad had just been put in."

"As his trips down the river became more prominent he had a special flatcar on the railroad that was operated between Galena and Branson--the sole purpose of which was to take back float boats to Galena. Barnes stated that they operated as many as 60 boats and it was common to have as many as 25 to 30 boats on the river at one time in operation. These earlier trips were conducted then much as they now are out of Jim Owen's operation at Branson, Mo. Complete outfits were brought along and tents were put up on the gravel bars. As time went on the trips became more and more extensive. Eventually their main trip was from Galena to Branson, which was considered a six-day trip, 125 miles in length."

(Author's note...That mileage is questionable, considering the distance between the two towns by Highway is about one-fifth that distance. But the distance advertised from Branson to Cotter Arkansas by boat was said to be 250 miles of river fishing.)

Lincoln continues as follows:

"According to Barnes the James River and the White were then pretty wild and both fishing and hunting was somewhat at a peak. The size of the fish taken on the average were very much as they are now, and a three and one-half pounder would be considered a pretty good bass. Barnes recalled, however, that he has seen bass taken by his parties on the river below Branson that would go to ten and twelve pounds. These bass, he

stated, were called slough bass, and were almost completely green in color and had no vestige of a black lateral line or stripe down the sides."

"The fishermen back in those days,' Barnes told me, 'were the worst fish hogs I have ever known. They would catch hundreds of fish and throw them away to rot. There was one place on the James River that became known as a dumping grounds where the fishermen would throw away the fish they had taken. The smell became so bad sometimes in the summer that you could detect it a mile away. Fisherman back then didn't know the first thing about conservation and if we made any kick about it we were laughed down. When I think back on it all it seems a wonder to me that the good fishing held out as long as it did."

"Barnes told me that he had never heard of John B. Thompson, "Ozark Ripley." He had never read any of Ripley's writings and, so far as he knew, this writer had never made a float trip with him. He remembered no writings that had been put out covering any of the trips that he had made, but it is pos-

Charlie Barnes and Robert Page Lincoln

sible that hundreds of writings must have found their way into the newspapers especially since the float trip business eventually became little short of an industry. I asked Barnes if the name "johnboat", as applied to this type of boat, was familiar to him and if it was known by this name in the days when he was operating out of Galena. He stated that the name was not familiar to him, indeed that he had never heard of it nor did he know how it originated."

"I do think I have heard the name as applied to these boats over on the Current River,' he said, 'but we have never used that name here. I wouldn't know the reason for the name. If Ripley stated that the float trip boat was first made and used on the Current River, he was wrong. We started in around the turn of the century and sport fishing in the Ozarks, from St. Louis, west, was practically unknown at that time. Later on, float trip operators started in here and there. One operator at Branson, who claimed to have invented the float trip boat, started building these boats and operating them well after we did. There were many imitators. Some of their boats were made with pointed bows and sterns, but they did not prove practical. We had early found that out. Float trip fishing became a great business over on the Current River. Some of our parties would go there and fishermen in turn from the Current River would come over to the James and the White.'"

"Charlie Barnes was in the float trip business 29 years, from 1904 to 1933 when he came over to Branson. His Galena business was taken over by L. 0. Stewart, although one Harry Dillard now runs it. Barnes went in with Jim Owen in 1933 and has been with him ever since. Under Jim Owen's guidance the float trip business was given its greatest impetus and instead of being confined in popularity to a Midwest range only, this manner of fishing is now known the length and breadth of the country."

"There are those who have complained that this float trip business is overrated; that it cannot live up to the publicity given it; and that the fishing is of a minor nature that can hardly be called worthwhile or dependable. If it is meant by this that all you have to do is throw your line and bait overboard and thereafter pull in fish, one after another, it is true that this cannot be done. You work for your bass on these Ozark streams, and sometimes you work hard. Yet where in the nation is it so easy to take fish in this advanced day. We could point out places to the north where your chances of taking fish, in fairly wild surroundings, is an even greater gamble than in the Ozark streams. Too, the complaint is made that the bass in the Ozark streams are small, and this is reasonably true since streams in the high country of the south are all about the same, ranging a pound to a possible two pounds in weight, with an occasional large bass making up the sum total."

"Possibly the charm manifest in float trips down these Ozark streams of Missouri lies in the youthful spirit of the thing, harking back to Tom Sawyer and Huckleberry Finn; a sort of sweeping adventure, just floatin' down the river and soaking up the glories of nature en route."

Charlie Barnes and Robert Page Lincoln

"We admit to many inconsistencies in this manner of fishing. For instance when our party last fall floated down from Beaver, Arkansas on the White River, to Viola, Mo., there had been no rain in the region for five months or more, and the stream was low, alarmingly so. The only water that came down was that produced by springs. This was a rather unusual condition inasmuch as the fall season generally sees a generous precipitation and an attendant rise in the river."

"As a result of the above lack of water we spent the greater part of our time pulling and shoving the unwieldy float trip boats over the rocks and riffles. With six inches to a foot more of water we would have sailed peacefully down the glides without even scraping on the bottom. For a float trip boat, while drawing little water, is of little use when the water is only three to four inches deep over the riffles. You cannot, in this case, expect the impossible."

"But whatever the drawbacks to float trip fishing on these Ozark streams may the fact remain that, year after year, the boys come back for more. They like to sit at ease in a camp chair in the boat and fish and dream. I believe that most of these fishermen are content with enough fish to eat. If they aren't they belong to the tribe Charlie Barnes told me about, who threw away their fish by the hundreds. Maybe the need in Missouri today is for more extensive hatcheries, more bass to be reared and more of them placed in the streams. In any event, float trips on the streams of the Ozarks must always remain among the most unique fishing adventures possible of achievement in the U.S. The idea and the locale are second to none in North America."

Townsend Godsey was a writer from the Branson area, and also a journalism teacher at nearby School of the Ozarks college in the mid-sixties. He interviewed Charlie Barnes in 1952, and quoted him as follows...

Charlie Barnes and Robert Page Lincoln

"The first boats I ever saw on the White River were about 30 feet long and 25 inches across the bottom...made for gigging. When the furriners started comin' into the mountains for float trips we had to make the boats shorter and wider. Needed that extra width so we could carry more campin' gear and let two men cast out of each boat. Used to buy number one pine for two dollars a hundred, now it costs more'n 30 dollars a hundred. Costs close to 50 dollars now to build one, and I get 65 dollars for a sixteen-footer, 85 dollars for a twenty-footer."

Godsey described the building of Barnes johnboat as such... "Time was when Charley charged two dollars rental on a boat and a dollar and a half for a guide fee. The Missouri Pacific Railroad fitted a flat car with side poles so Charley could ship sixteen boats at one time. It cost him a dollar and twenty cents to ship a boat via rail, with a fifty cent loading fee and a twenty-five cent unloading fee. Today (1952) things have changed except the simple procedure he follows in building a johnboat. A hammer, saw, plane and screwdriver are the only tool he uses. He works on a pair of sawhorses, and fits the bottom tongue and grooved boards together as a starter. Then the iron braces are bolted to the boards. Next, the end pieces are put in place, the sides fastened to these blocks and bolted to the iron braces. The sides are nailed to the bottom with number eight box nails. The seats are installed, the boat turned over and the bats nailed to the bottom. The boat is given two coats of paint and then one bolt is fastened to the prow of the boat for the eight foot anchor chain."

Note from the author...... When Charley Barnes said that float fishing began on the White, he sincerely thought it did. But he was probably wrong about that. No doubt there were organized float trips on the Current in the 1880's and probably before. In doing research for this book I talked to one old timer who knew Charlie, and had guided with him on the White. He said that he was absolutely sure that Charlie bought an old wooden johnboat just after the turn of the century that was near-

58

ly worn out, from a guide and boat builder over on the Current or Eleven Point, and brought it back to Galena, where he and his brothers dismantled it and built their first boat from what they learned. But the metal wheel rim braces may have originated with Charlie, as the Current river boats had wood braces.

Charlie Barnes and Robert Page Lincoln

Plans for Charlie Barnes johnboat

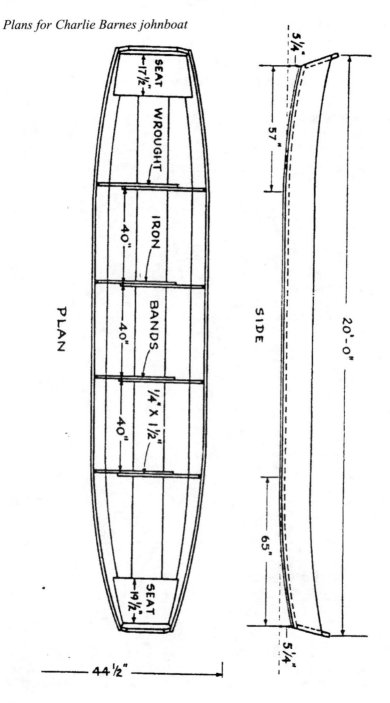

Plans for Charlie Barnes johnboat continued

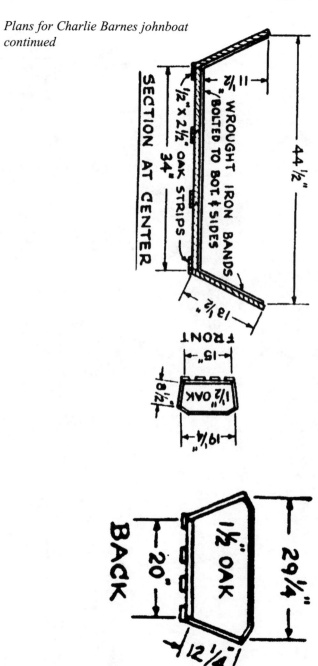

5
RECOLLECTIONS OF AN OZARK FLOAT TRIP GUIDE... BY TED SARE

Ted Sare was a guide for Jim Owen's float service in the 1940's on the White River. In the 1990's he wrote a 56-page book about his years as a guide, the people he knew and his anecdotes and experiences. Ted passed away in 2002, but his wife Vernetta still sells his book for $10. per copy. It is a great book, providing insight into the lives of the White River guides, plenty of nostalgia and humor and old photos. We have printed a small section of his book here, with permission from Mrs. Sare. We hope you have a chance to read it in its entirety. To order Ted's book, "Some Recollections of an Ozarks Float Trip Guide", write to Vernetta Sare, 3027 W. Farm Rd. 38, Willard, Mo. 65781 and submit a check or money order for $10.00, plus $2.00 for postage.

Recollections of an Ozark Float Trip Guide... by Ted Sare

Ted Sare (center) is the author of the following chapter. He is pictured here with Little Hoss Jennings seated left, Tom Hembree seated right, Clint Carr standing left, and Lee Matlock standing right.

The White River, from its beginning near Pettigrew, Arkansas to its end at a place in Southeast Arkansas called "Big Island," where it runs into both the Arkansas and the Mississippi rivers, was as important a part of the Ozarks as the hills themselves. Along with its tributaries, it drained nearly all of the Southern Ozarks. From its head waters it meandered north into Missouri, stayed there for a distance, then turned back in to Arkansas, then back again into Missouri, then again back into Arkansas and on thru the hills to the flat lands of Eastern Arkansas. This enchanting part of the Ozarks was "White River Country," very scenic, and very good fishing.

When I came on the scene as a float trip guide working for

Recollections of an Ozark Float Trip Guide... by Ted Sare

Jim Owen who owned the Owen Boat Line at Branson, Missouri, the White River had only one impoundment in its entire length, that was Lake Taneycomo made by a dam at Powersite just up the river from Forsyth. Powersite Dam was a low dam that raised the water in the lake to just about bank full most of the way up to a little below the old original Table Rock, a big flat rock on top of the bluff on the south side of the river a mile or two above Point Lookout where now stands the "College of the Ozarks." All the rest of the river was unimpeded, free flowing. That portion of White River that was above, or upstream, from Lake Taneycomo we called "upper White." That part below, or downstream, from Lake Taneycomo we called "lower White." (Taneycomo is a contraction of Taney County Missouri.)

The float boat was about twenty feet long, it was made from clear twenty foot pine lumber and the ribs were made of wagon tires, also called wagon rims. Wagon rims are metal, flat on the inside, convex on the outside, that covered the outer surface of a wooden wagon wheel. These pieces of wagon rims were shaped so that they ran from the top of the boatside down the side and across the bottom of the boat to the other side. The corresponding piece of the rim down the opposite side of the boat was done the same way so that the two overlapped side by side on the bottom of the boat but were not joined. All this was, of course on the inside of the boat, and maintained the proper shape of the boat. There were several ribs in the boat since the shape of the sides were not the same throughout, the center flared more than the ends. The boats had some "rake" in them, that is the front turned up just a little, the back even less. The back of the boat had an ample sized seat that filled in the back twenty-eight to thirty inches and was down from the sides about three inches and four and one-half to five inches below the top of the transom. Most guides folded up a canvas tent just to fit on the seat. That not only made a place to haul the tent, but raised the guide up a few inches which gave him a better view

Recollections of an Ozark Float Trip Guide... by Ted Sare

of the river.   Our boats, that is the Jim Owen boats, had a small seat in the front, no doubt there to aid in the rigidity of the front shape, but also used as a seat or step. I have seen some boats without this front step in them.

It is interesting that the shape of float boats varied with the type of river that they were to be used on. They were all about the same length, twenty feet or so. On the James River and upper White the boats were narrower even though of the same basic design. This narrowness made them easier to get through narrow places on the shoals of smaller streams. The boats of Galena Boat Company at Galena, Missouri on the James River and those of Bill Rogers located at Kimberling Bridge on the upper White, were about the same narrow design. Jim Owen's boats and those of Wilbur Hicks at Forsyth, Missouri on the lower White were about the same middle width design. The boats of Elmo Hurst at Cotter, Arkansas were really wide since down there the river was bigger, wider, and usually more shallow and the shoals were wide and shallow and slower rather than narrow and rushing. I believe I have seen some of those wide boats with wooden ribs rather than the space saving wagon tire ribs. Jim Owen's boats were all made by an old man named Charley Barnes, sometimes called 'Jason' and he was an old time river man.

Our boats, like most others, had a slatted thing made of one-by-three inch lumber called a "false bottom" that was loose and could be taken in and out. Its purpose was to keep the water out of boxes and anything else stowed in the boat. It seems there was always a little water in the boat and if it got as high as the top of the false bottom, it had better be bailed out. The length of twenty feet was just about right for a float boat. A shorter boat tended to spin too much when paddled hard and of course wouldn't carry as much load. A longer boat was more subject to the wind and became hard to hold in position in the wind. A loaded twenty foot float-boat could carry an immense load, and was surprisingly easy to run with only a boat paddle when you

66

Recollections of an Ozark Float Trip Guide... by Ted Sare

got the knack of it. A guide sat in the back of the boat, paddled on one side only, never swapped sides with a paddle except perhaps in an emergency. He controlled the direction by feathering the paddle blade, or simply by pulling to or pushing from with the paddle. The paddle was usually six feet long and made of ash wood, although some of the early boat paddle makers used other wood. Mace Tilden is said to have made paddles from the wood of the linden tree, while Randa Layton used the wood of the sassafras tree. A guide always carried two paddles in case one got broken or lost. We usually called the boats "float-boats," although they were sometimes called johnboats.

Our equipment included just about everything needed for a nice comfortable camp. We took tents and cook flys with us on all trips. Cook flys are like the roof only of a tent, no side walls. Being much larger than a tent, they were used to cook under when it rained and on some rainy nights the guides would sleep under them although normally the guides would just sleep anywhere on the gravel bar that suited them. The guides bed rolls were usually covered over and under with a piece of waterproof canvas with any personal things such as a toothbrush, aspirin, or whatever, rolled up inside, or else carried in a small satchel. In case of a swamped boat, a bed roll would float for a long time unless it hung up somewhere. Folding camp cots were taken for and used by everyone. Sleeping on a cot was not only more comfortable than sleeping on a gravel bar, but it also kept snakes from getting in bed with you. At night a guide usually folded up his pants and shirt and used them for a pillow. On the gravel bar under his cot were probably a raincoat, light jacket, hat, and tennis shoes. All summer we wore the old-fashioned, inexpensive tennis shoes since we were in and out of the water a lot. When the river got cool in the fall, we would wear hip boots. We always were careful in picking up the things under our cots the next morning because sometimes there would be a snake curled up under something. It seem that copperheads were a little more apt to do this than the plain old water snake.

67

Recollections of an Ozark Float Trip Guide... by Ted Sare

We really didn't have a problem with snakes but they did seem to sometimes prowl around the camp at night.

The "party," that is the fishermen who were paying for the trip, slept in tents which the guides put up. Too, the guides set up the folding cots and put on the blankets. Everything was done for the fishermen. All they had to bring was their fishing tackle. Usually they would bring their own Scotch or Bourbon and if they wanted beer or soft drinks we'd find this out and load whatever they wanted before we left town. We had folding camp chairs, the ones with light canvas bottoms and backs and with arms. I think they now call them producer's chairs.

We had one of those for each person in the party. They would sit in them in the boats as well as in camp at night. In addition to all this, there would be ice boxes, cook boxes, grocery boxes, bread boxes, minnow traps in boxes, Coleman gas lanterns in boxes, a can of white gas for the lanterns, ridge poles and upright poles for the tents and cook fly, metal stakes for the tents and cook fly, and a "pole axe", that is a single bitted axe, the hammer side of which was used for driving tent stakes. The ice boxes were made of lumber (we hadn't even heard of Styrofoam then.) To insulate the boxes, we would lay down a generous layer of newspaper, put the block of ice on it, then completely wrap the sides and top of the block of ice with many layers of newspaper. All this was done at the ice house in Branson in the morning before we left for the river.

There would be a big ice box with a big, probably two hundred pound block of ice in the commissary boat, and a smaller ice box for each fishing boat with a fifty or one hundred pound block of ice in it. The size of the block depended on the length of the trip. All of this was loaded on one or two trucks to be hauled to the river. Each truck would haul four boats, two wide and two high with all the boxes, cots, tents, cook flys, chairs, bed rolls, and everything else I've forgotten to mention stacked on the top boats. The Owen Boat Line had two trucks and a pickup with a boat trailer so there could be many combinations

68

Recollections of an Ozark Float Trip Guide... by Ted Sare

to suit the need. All this would be hauled to the river at whatever our "put in" location was and also hauled back from our "take out" location. Sometimes the fishing party would ride the trucks to and from the river. Sometimes they would use one or two of their cars to and from, which of course required a driver to bring the car back to town then back to the river.

A typical float trip would consist of a boat for each two fishermen sitting in their chairs with an ice box sitting directly in front of the guide. This ice box held whatever drinks the fishermen wanted. It also would hold whatever fish they caught. The fish were kept on stringers through the day but each evening the guides would gut and clean the fish and ice them down. That same boat would carry the guides bed roll, a few items of the general camp equipment, and of course the fisherman's own tackle and whatever personal things they brought along. In addition to the fishing boats, there would be a commissary boat.

This boat hauled the big ice box, the cook box, the grocery box, bread box, and most of the general camp equipment, but typically, no fishermen. It also carried the camp grate which I forgot to mention earlier. It (camp grate) was made of wagon rims, strips of metal side by side and about one and one half inches apart, fastened on each end to another strip that turned down on the end to form legs. The whole grate was about two feet by three feet with four legs. This was used over the campfire to cook on. We never took any stove, all the cooking was done over a camp fire.

The guide that ran the commissary boat was the head guide, or boss, of that trip. He decided where and when to camp, did most of the cooking and was, in general, in charge of the trip. Camp was always made on a gravel bar. There were several reasons for that. It was clean, no mud or dirt to contend with, no trees in the way of setting up tents, the gravel was easy to drive tent stakes in, and the more you could keep camp away from trees, willows, and brush and weeds in general, the less the mosquito problem would be. The party wouldn't appreciate

Recollections of an Ozark Float Trip Guide... by Ted Sare

being exposed to ticks, chiggers, and poison ivy.

The commissary men knew all the good camp sites, so some gravel bars were used repeatedly and others hardly at all. The commissary man would be the first boat to get to the campsite. He would gather wood and start a fire, unload a part of his boat and get camp started. When the first fishing boat got there, that guide would help him unload the cook box and grocery box: they were the heavy ones. The big ice box stayed in the commissary boat. For the first night we took meat, either steaks or chicken (the parties choice) to eat. Every night after that, we ate fish. Yes we always had enough fish for supper. If sometimes it looked like we might be short of fish for supper the guides would get busy and catch enough to do us.

The cook box held all the pots and pans as well as skillets, dish pans, coffee pots, plates, cups, and everything required to cook and set the table with. Our plates, cups, etc. were the "granite" porcelain type. Every guide that was usually a commissary man had his favorite cook box that he would use trip after trip because he knew how the dishes had been washed, how everything was stowed in the box, and what incidentals, like sealed salt and pepper shakers and sharp butcher knives or waterproof matches were there. The grocery box, of course, held all the groceries, except bread and crackers which were in the bread box. We had a way of setting the cook box and grocery box back to back and about five feet apart near the camp fire. Then we'd push a short stick in the bar and open the lid of one box onto the stick, then open the other lid onto the end of the first lid. This would provide us with an ample table to work on to prepare the meal.

Our suppers normally consisted of a salad, meat or fish, french fries, two canned vegetables like green beans or mixed vegetables or whatever, bread and butter and jelly, and canned fruit for dessert. Of course, we always had coffee, but for supper most fishermen preferred to drink a soft drink, beer, or water. We usually carried along a five gallon can of town water,

70

Recollections of an Ozark Float Trip Guide... by Ted Sare

or preferably spring water, for drinking. Our coffee was made of river water, we just dipped the coffee pot in the river and filled it to the desired level, and then set it on the grate over the fire until it boiled. We let it boil a few minutes, poured in the right amount of coffee, and then set it off the fire to stop the boiling. As soon as it quit boiling and grounds settled to the bottom, it would be put back close enough to the fire to keep it hot, but not enough to boil again.

We had a rather unique arrangement for a table. A piece of canvas about thirty inches wide and seven feet long had wood lath tacked to it crossways and about one inch apart. With it rolled out on a camp cot, lath side down and covered over with a clean oil cloth, it made a nice table. When not in use, it was rolled up in a six or seven inch roll which was small and easy to haul.

For breakfast we fixed bacon, eggs, and hot cakes. The hot cakes were made from Aunt Jemima's pancake mix mixed with Pet milk and water; the syrup was Aunt Jemima's too. We'd have orange, tomato, or V-8 juice and of course a big pot of coffee. Sometimes if one of the fishermen shouldn't have much

Recollections of an Ozark Float Trip Guide... by Ted Sare

grease, I'd usually poach as many eggs as he wanted.

Of course, the fishing party always ate first, then when they had all finished and the table was cleared, the guides would eat using the same table. Before the commissary man sat down to eat, he would fill two dishpans about half full of river water and set them on the fire to heat. When he had finished eating, the water was plenty hot in which to wash and rinse the dishes. The commissary man would pick a guide to help him with the cooking and dishwashing. The other guides would set up and take down tents, cots, etc. Every guide knew what had to be done and they would make short order of either setting up or taking down camp. It could all be done in a few minutes.

The commissary man would be the last boat to leave the campsite gravel bar. After the fishing boats had gone, he would check over the campsite, burn any trash, be sure all the tin cans were picked up, etc. Any food scraps that were left were soon devoured by buzzards or raccoons.

Oh yes, one other item of camp equipment that I failed to mention was what the guides called the "White River Special".

Recollections of an Ozark Float Trip Guide... by Ted Sare

It was the seat part of a bathroom stool fixed so that four pipe legs could be attached to it so that it made a standing toilet stool. One of the guides would set it back in the brush when camp was made in the evening, then it had to be picked up when breaking camp next morning. The guide that tended to it always threatened to forget it. Even though the commissary man was the last to leave the gravel bar and had the heaviest loaded boat, he would soon pass the fishing boats, since he would get right out in the current and move on down the river. If he hadn't already done it, he would tell the other guides as he passed them where he would be at noon. The site picked for lunch would usually be on a nice clean gravel bar and in the shade of a big sycamore tree. The table would be set up and a lunch of lunch meat, cheese, pork and beans, bread, crackers, pickles, onions, a variety of sandwich dressings, and drinks were the menu.

Again, the commissary man would be the last to leave the lunch site and the first to arrive at the night campsite. He would tell the other guides where camp would be that night so they would know how to pace the remaining part of the day. A guide could "make good time" or "poke along" as the need might be without the fishermen being aware of it or being deprived of any good fishing chances.

Casting is done toward the bank side of the river, not the shallow or gravel bar side. The guide was always careful to run the boat just the right distance from the river bank or the area that the fishermen should be casting into. Nearly all the fishing was done with artificial lures thrown by a casting rod and with a level wind reel. At that time, no one had spinning reels. I don't think they were even available. There were several good brands of reels, some of the most popular were Shakespeare, Langley, and Pflueger. In that day, the ultimate reel was the Pflueger Supreme. Casting rods were mostly solid steel or tubular steel. Glass casting rods were just being generally accepted while I was guiding; 1947 through 1950.

73

Recollections of an Ozark Float Trip Guide... by Ted Sare

Most of our fishermen were genuine sportsmen and true fishermen. They came to fish, and they brought with them some of the best tackle available, and by and large they knew how to use it.

Ralph Foster, a well known Ozark sportsman fished often with Sare and other White River fishing guides.

Right here I'd like to say that Glenn Henderson was the man that made it all happen like it should. He was Jim Owen's right hand man. He was in charge of seeing that everything was done

Recollections of an Ozark Float Trip Guide... by Ted Sare

right and at the right time. He hauled boats and equipment to and from the river, knew where every fishing party was, where and when they would take out. He knew where all the camping equipment was, who had it, and what needed to be repaired. He got drivers for the fishermen's cars when needed, extra drivers for the trucks, and kept everything running smoothly. I don't think he wrote anything down, he had it all in his head. The rivers that we floated were the lower White in both Missouri and Arkansas, the upper White and James in Missouri, and the Buffalo and occasionally the Kings River in Arkansas and a little bit of Kings in Missouri. Each river had its own character. James River, or "The James Fork of the White River" as it was sometimes called back then, was floated a lot. Not just by Jim Owen's boat line, but mostly by Galena Boat Company of Galena, Missouri, Lyle Chamberlin of Cape Fair, Missouri, and by Bill Rogers Line of the old Kimberling Bridge on the White. The James had one feature that occurred so much, it was worth noting. That is, on many of it's shoals (shoals are what you might call "rapids") the river divided. Some of it went on each side of an island and the shoals usually curved so that you couldn't see all the way through them, so if you weren't pretty familiar with the river you could easily take the wrong chute. The James was a smaller river than the White. The holes, (you might call them "eddies") for the most part were not very long, so the shoals were fairly close together. Most of them, the shoals that is, were fast and deep and some of them could be difficult to run especially if you took the wrong chute. A float-boat was hardly ever turned over, instead, if a mishap occurred, the boat was "swamped." That is, the water came in over the side or back until the boat filled with water and sank. When a river was low, it was harder to run than when it was full. The James was a nice river to float, lots of movement, a good small-mouth bass stream, not too many "lineside" bass (we usually called largemouth bass "lineside"), and it always seemed to have more goggle eye than any other stream that we floated.

75

Recollections of an Ozark Float Trip Guide... by Ted Sare

There were many holes of deep water with huge boulders in them and these seemed to always produce some goggle eye. Too, I don't recall smallmouth bass jumping in the boat on any river but the James, but there it happened several times. I don't know if this was coincidence or a feature of the fish of that river. As I recall the fish in James River jumped in general more than in other streams. The upper White was some bigger than the James. When you were on the James and floated out onto the White, it seemed like the country opened out on both sides of the river, with not so much of a closed in feeling. The holes of the river were decidedly longer and wider, the shoals were more open and not so rushing and twisting and you could see all the way through them from the upper end. Fishing was about like that of the James river except if you jug fished, still fished or trotlined at night, it seemed to have more catfish than the James.

Before I started guiding, I would sometimes camp at the old Kimberling Bridge and would motor up the river for a few miles, then put out eight or ten 'jugs" for jug fishing. This was done by tying one and a half or two feet of fishing line onto the jug" which could be anything that would float good, like a capped empty tin can, a gallon jug, or fruit jar. If a glass jug or fruit jar were used, they needed to be painted or they were quite hard to see any distance away. Tie a hook on the line, bait the hook with either live or dead minnows, or any good catfish bait, throw them out in the river, give them a little head start, then float slowly after them and cast for bass while you watched the jugs. When any of them bobbed and disappeared for a while, you knew you had a catfish hooked. Now that was fishing! We could float from Viola or Shell Knob or even as far up as Eagle Rock to Branson. But usually the floats were from Kimberling Bridge, on the old Wilderness Road, to Branson or maybe from Galena on the James to Branson. On these trips that ended in Branson, we didn't actually float all the way to Branson since it was on the backwater of Lake Taneycomo. We would stop at a

76

Recollections of an Ozark Float Trip Guide... by Ted Sare

place called Acacia Club four miles or so above Branson and just about where the backwater began. Glenn Henderson would meet the party there with the pickup and maybe a car or two of the party's and take the party, all their belongings, and the rest of the guides on into Branson. He would bring along an outboard motor, and if I was on that trip, I would put it on my boat, tie all the other boats to mine and motor the rest of the way into Branson where Glenn would meet me again with enough help to get all the boats and camping equipment to the boat house. At that time, the Owen Boat Line had a few five horse and larger outboard motors, a ten or twelve horse Johnson, and an eleven horse Evinrude, which I preferred. When I had a choice, I would use it. One interesting thing about the upper White, if and when someone would catch a jack salmon (wall eyed pike), it probably would be in a wide rocky hole just below the mouth of Long Creek, on a deep running bass plug. They were at times caught at other places, but this is the only hole that I ever saw them caught in--and several times, too.

The Buffalo River was an extremely pretty river to float. It started in the Boston Mountain section of the Ozarks and stayed in very rough country all the way. Consequently, it was a fast stream and small as rivers go. It needed to have a little "rise" on it, that is, it needed to be full to have enough water for our heavy loaded float-boats to run it. The Buffalo river claimed more swamped boats than any of the rivers that we ran. It changed from summer to summer, so it had its share of surprises and had a lot of just plain mean shoals to run. With a heavy loaded twenty foot float-boat, it could certainly be a test of boatmanship. Also, when it was up or down six inches, it was entirely different and even more so with one foot more or less water. It looked altogether different to a guide, depending on the stage it was in. At any rate, it was fast moving with short holes and with rough, frequent shoals. It was too narrow to offer good casting distance from the boat. It had a lot of medium sized to small, smallmouth bass, which the natives called

77

Recollections of an Ozark Float Trip Guide... by Ted Sare

"trout." They tended to be darker in color, some almost black, than the smallmouth bass in other streams, and when you hooked one, he sure put up a fight.

The scenery was outstanding on the Buffalo. There were rock bluffs of varying height, color, shape, and texture, first on one side, then the other and some of the views way back from the river to the tops of mountains were really outstanding. As a fishing stream in my day, I would classify it as "fair."

The Kings River we floated only occasionally. It had to have a little rise on for us to float it. It was every bit as difficult or maybe more so to run than the Buffalo. I had heard a lot of wild stories about the Kings River so when I was scheduled for my first trip on the Kings, I asked an old guide who had been there what the Kings river was really like. He said, "She's a wildcat with a bell on." When I got there I found it didn't even have a bell on. It was small, fast, and with a lot of twisting, mean shoals. But the worst thing I found, and this occurred over and over, you would zoom around one of those fast, deep, crooked chutes to suddenly be confronted with a tree lying all the way across the river. If you couldn't get your boat stopped with the boat paddle, then the only choice was to bail out, grab the tail rope and try to get it stopped by main strength and awkwardness. If it hadn't been for those trees, it would have been kind of fun to run because it was sure a challenge. As a fishing stream, in those days, I would class it a little above the Buffalo. It seemed to have more smallmouth bass and definitely larger ones than the Buffalo River.

One time many years after my guiding days when Table Rock Dam was completed and the water was backing up, I went to a place on the Kings River just about on the Missouri-Arkansas line and was casting from the bank. I got a strike on every cast. I wasn't seeing how many fish I could catch, but how many "doubles" I could catch. On every cast I would get a smallmouth bass and there would be three or four more trying to fight the same plug, resulting in a lot of doubles. Except for

78

Recollections of an Ozark Float Trip Guide... by Ted Sare

enough for one meal, I turned them all back to the river.

The Kings would have been a dandy river for one day floats where you didn't have a boat loaded down with camp equipment but it was too far from Branson for us to haul for one day floats. The Kings would have been a dandy river for one day floats where you didn't have a boat loaded down with camp equipment but it was too far from Branson for us to haul for one day floats.

We guides had to have guide licenses in both Missouri and Arkansas since the White River was in both states as well as the Buffalo and Kings river were in Arkansas and the James was in Missouri. There wasn't anything to getting them--no test, no questions--just pay the money.

Can you believe when I went to work as a guide in 1947 the pay was $6 a day and keep. When I quit guiding at the end of the 1950 season the pay was $8 a day and keep. In addition to this we usually received a tip from the fishing party, normally about $20, but it could range from $5 to $50.

Most of the first year that I worked, I ran fishing boats but was usually asked to help the commissary man. Most of the next three years, I ran commissary boats.

The lower White River was by far the most floated, most fished, and most productive river of them all. It was just the right size to float, the right distance from the good spots to cast a bass plug into. The bass species were almost evenly divided between smallmouth and largemouth, probably just a little more than half smallmouth, and big fish of both kinds were abundant. As I look back on it now, it just doesn't seem possible that so many bass were taken from that part of the White River.

6
IN QUEST OF THE RED-EYES – J.B. THOMPSON

This article is taken from the August 3rd, 1912 issue of Forest and Stream Magazine. J.B. Thompson, the author, also wrote under the pen name of Ozark Ripley. He was also a Missouri game warden.

It has always been my practice in spring, after the last cold spell, or at least after what is imagined to be the last, to make my obeisance to the small-mouth of Current River, Missouri. This had so long been the case that I considered it really a necessary procedure in order to propitiate the fish gods in my favor. Personally, I have always believed it to be the best red-eye stream I have come in contact with, while its fish were the strongest battlers I had ever engaged with, its waters the coldest and by far the clearest, and the fish ran larger in size. I have had only one complaint to register against it--the late period in spring before the bass rose to flies; sometimes they remained until the latter part of May before offering battle with the light fly-rod.

In Quest of the Red-eyes

Other nearby streams offer fishing a month before, but as with the exception of Eleven Point they contain the less belligerent big-mouth. They have been unable to lure me from my favorite. But my favorite stream takes the melting snows from so many formidable chains of hillsides. The water is very late before it has enough warmth to bring forth the little bronze warriors from their lair of rock. However, a month's idleness from a stream in spring is unthought of by the angler, so I planned a little sortie to one of the tributaries, reasoning that where the water warmed earlier, fishing would be of some consequence.

Nevertheless I had to think of an ideal place. There were Buffalo and others, but too many big-mouth in them to suit me. Then I began to count over acquaintances of the kind from Current River's source, and I knew only one creek would fit my wants. It must of course be a tributary of Current River, have its start from springs in the mountains, rock and gravel bottom, fairly deep and particularly swift nearly all its length, as a mill race. Then as suddenly came to my mind a small stream way up, cutting through mountains, right in the maple sugar camps of Shannon County. Big Creek; that is the one.

I remembered once a visit there without rod or fishing tackle of any kind. Yes, that was the place where I cast the early grasshopper on the hastening waters and the great rush of red-eyes after it. In a few days I had arrived at Eminence, the county seat on the Jack's Fork of Current River.

While I had gained this little town, plastered by some miracle on the side of a hill, and by a greater miracle it remained there, I had only passed a few of the terrors incident to the journey. The undesirable train service looked almost like comfortable traveling, when I realized that the remainder of my journey was to be made on foot over steep acclivities, numerous waterways, an not the least among the native element hostile to visitors if they bear any resemblance to their conceptions of certain State officers. Unfortunately I came within the latter classification and the well-meaning prosecuting attorney had warned

In Quest of the Red-eyes

me at the last moment against exposing my identity and protested strongly my making the trip on foot and alone.

But an angler has little consideration for other than the subject of his quest. I was anxious to be off. However, Jack's Fork had taken a sudden rise and was too deep to ford and not a boat in sight, so I remained a day in the terrace-situated town and watched a snow storm chill my prospects, but not my ardor.

Fortunately the following day broke clear, and in an hour the sun, under the influence of a warm southern breeze, had vanished. Somewhat restless I took a stroll down the stream and found a small boat moored to a clump of leather wood. There was only one way to acquire its services; that was to appropriate it without asking. So I ran hastily to town, gathered my scanty luggage threw it in the craft and after a hard struggle, poled her across the rapids. I left her fastened for some other wayfarer.

Knowing the depths of the main streams, I decided to avoid them. Keeping close within touch of them I could tell my whereabouts wherever I happened to be. I knew the river routes well, but back in the untouched wilderness of the pine, where houses were not to be met up with, I was dependent on those signs of direction which nature posts in the wild countries. I got my course as I passed the last farm and swung along the bluffs for a short distance and left the stream right at the point where the river makes its horseshoe bend.

A trail was discovered across the first hill. It was followed to the northeast until it reached a rapid creek, whose bed of flat rock made quick falls in its haste to the river. It was Sheldon Creek. While its water was clear and it possessed the desirable swiftness, it lacked the depth of the typical small-mouth stream. I pursued it for a mile or more before I discovered a crossing.

Evidently the cold had still a grasp on the shaded areas of the northeast face of the bluffs. Icicles clung to the shelving rock.

An hour before dusk I espied a small clearing in the distance

83

In Quest of the Red-eyes

and gazing beyond a well known landmark on the east approach of the river--the large bluff of rock called Bee Rock. Yes, I had reason to remember it, for only the spring before I saw a four-point whitetail leap to his death on the gravel bar--a palpable case of suicide. It was in the little valley upon which the rock frowned, and where the blue smoke of green wood fire curled up, that I realized was one place where I could remain for the night. The character of my host was doubtful as the vindictiveness of former feuds in the valley remained, and a certain intangible hostility against a man from the city was still there, and I doubt if this feeling will ever be eradicated. A certain apprehension took hold of me as I dropped to the flat to apply for a night's lodging, and more than that, if fishing was good, a week would find me there, but the owner of the small farm was a dangerous citizen when aroused, and I thought caution was necessary.

Through the second growth hickory on the outside of the fence a man and a woman pulled laboriously a cross-cut saw. I walked over to them and offered the conventional "Howdy," responded to in the same tone as offered, possibly a little brusher and slightly tainted with curiosity as well as suspicion. I seated myself on another log, showing no undue eagerness to enter into conversation, and watched the slow severing of the hard wood. We remained under this spell of uncommunicativeness for at least thirty minutes and the subject uppermost in my mind, a sleeping place for the night, as yet remained unbrushed.

Two children came to the clearing--dirty little bare-headed urchins. The older, a girl about eight years, was leading a younger one, a boy. I noticed that the left hand of the boy had a repulsive bandage around it, and the owner flinched as he stepped gingerly over strewn limbs.

"What's the matter with the little chap's hand?" I asked of the father.

He turned to me with an expectant look an explained: "Poor little devil got three fingers chopped off; got hold of my tie-axe

84

In Quest of the Red-eyes

and tried to chop some pine knots. Do you know he ain't slept any since it happened."

"How long since it has happened?" I asked.

"Three days."

"Have you done anything for it?"

"Yes, wrapped a piece of fat meat on it after we got the bleeding stopped, but he's still pretty sore. I guess I'd better take him to a doctor next week if we go to town, but the river's done been too high of late to ford; Dunno when I'll get a chance."

"If you don't mind I'll dress his hand," I offered. "If you have some hot water at the house I'll fix the little fellow up," I added.

There was in my tramping clothes an emergency outfit which I always carried, and told the big man of it. He immediately picked the youngster caressingly in his arms and struck out for the shanty, visible at a distance of 200 yards on the ridge. His wife and I followed.

His house was a large log house of one room crowded with beds, stove, tools and in confusion of dirtiness. But there was one agreeable prospect--the large open fireplace, and on two smoldering logs steamed a kettle. I took the little fellow in my lap and proceeded to unwind the covering. From a bowl of warm water the mother had placed within easy reach, I saturated the hand and was able to unwrap it without much pain. What a sight met my eyes as the last remnant of cloth came from the wound! A dirty, repulsive, festering, gangrenous sore.

"You are a brave fine fellow," I said to the unflinching young one as I washed it with antiseptics and followed with a dressing of absorbent cotton. Aside to the parents who were over looking my amateur efforts at surgery I remarked: Jessie, I want to take a picture of him, the bravest boy I ever saw, and I'll do it tomorrow if you will only keep me over night."

The parents stepped back amazed at my knowledge of their names, and the boy laughed out: "Pap, my hand ain't hurting

85

In Quest of the Red-eyes

none now," At the same time he threw me such a grateful look.

"How did you 'un know my name?" drawled the father in surprise. The description offered to me in advance of him had been too accurate to mislead, and I also remembered his face as one of the cedar rafters that occasionally visited my town.

"B.," I exclaimed, "I want to stay awhile. Now don't get a false impression about me. I'm a game warden; I have nothing at present, strange to say, against your crowd, but I want to do some fishing on Big Creek. I have a week to myself, and I want to make the most of it. So it's up to you to say get or stay." I could see amazement, hatred and kindred facial expressions melt under the rapidly growing warmth of gratitude. He lowered his soft brown eyes and extended his hand to me, and his wife gained confidence and blurted in with the big mountaineer.

"Well, it's a case of stay as long as you want to, and I'm sure everyone's gwine to treat you right." We both laughed, and from that moment I felt comfortable, and it might be well to say that all the natives showed me marked respect, and did everything in their power to make my visit a memorable one. While the men of the hills had slight respect for the game laws, and prior to this visit, I was continually in conflict with them, I had no need to be on my guard against the customary pernicious nagging that undesirable visitors are subjected to. I had his word and it sufficed for me. Across Current River I was fairly familiar with the country. I had tramped it before to the extent of the small village of the Rat post office, and during the jaunt had become acquainted with the promises of Big Creek.

Morning came with its transcendent glow of pine, and as it touched the yellow sedge-clad hills and flashed back a light of gold, a marvelous transformation had taken place; the unkempt hut was now clean, the food was good and I reveled in comforts unlooked for the day before.

Climbing into the hollowed pine log canoe I pushed across the swollen river to the mouth of Brushy Creek, took the waterway and followed it about a mile, where a fallen maple log

86

In Quest of the Red-eyes

made easy crossing. Then I changed my route to one due north and climbed an immense hill; an hour elapsed in going over it. At its base flowed swiftly Big Creek, while in the eastern divide of the hills I discovered all of the branches to be clear and in a normal condition of flow.

On the side I had passed the day before, unprecedented rains at the head of the Jack's Fork had given the water an ugly appearance. I figured from my present location I could have five miles of fishing water to the river, and believed that I was to be the first person who had ever cast a fly on the transparent stream. I was in a narrow valley and could see the maple trees dripping slowly in the crude cups their sap; it was the maple sugar district of the county.

It was not necessary to select a particular pool. All the water course looked likely. Assembling my rod I dressed my leader with a trio of royal coachman. I made my first cast across to the opposite bank under a leaning birch. I had acquired the right side and found few trees or entangling growths on the other side.

My first offering received immediate response, possibly thirty small red-eye charged angrily at my flies. Two not over eight inches impaled themselves on the hooks. It was such a motley gathering of black bass that as I released the lucky pair and returned them to their home, I felt encouraged. Working slowly down stream I drew a two-pounder from under a rock and had quite an exciting tussle in keeping him away from the numerous large rocks in the stream.

Another cast behind the same rock brought a double of about the same weight. I coaxed them to within ten feet of the bank when one tried an upstream route and the other, just as determined, frantically plunged down stream. Unfortunately, a small boulder of flint, peering a inch above water, obstructed the leader. The up stream fish gave a leap and took with him the second dropper fly. As chance would have it, the other fish seemed content to use open water for his battle, finally to yield

In Quest of the Red-eyes

gracefully to the persuasions of my tackle.

I left the stream for a moment on account of its narrowing and numerous obstructions, but eventually turned back to a broad stretch of water. It was fairly fast, and I should judge eight or ten feet in depth.

Many good size fishes were caught invariably on the trailer. The dropper, during the combat, was attacked by hundreds of smallmouth not over six inches in length. It proved to me conclusively that in March the bass were making the run of the smaller waterways of the mountains. By noon I had fifteen fish averaging from a pound and a half to four pounds and saw that all the muscle I put to crowding them in the creel could not make it contain more. Nevertheless this would prove sufficient for the family and myself. I wandered on through the sugar camps, finally to a confluence of creeks, climbed a ridge, descended and found my boat.

I had discovered in my contests with the Big Creek smallmouth that the light rod I carried was entirely out of place here. The fish were such gallant fighters, the stream so promiscuously strewn with sharp boulders that I had lost many, as in the limited fighting territory frequently I could not turn them quickly enough from dangerous quarters. But I had no complaint to make; I had fully enjoyed the day and now was anxious to see my intrepid little patient.

Jessie greeted my arrival as he accepted the heavy creel: "We sure will have plenty of fish; they ain't none of them trout caught here unless we gig 'em. My leetle chap feels mighty pert since you fixed him up."

The little one just then peeped from the doorway and I advised him that it was time to renew the dressing on his hand. Again the youngster exhibited his bravery, this time scarcely flinching while I bathed the wound.

"Did you meet anyone?" asked the father.

"No. Why?"

"Some of the boys planned to go out tonight and gig some

In Quest of the Red-eyes

fish if you didn't ketch enny, but I 'lowed you might meet someone."

"No, I passed through the sugar country and saw no one."

"I'll blow the horn, then they'll know you ketches enough, and as thems plenty fur all, I'll have the McIntyre boys over fur supper."

Little Jessie had become very much attached to me, and while seated near the fire found my knee an irresistible seat. He was a charming child, intelligent and promised much under other associations. The MacIntyres came for supper, shook hands, asked about the boy, and the hard uncommunicativeness of their kind mellowed under the warming influence of Jessie's attitude to me.

"If you'll only fish at the lower end of them little rock dams you seen on Big Crick, I'm sure you'd get some crackerjacks," offered the older of the visitors, who spoke for the first time. "While down at my sugar trees the other day I seen some whoppers a-jumping."

I had wondered to myself during the day the wherefore of the innumerable dams on the short stream; two or three to each mile, so I interposed. "What's the reason for so many dams on the stream? It seems to me rather out of the way for much grinding to be done."

McIntyre blushed visibly, but finally managed to say not without exhibiting suspicion at the purport to my question: "Ah!" I guess a person can set a mill near water if they wants to, and them that wants to grind can do it when they pleases."

I shifted subjects at once, for inadvertently I had blundered on an occupation of the natives that was quite risky to make mention of. At least, if circumstantial evidence was to be considered, indications of activity in the mountain dew way were in evidence on many sides. But as I had no interest other than curiosity, I subsided into another lead. However, my faux pas went unnoticed, and we parted good friends.

My last morning found me on the stream. Great banks of

89

In Quest of the Red-eyes

clouds hovered threateningly in the east. The lessons of the day before had been of some service. So as not to be bothered with the smaller fishes as I had been the day before, I placed my faith in the superior powers of the black gnat. Stepping cautiously along the rocky bank I placed my first cast below the fall of an old dismantled dam. Nothing came; again and again I worked along the decaying timbers, perfectly bound up in the estimate, that no place could be more promising without results. Stepping below a rock that jutted midstream some ten feet from the dam, I cast upstream, the flies glancingly scraped the rock, then dropped lifelessly on the water. Just as I began a quick recovery there came from under the huge boulder a flash of gleaming bronze, hurling itself with fury at the dropper. It seized it at the first rush and dashed fiercely with it down stream, until it gained the opener water which was free from obstructing boulders and logs.

I had no conception of its size. Suddenly from out the water as it felt the first inhibitive prick of barbed steel it leaped for freedom, and to my eyes came through the haze of morning a momentary vision of one of the largest smallmouth I had ever seen. He plunged for the opposite bank where a few logs offered release. Luckily he turned hastily as one of the MacIntye boys happened at the moment to pass on his visit to his sugar trees, and realizing the danger to my tackle began shaking a willow on the bank. the fish saw it and tried to bore for the deep water. This put me at my wits' end, for they have a peculiar habit when hooked to making gyrating dives for the bottom, if perchance, as there usually is, some obstruction offers an opportunity for escape. Nevertheless, I gained confidence. Finding that I had open water nearly all of the way down stream, the creek fairly wide, I could risk roughing it with him if I could only deter him from charging to the bank opposite me.

Unsuccessful with his diving experiments he went into a series of spectacular leaps, but between each, shaking and tear-

In Quest of the Red-eyes

ing of the line with the relentless determination of an infuriated bulldog.

The Ozarker shouted as the fish lunged for the first rapid: "If he gets in that swift water, he's sure a goner!"

"No," I replied with confidence, "he'll go straight through, and I'm going with him." True to my words, as I saw I could not check his strong rush, I leaped in the water as he gained the first riffle. I could feel the strain ease some and thought possibly the line had been severed. I began to reel slowly, then I knew the cause as the giant broke water once more. He had backed into one of those upstream currents and I was only too glad for the rest of my hand. He took the swift water again, and

In Quest of the Red-eyes

with chilled limbs I followed in is wake. Occasionally he attempted a frantic upstream effort, but the current favored not.

Finally he dove for another deep pool and the gyrating dives were again begun with desperate intensity. But the little rod responded nobly, and McIntyre on the bank, shouting inarticulate orders and gesticulating wildly, assisted me greatly in turning him from the brushy bank. The fish eased slightly as I took the bank, for the stream was now too deep for another rapid--a very short one. I permitted him to back slowly into the quiet pool. I could perceive that his rushes were weaker and he made them in heartlessly small circles. Now it was my turn at the initiative.

I gave him a taste of roughing it until he went into a succession of feeble leaps, then I coaxed him into a smooth eddy where the bronze warrior backed reluctantly into the landing net, his red eyes flashing belligerent lights.

McIntyre came to me and I held my hand out to him, and he, accepting it, was the first to speak: "That sure was some fighting, wasn't it?"

"You bet!" I explained. "If it had not been for you on the other side frightening him from the bank I never would have landed him; he was so strong I simply couldn't turn him."

"He'll weight six pounds sure as a fiddle," announced my friend admiring my prize. "He's certainly a son of a gun of a yaller bass!"

"Any way, I have had the experience of my life. I will present him to you, but I want you to tack his head up an save it for me," I said.

Mack smiled all over, and after urgent solicitations accepted my gift. I afterward learned from a card sent to me by the recipient that the fish weighed five and a quarter pounds and was twenty-one and a half inches in length.

With the capture of the big fellow the black gnat lost its potency. Finally after offering several deceits with only ordinary success I gave my old favorite, silver doctor, a chance to

In Quest of the Red-eyes

display its effectiveness. That it had attractive powers was immediately proven. In a short time the weight of my creel drove me to the Jessie homestead. Even if it had not, the ominous growlings of a near thunder storm would have hastened me to shelter. I had only gained the west side of Current River when the storm lashed forth in all its fury, and by the time I reached the warm fireplace I was soaked to the skin.

I borrowed clothes from the head of the house, though they could easily contain two of my frame. I felt comfortable and remained before the radiant fireplace watching my garments pouring a cloud of steam throughout the restrictions of the room, and knowing well that the terrific downpour of rain would ruin the fishing for a week or more. Still my mind reverted longingly to the small stream hidden in the hills, and I sensed that the lure of its pleasures was so strong upon me the another try at the red-eyes of Big Creek would follow soon.*

*In writing the article, I have purposely withheld from giving the name of my host, Jessie; as he is a rather dangerous animal and the valley is full of lawless feudists, I would not care to have some of your readers run in there for a trip and meet with disaster. That district has been noted for its monthly killings of the most cold-blooded kinds.

I think you will be pleased to learn that I secured conviction of the notorious duck shipper in the Sunken Lands, DeLisle Godair, for attempting to ship 100 woodducks. This has about cleaned up the last shipper on the Missouri side of the big overflow.

7 CURRENT RIVER COUNTRY

There isn't much doubt that float-fishing in the Ozarks began on the Current river. That is, the practice of using hand-made wooden boats to travel downstream fishing the shoals and eddies as you went. The boats were often made right on the river, used one time and left where ever the fishing trip ended. They were crudely made, but began the pattern for the type of float-boats which were to become known throughout the Midwest. They ranged from 20 to 26 feet in that day, though not much wider than today's shorter johnboats. According to old accounts, the 'upper river' johnboats, those used above Van Buren and in the Jacks Fork tributary, had a rake of six feet on the end, while 'lower river' boats had eight feet of rake. And often, the men who built the boats handled them, paid by city clients who wanted to fish.

That likely began ten or fifteen years after the civil war, maybe even before, whenever people came to the region who could use fly-rods, and therefore make casts from a boat. The Current was, after all, the earliest settled of the rivers, and there were records of recreational activities there because in the late 1800's, hunting and fishing lodges were formed which accounted for trips taken by members.

Those accounts are colorful and revealing. The Carter County Fishing and Shooting Club was founded in 1888 by four Springfield, Missouri men who were officials of the Frisco RR. They built a clubhouse seven miles south of Van Buren while they were building the Willow Springs-Grandin Railroad Branch which skirted the Current for many miles. Their Clubhouse sat on a bluff near Van Buren.

This is the Carter County Club House about the turn of the century. Notice the two turkeys hanging from porch posts. Photo provided by Larry Kester.

At one time there was a total membership of about 80. Members made a habit of signing in and recording their catches. This practice continued for more than forty years, until 1930. Many poled upstream, but a 1907 railroad spur crossing the Jacks Fork for moving timber enabled fishermen to move their boats on railroad cars.

On Sept 23, 1892 the four founders of the Carter County

Current River Country

Club, G.W. Horton, C.B. McAfee, Col. H.W. Diggins and Lewis Sutter, and seven companions recorded a two and a half day catch of 452 fish, stating the average of 16 1/2 fish per man per day to be "the best on record". It is likely they are only recording the fish they kept, because that's not a lot of fish to be caught in one day. That is reinforced by the fact that Colonel Diggins and his company reported 21 bass on Sept. 19 and the smallest was said to have been 2 3/4 pounds. Surely there were smaller fish caught and released. But you can't help but wonder if the fishermen of that time were like fishermen today. Maybe there were lot's of 2 and 1/2 pound bass which got rounded off to 3 pounds. Diggins and Horton reported 36 jack salmon (walleye), ten bass, five eels, (see page 238 for more about eels) one goggle-eye and one dogfish in April of 1896.

Eleven years later, on Sept. 7, 1907, four sportsmen from Carthage Mo left the following record at the lodge...

"Log train from Winona to Jack's Fork, beginning Monday through Saturday, caught 175 bass with ten grandpa's weighing three pounds each. E.B. Jacobs had two doubles, one three pounds and one two pounds. Bill Logan caught the largest black bass taken from the river in the last four years. It was a smallmouth caught on a four and a half Skinner spoon and weighed four pounds, seven ounces."

And there were reports on other activities besides fishing. In 1890 a club member reported an on-the-river poker game as such... "Largest game ever known...$200 to sit in, $5 ante, largest loser $1,025, largest winner $1,764."

The club was visited by state legislators and a Governor. One politician left these remarks on June 17, 1920. "Stopped at Van Buren and learned that Harding and Coolidge had been nominated.. Hurrah!"

According to the records, sometimes timber being rafted down the river would create a jam-up and the Current would remained blocked for some time. Until a big flood washed it out, or until some of the jams were dynamited, floaters would

97

Current River Country

have to carry around the jam and with these heavy boats, it was tremendous work through the brush or over gravel bars up to 50 to100 yards.

Sometimes the fishing wasn't all that great. Six Springfield men, reported this June 14, 1893 trip from Klipsink(?) Mill on Jacks Fork: "Tipped over twice on snags. No fault of any except Fairbanks and Culley who were never too good as lookouts. Lost one rifle, two shotguns, fishing tackle, 6 gallons of whiskey. We will go home tomorrow as we are out of whiskey."

In June of 1902, there was this report. "A true fish story - come down from Round Springs and caught nothing. River in no condition due to rains."

In 1946 The Missouri Conservationist Magazine analyzed the reports of the Carter County Fishing and Hunting Club and come up with the following comparisons.

"From 1891 to 1900 the average good day of fishing on the Current yielded 13.5 fish. From 1901 to 1910 the average dropped 45 percent to 7.3 fish per day. From 1911 to 1920 that average rose again...8.8 percent fish per day. From 1920 to 1930, the average dropped drastically to 5.9 fish per day.

In November of 1890 a writer identifying himself as one of a group of 17 "Warrensburg Nimrods", floated down the Current and into the Black River to Pocahontas, AR. The writer stated that Mr. Carter, the father of Carter County, met them at Van Buren and built boats there on the bank, one being a six by 32 flat barge.

The party had all types of mishaps, as many members lost guns and gear and comfort. In the entire account, only one deer was killed, and the party lived more on squirrels and fish than anything else. The difficulty of the trip resulted in six of the men quitting and walking out to find civilization and any way home they could find.

One part of his account was especially amusing. He wrote, "Occasional dunkings were all fruitful source of much fun, and

Current River Country

the last one was no exception to the rule in spite of our sorrow that Griggs lost his splendid new gun in the incident.

The rest of the day would have been largely uneventful had not Dode Caldwell and Matt Brown mistook a black calf in a cane break for a black bear and shot at the poor thing vigorously. It was fortunate for them that they missed it, for the owner --an old woman-- was standing in the door of her cabin not far away."

Reading about the Current River doesn't give you any comprehension of what it really is. I'm not going to go about trying to compare rivers here because I don't know that the White, in it's day before the dams, had any equal, and there is nothing greater than the 300 mile Gasconade, with the Big Piney river as it's sidekick. But on a scale of one to ten, the Current river is also a twenty. And it is what it is because of the springs which make it. The Current, the Jacks Fork and Eleven Point are all sort of birds of a feather, sister streams which are very very similar. But it is the Current River which carries the volume, and gets the most attention.

The two largest springs in the state of Missouri are found on the Current, (Big Springs flowing an average of about 280 million gallons of water per day) and the Eleven Point, (Greer Springs, flowing about 250 million gallons per day). In fact, Big Springs average gallons output per year makes it the second biggest spring in the U.S. While most of the large springs in the Current River system and on the Eleven Point were used to power grist mills, Big Springs is preserved in the Ozark Scenic National Riverways completely natural and without any structures. If you have not seen it, you need to visit it, because it is unbelievable in its beauty. I can sit for hours and look down at the bubbling boiling springs, so blue it is difficult to imagine the color unless you see it. Like other springs, it has a mesmerizing effect, if you look into the crystal clear waters long enough.

Just as beautiful in another way are the two big springs

Current River Country

where grist mills were built and still remain, operated as historic sites at Montauk Springs, which is actually the very beginnings of the Current, and Alley Springs which contributes about 81 million gallons of water to the Jacks Fork, about 13 miles above the point where it joins the Current.

On the Big Piney, where I grew up, the biggest spring on the river is Boiling Springs, not all that far west of Montauk Springs. The Current river originates and flows southerly, while the Big Piney flows in a northerly direction, with a high ridge of ground between them. The Piney and other Ozark streams have a number of springs of course, but nothing close to the size of the dozens of huge springs along the Current, Jacks Fork and Eleven Point. The difference in these two river systems, which are only separated by a few miles as the crow flies, is remarkable. And yet there are so many things which make them alike as well. To the west edge of the Ozarks, springs are few, and small, but to the east edge, the springs are many and magnificent. While springs produce about 60 percent of the summer flow of the Current and Jacks Fork and Eleven Point, the Big Piney and Gasconade probably have only about 30 to 40 percent of its water originating from springs in the summer. In northwest Arkansas, the Ozarks streams may receive only 10 or 20 percent of their flow from springs.

The early settlers to the Ozarks were no doubt drawn to center around the springs, and the grist mills which were built there were centers of activity all through the 1800's and early 1900's. And there were six sawmills on the Current River valley before 1860, powered by dams on creeks which fed the river.

Writers Henry Schoolcraft and George Featherstonhaugh, described crossing the river between 1820 and 1835 in scows or on flat ferries. They first described 20 to 30 foot dugout canoes, and then before 1850 a plank built gigging canoe. The first of the johnboats in the Ozarks, whatever they were called, or whatever they looked like, were built there on the current between 1835 and 1850, from boards sawed from those early

100

Current River Country

sawmills.

There was a small trading post-store at the mouth of the Jacks Fork by 1850. The first of the white settlers beginning coming to the Current River country just after the Louisiana Purchase, which included the Ozarks, in 1803. At that time, there were said to be Osage Indians to the west, but no Indians of any concentrations in the Current river valley. Then eastern tribes began to move into the area.

I am going to resist the temptation to go into detail about the immigration of the Cherokee, Delaware, Choctaw and Shawnee Indians to the region, and the difficulties arising from that, even though it is extremely fascinating, as is the record of the first settlers and how they lived. You may find all of that in another book, and I recommend that if you are interested in the history of the Current River Country you obtain it and read it. It is entitled "A Homeland and a Hinterland", written by a National Park Service Historian, Donald L. Stevens and so full of interesting information I couldn't put it down once I started it. It is a large book with about 250 pages of fascinating detail as to the history of the river and and the region around it, with lots of maps and old photos. The book sells at the NPS headquarters of the Ozark National Scenic Riverways in Van Buren Missouri for $7.00 at the time of this writing, and it is a bargain. There is tremendous detail of all aspects of the Current, from ancient times to the mid 1900's, and there are numbers of old photos which show all the aspects of early life in the current river valley, and indeed, the photos are worth thousands of words.

From that book I learned that the first decades of the 1800's saw several immigrations of eastern Indian groups, but about half the Indian population was said to be Shawnee. They seemed to get along with white settlers fairly well, but not so much with each other. Then during the war of 1812 they stopped fighting amongst each other and sided with the British.

The first folks to come into that section of the Ozarks were

101

Current River Country

predominantly Scotch-Irish, hard working but volatile people from the Appalachians of Kentucky and Tennessee, and the Carolinas. Historian Will Sarvis wrote of them...."They came from the Southern Appalachians.... Irish, southern Scottish, northern English ethnic stock....The cultural traits of these peoples included a strong sense of independence, low rates of formal education, adherence to a mostly Baptist sect, and a warrior mentality that manifested itself in a tendency toward combativeness."

The first white Settler to the region was said to be Isaac Kelley, who came about 1805 and began to trade with the Indians. He developed a farm along the river above Van Buren, and Zimri Carter, after whom Carter county was named, built a farm across the river from Kelleys. Two other early settlers to the area were Thomas Boggs Chilton and William Ashley. Ashley came from St. Louis in 1814 and discovered an abundance of saltpeter in caves at the Currents headwaters. In one of them, known as Ashley Cave, he mined large quantities of saltpeter and developed a lucrative gunpowder industry. Within ten years he branched off into fur, developing a new method of fur trapping which helped him to become prominent in economics and politics.

The Current River country was ravaged by the civil war. It wasn't so much the conflict created between confederate and union armies which clashed all through Southern Missouri and Northern Arkansas. Most of the suffering was created by a lawless element of guerrillas, ambushers and bushwhackers. Political rivals killed each other, and many innocent people as well. Most of the bushwhackers and guerrillas were southern sympathizers, and those who favored the Union were in for hard times, In fact it continued well after the war ended. You can read all about that difficult time in the book "Homeland and Hinterland" which goes into great detail about the civil war years in Current River country.

After the war, the building of railroads and railroad spurs

Current River Country

contributed to the mass clearing of forests in the valleys of the Current, the Jacks Fork and the Eleven Point. From what I have read, and photos I have seen, the 1800's turned one of God's greatest creations, and one of the most beautiful regions in the entire Midwest, into a ravaged land. Mining and timber cutting interests did what they wanted, and the Current River and it's watershed, including that of the Jack's Fork and Eleven Point was laid to waste, huge sections denuded of pine and oak timber, the steep ground eroding with seasonal rains.

The worst of it took place between 1880 and 1920, in Carter and Shannon counties. In 1890 the largest sawmill west of the Mississippi was at Grandin, MO which was turning out 285,000 board feet of lumber per day."

Writing in the 1946 Missouri Conservationist, Charles Callison said, "The timber was removed as clean from the land as if cut by a giant scythe, and then afterward the hills were burned annually, turned into farmlands, overgrazed and plowed, laying the land bare to erosion. Millions of tons of topsoil and then the underlying layer of gravel swept down the hillsides and into the streams destroying the spawn, the habitat and the food."

In 1870, there were 23 steam operated lumber mills in the region producing five and half million board feet of lumber that year. In 1880, there were 47 mills producing more than 40 million board feet of lumber. In 1871, a group of Pennsylvania lumbermen and investors purchased 30,000 acres of timberland in Carter County for one dollar per acre.

No one who sees the Current today can ever understand the way it was before 1850, but there are places now protected within the boundary of the Ozark National Scenic Riverways where you can see maturing timber in tracts of land which might resemble the way it was 200 years ago. But the river will never look as it did back then, because there has been so much filling with gravel washed from the hills around it.

By 1920 it became apparent that if some people had their

103

Current River Country

way, it would have been buried beneath a series of dams. The state of Missouri established 8 state parks in the early 20's, and three of them were the well-known springs on the Jack's Fork and Current, Round Springs first encompassing all of 75 acres, then Alley Springs including 425 acres, and then Big Springs, a whopping 4,258 acres.

In the 1930's, much of the bedraggled, scalped, and scarred forestlands of the Current and Eleven Point were placed under the management of the National Forest Service, 44 percent of Carter County, 35 percent of Ripley and 19 percent of Shannon became National Forestland. During the depression, the National Forest Service established Civilian Conservation Camps, one of the best things which ever happened to Ozark country parks in both southern Missouri and north Arkansas. CCC workers built some of the most lasting and picturesque walls, trails, buildings and camping areas ever seen in the Ozarks, many, indeed most, lasting today inside the state and national parks of this region. Another depression era attempt at putting men to work in the Midwest was known as the Works Progress Administration. Thousands of forest workers in the Current River and Eleven Point river valleys built roads, and replanted forests under the direction of the WPA.

The first threat of dams on the Current and Jack's Fork came from private power companies. By 1930, private companies had built Bagnell dam on the Osage River, and Powersite Dam on the White River. In 1933, the Kansas City Power Company received a license from the Federal Power Commission to survey the Current for three power-producing dams. About that same time, Congress authorized the Corps of Engineers to build fifty dams in the state. It was becoming apparent that if the dam builders had their way, the Current, Jack's Fork and Eleven Point would be buried forever.

In 1941, Wapappello Dam was built on the St. Francis river, and the Corps turned its attention to the Current, with plans for two huge dams, one at Blair Creek and one at Doniphan.

104

Current River Country

A crew of Civilian Conservation Corp workers in the 1930's begin construction on roads and rock walls at Alley Springs. NPS Photo.

Current River Country

Perhaps only World War II kept that from happening, but after the war, stiff resistance began to build. Governor Forrest Smith threw in his opposition with this statement in 1949...."There are streams with natural attributes which, in their total, are so unique as to warrant their preservation simply because they are unique....it is apparent the Current River is such a stream. The state contends that the reservoirs would not be justified under any circumstance."

In 1950, the Corps dropped it's plans to dam the Current, and as early as the 1950's people began to talk about ways to protect the stream. In 1960, the National Park Service proposed making the three rivers a part of the National Park System. There was friction between the Forest Service and Park Service, naturally. The National Forest Service wanted to see the water-shed opened to logging and the Park Service would preserve those forests.

In the book "Homeland to Hinterland" those years of strug-gle to determine the future of the Current River country are well documented, with tremendous detail as to who sided with who, and what a divisive battle it became. Something of a compro-mise was reached. The Eleven Point would remain under the jurisdiction of the National Forest Service under the Wild and Scenic Rivers Act, and most of the Jack's Fork and Current would become the Ozark National Scenic Riverways, about 80,000 acres of watershed under the jurisdiction of the National Park Service. President Lyndon Johnson signed the legislation on the Current in 1964, and congress passed the legislation on the Eleven Point in 1968.

That protection ended the uncontrolled burning of the forests, the free-ranging hogs and cattle, and the building of pri-vate roads and structures. It did, in fact, make the future of the river somewhat brighter, in that generations to come will be able to see the flowing water, the forests, springs, caves and wild creatures something like it all might have been hundreds of years ago. But it created what is known as mass recreation,

Current River Country

and opened the river to thousands upon thousands of people who prove through their actions that they do not deserve to enjoy what has been preserved for them. Perhaps it is because most of them live so far from a natural world they do not understand it...perhaps it can be chalked up to ignorance, but it becomes apparent, where ever you see these thousands of suburban visitors descend on any river, whether it is the Current, the Niangua, the Buffalo, or others where canoe outfitters come to make their fortune, that they are there to get wet and get drunk and the faster they can go with the current the better. Some of them seem to be hordes of living creatures without souls. They have no outdoor skills, no outdoor knowledge, no love and no appreciation. They have no understanding, and most of all, they have no reverence. And that is the one thing that hurts the most. Those masses have learned something in their lives wherever they come from which goes against the grain of those of us who love this land and these rivers....they live their lives motivated by quantity, with little thought of quality, and they are less concerned with what they leave for others than what they take.

The river might look the same as it once was, but for hardened, barren ground where countless feet have trod, but for the eroded muddied ground where ATV's marred the river and the banks, but for the shiny trail of aluminum beer cans, but for the litter and toilet paper on every gravel bar. And it might sound the same, but for the bang of canoes, the loud shrieks of the throngs who drift with the current, and the roar of the motors which ascend the river against it. But I know all people who come to see this magnificent river are not like that. Some come in reverence and respect, admiration and awe. Some take with them the refuse others have left. Some are here and gone, unnoticed. Some fit this river and this land, some find the treasure hidden here which few others ever know about. But they are not many, and they are growing fewer each year.

It would not do to end this chapter without giving credit to

Current River Country

those who have been a part of the Current river and passed on. One of them was a politician, but had to be something different than what we consider politicians to be today. His name was David Bales, a State Representative from Eminence who was elected to the State Senate in 1930. He was a leader in creating state parks at Alley, Round and Big Springs as a Representative, and a staunch advocate of conserving and preserving the river. When private power companies began to plan dams on the Current, Bales introduced legislation to regulate them in 1933 as a Senator.

Bales son, Walter, began a johnboat guided float-fishing business in 1927, operating on the Jacks Fork from his store at Eminence, but offered deluxe guided trips on the White, the Eleven Point, the North Fork, Current and Buffalo. He called his business the Bales Boating and Mercantile Company. But in a spring flood that year, he lost all of his johnboats, and had to start anew in 1928. One of his guides, Tommy Rowlett, built a dozen new ones. Both Walter and David Bales were ahead of their time as far as conservation consciousness, and writer Leonard Hall quoted Walter Bales as saying, "A fish in the stream has a value equal to or greater than one on the stringer." It is said he switched from bait fishing gear and large treble hooks to fly-fishing equipment and single hook, just to allow the release of fish he caught back into the stream in a healthy state. Walter Bales died in an auto accident in 1950, but the Bales Boating and Mercantile company was kept going by family members until 1964. Many of the guides who began their own businesses on the Current started with Walter Bales.

Leo Drey, a St. Louisian and noted conservationist, was said to be the largest landowner in all of Missouri, and he had 130,000 acres in Shannon, Reynolds and Carter Counties. He had 35 miles of river frontage on the Jacks Fork and Current, which he managed to stabilize the watershed. Drey managed timber through selective cutting and transplanting, and identified and preserved certain natural areas. He loved the rivers

108

Current River Country

and he loved floating, and he never cut trees along the streams. But he opposed the National Park Service plan for the Current and Jacks Fork because he felt that the influx of huge numbers of visitors would ruin the stream. Drey said often that the wilderness was gone forever, and what the streams could offer was "the illusion of wilderness" and should be used to afford that as best as possible through the multiple use plans the National Forest Service wanted. Drey always was a supporter of the National Forest Service, and opposed strongly the setting aside of the river systems for management as a National Park.

Leonard Hall, a writer and naturalist was a friend of Drey who originally agreed with his perspective, but later changed his mind and supported the National Park Service idea of single purpose management. He believed, as many did and still do today, that with the National Forest Service might tout multiple use, but when it came down to it, their main goal would be the building of logging roads and the harvesting of timber first and foremost, and recreation and preservation, and fish and wildlife management would come only when it didn't interfere with the production of board feet of lumber. Hall eventually changed his mind about the National Park Service when he began to under-stand what mass recreation would do to the waterways. In 1958, Hall wrote a book entitled "Stars Upstream" which con-cerned a float trip on the Current River, and he gained promi-nence as the book became increasingly popular as a tool to pro-tect the river. Hall and his wife moved from St. Louis to a farm near Caledonia, Mo. in 1945 and began to live off the land as much as possible, raising garden produce and chickens and cat-tle, keeping bees and other farm animals. In 1958 he wrote that Ozarkians were the best of people and the areas most valuable resource. But he changed his mind about that also as he grew older, and saw how much local people objected to preserving the river.

In 1960 he said that Ozark people had too many self inter-ests which would keep them from ever wanting to preserve the

Current River Country

river. He stated that he believed they were too ignorant to appreciate the aesthetic properties of the river. He wrote, "Regardless of their competence as canoemen, they know too little about ecology, conservation, and the economics of the region to discuss these matters with much intelligence, and will have to be discounted in any serious planning for the region."

He went on to say that the local people had known little else but destructive farming and forestry practices, and had a conviction that the world owed the area a livelihood through subsidies. He came to believe that mass recreation for the Current River and it's tributaries was a poor option, but the only one which could save the streams and the watershed.

Ozark National Scenic Riverways superintendent Art Sullivan, who served in that capacity from 1976 to 1995, once said after leaving his post, "It was so difficult to get anything done, particularly seeing that there was always a small core of local people that would object to any plan that the Park Service would come up with."

A long time Park Service employee, Alex Outlaw, said it best perhaps... "To me, a lot of things could have been resolved, all the way down the line, from the first superintendent (a controversial figure) on down to the horses and the trapping and the motor boats, if they had just had a meeting of the minds, and had communicated, and tried to understand each other. Everybody was trying to be understood, but they were just all talking, and no one was listening."

It's not hard to understand what the problem is.....so many millions of people, so small the treasure. Everyone wants something different from the river and the land, and there just isn't enough of it. When hundreds of people swarm to a patch of beautiful wildflowers, how does the wildflower survive the descending rush. How even, does the grass keep from withering and dying from the weight of the intended good attention. Until some time in a distant future when mankind becomes wise enough to control his numbers, or until nature does it for him, there will never be less timber, less water, fewer resources, to go around. And no matter where the river is found, or where it flows, it will not hold all the canoes that are to come. It is a rarity, a precious stone, because so many like it which we once had, have been buried beneath dams, or muddied, or tainted with poisons and toxins and wastes. In some manner, we saved the Current, and the Buffalo, and a few others.

But we saved too few.

8
GIGGERS AND TIE RAFTERS

Gigging has always been a popular method of taking fish from Ozark streams, both for recreation and for profit. But in the Current and Jacks Fork, it was always bigger than anywhere else, and still is. Before laws were established to make the taking of game fish illegal and outlawing the sale of fish taken by gigging, it was a method used to produce income for river families in the Midwest. As far as the Ozarks is concerned, gigging certainly originated on the Current and Jacks Fork, with the migrant Delaware and Shawnee Indians who brought the art of spearing fish, and shooting fish with arrows, from their Eastern lands. The Indians used long, sturdy arrows made from secondary growth hickory or ash or even cane, each with only a single spike point.

In the early part of the 20th century, bow-gigging was still very popular, and rivermen in Current River country were forging metal points with two or three tines, attaching them to arrows up to six feet long, and shooting them into fish with strong bows which they fashioned themselves. The practice of bow-gigging was outlawed in the mid thirties, and shortly afterward, all gigging was regulated by the newly formed Missouri

Giggers and Tie Rafters

Conservation Commission, restricted to the winter months and allowed only at night.

It was the wooden johnboat which made gigging so popular. The boats were built long and stable, and a man could stand in one and do all sorts of work without capsizing. Gig makers, men who could forge the multi-tined gigs became well known in the 20's and 30's. They made gigs out of several kinds of metal, but old auto springs became the most popular material. Handles on those gigs might be 18 or 20 feet long, and the gig itself was so strong, they were often used to pole the boats upstream. Some giggers got so good at what they were doing they could actually throw a gig at a fish in the outer glow of the lights, and consistently hit their target. Cords around the arms were attached to the gig handles.

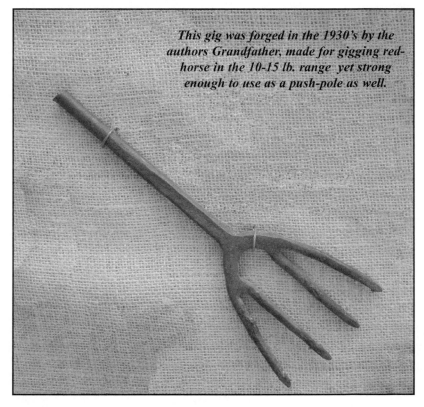

This gig was forged in the 1930's by the authors Grandfather, made for gigging redhorse in the 10-15 lb. range yet strong enough to use as a push-pole as well.

Giggers and Tie Rafters

The light needed to see into the deep clear water came from burning pine knots in the early days, and eventually carbide lamps mounted to the boat and directed toward the water, shielded from the giggers eyes. When pine knots were burned, they were usually held out away from the boat by heavy wire baskets or metal baskets made from wagon rims, attached to the boat. Sometimes clay was used on the johnboat floor to keep any falling embers from burning the bottom.

Johnboats on the Current were indeed used for fishing, for trapping, for hunting and just crossing the river, but they were of no more value for any of those things than they were to the gigger. And certainly, in those days there were many johnboat builders. One who was especially well known was Ed Murray, who made a number of them spanning 40 or 50 years.

I spent some time talking to Ed Murray's son, Cecil Murray about the Current River. Born in 1940, Cecil is not one of the old-time rivermen, but he is one of the last of the johnboat makers, and proud of the precise measurements and carpentry that goes into the boats he makes, which may take four to six days of work to complete.

Giggers and Tie Rafters

He acknowledges that the early johnboats were fairly crude, often built in one day right on the river where the fishing trip was to begin. Most weren't used more than a season or so, sometimes only for one three- or four-day trip. Cecil's grandfathers brother was John Murray, who lived on the river in a handmade boat house where he raised seven children, and whom some believe gave the wooden river boat the name of 'johnboat'. Cecil's father, Ed Murray, built a large number of the Current and Jacks Fork johnboats in the twenties, thirties and forties. They were certainly well-made, but with a lot less time involved, to be used for a few years and then replaced. Cecil recalls that most of them were from 18 to 24 feet long, and most were made to hold small motors of 5 horsepower, or to be poled or paddled. His uncle Earnest made a few johnboats and paddles as well, and Cecil talks highly of his uncle.

Building a Current River johnboat... Ed Murray far left, Cecil Murray center, and Ernest Murray far right, show apprentice Steve Cookson the techniques at a Columbia, Missouri arts program in 1993.

"Dad had a family to raise," Cecil told me, "long hours of work to keep everyone fed and clothed. But Uncle Ernest was single and I tagged around after him while he hunted and fished and taught me everything he knew. I learned so much from him, I just thought the world of my uncle. He made lots of paddles, but not as many boats as dad. The ones he did make he spent lots of time on them and did a very good job." Murray showed me an old paddle in his family collection, and a picture of his uncle in a johnboat with a small axe on his belt. "He made this paddle," he told me, "from a board he found on the river on a 1930's fishing trip...and from that axe on his belt."

Giggers and Tie Rafters

Cecil Murray with a sassafras set paddle under construction.

One of Ed Murray's old johnboats is on display at the Current River Museum in Doniphan, Mo. One of the area's foremost historians, Ray Joe Hastings, has assembled a very interesting museum of the area and the river people. There is a large number of old gigs to be seen there, and old handmade paddles, set paddles and pushpoles of all kinds. Also found in

Giggers and Tie Rafters

the museum is the fishing paraphernalia from the days of wooden johnboats, old pictures, plus items used by tie hackers and tie drivers, Indian artifacts and the items used 100 years or more ago by the river people of the Current River area.

Cecil Murray remembers a river and a way of life that todays generation will never completely understand, because the fifties, when he guided fishermen on the Jacks Fork and the Current, afforded some excellent fishing, and a secluded, quieter, more peaceful river than is possible to enjoy today.

"The National Park Service came out and asked me my opinions about the motors on the river," he told me. "And I told them that the high horsepower motors and the shoal-runners and jet boats are ruining the river, eroding the banks and destroying the spawn and creating all kinds of problems. A while after that one of the local boat and motor salesmen came out here mad as he could be. But a while back, I sat on the bank and counted 45 high-powered boats roaring past in 15 minutes. Where will that end?"

Murray says he stays off the river on week-ends during the summer. He says the people who come on week-ends are there to get wet and get drunk, and there is no hope of spending a few hours fishing until perhaps mid-week.

"I'll get back to the river in the fall, and that's when the fishing will get good again," he said. "Whenever it gets cool enough that people have to put on clothes to stay warm and it's too cool to get in the water, the crowds will stop."

Surprisingly, Murray isn't so excited about the walleye and bass fishing as he is the winter fishing for grass pickerel. "They get into the bays and sloughs in the fall and winter and I catch them on top-water lures, mostly bass-oreno's or large topwater rebels."

Grass pike are not found in the western Ozark streams, they are often found in the delta-type waters of flatter regions to the south and east. And usually, they aren't very big, averaging only a pound or so. But Murray says he catches some up to four

119

Giggers and Tie Rafters

pounds and has seen seven pounders in the Current. He also says that he has seen a gradual decline in bass and goggle-eye numbers, and that walleye fishing is best well down the river, near the Arkansas border.

He showed me some of the old paddles used on the river when he was a boy, something else you do not see on streams to the west. Set paddles, as they are called, are hand-made, and fitted with metal grabs on the bottom something like an oversized saw blade or a pair of spoon blades. They are used to hold the boat on underwater logs, or in gravel shoals where the cur-

From Cecil Murray's collection - an old tie-rafter's pike pole, left, a push-pole made by his uncle Ernest in the 1930's, center and a fifty year-old handmade sassafras set paddle, right.

Giggers and Tie Rafters

rent is swift.

Murray says that he guided mostly on the lower part of the river between Van Buren and Doniphan, beginning in the late 1950's. That was the beginning of the coming of motors to the Ozark streams. After World War II rivermen began to acquire 5 to 6 horsepower motors, and eventually 10 horsepower motors. Murray recalls taking fishermen upstream several miles by motor, then slowly fishing back downstream. The lower Current's size allowed that, as it now allows the 200 horsepower boats which have made any fishing difficult in the summer on those same waters.

The shoal runner boats have 350 cubic inch V-8 inboard motors, and they will swamp smaller johnboats and canoes at times. It is a far cry from what the Current was a hundred years ago. But in some ways, things are better. In the early 1900's, the entire valley was being systematically denuded by loggers and timber companies, cutting every stand of pine and oak they could get too, and the river made it easier to do.

Between 1880 and 1930, millions of logs and railroad ties were floated down both rivers to waiting sawmills or flatcars at Van Buren and Doniphan. Logs were cut from standing oaks into eight foot sections, and then tie hackers would use a broad axe to shape the logs into seven-by-nine or eight-by-eight inch railroad ties. They were marked by the tie hacker with his own mark, so that later he could be paid for them when they arrived at the loading yard. A good tie hacker could cut about thirty ties per day, and in the early years they were only being paid about 5 to 10 cents per tie. The price rose some in the twenties, but not by much. About the best money a tie cutter ever saw was 25 cents per tie. If he was really good, he was making about a dollar and fifty cents in the early 1900's and he could make about seven dollars a day in the mid to late twenties. It was dangerous work, because late in the day, when a man became tired, he might chop off a toe, or suffer a deep axe wound to the foot.

121

Photo - courtesy Moss Tie Company

When the ties cut in the winter were dried, and that was important because green oak ties tended to sink, they were placed together in blocks of maybe a dozen to two dozen ties, and nailed together by use of hickory poles or boards. When the rafts were formed, there might be enough of them to reach half mile down the river, and each raft, or block of ties, was connected to the one ahead or the one behind by a long green hickory pole nailed on each end so it would swivel.

Giggers and Tie Rafters

On the Current, some of the tie raft trains were said to be a half mile long. On the last block of ties there was a hickory snubbing post which stuck down into the water and dragged along the substrate, or into the gravel shoals to keep the long snaking tie raft slowed enough so that the back rafts didn't put pressure on the ones in front. On the front block of ties and also on the very back block, a long pole with a 12-or 15-inch board attached as a paddle or keel attached perpendicular to the water, was used to steer the floating snake of rafts to the middle of the river and away from the bank or in-stream obstacles. Other tie rafters spread out along the rafts using what is known as pike-poles to keep the whole procession going straight, and pry off of rocks or gravel bars along the way.

In the September 1990 issue of the Missouri Conservationist magazine, forester Robert Cunningham wrote about tie rafting on the Current. He said working on a rafting crew at its heyday earned a worker about 4 dollars per day, and it might take several days to work the raft of ties down the river. He said crews with camp gear followed the rafts in johnboats,

Giggers and Tie Rafters

setting up camp and preparing meals. At night, the tie raft train was secured, and at dawn the men were up and fed, and off again. On the Current, a raft of 1500 ties moved about 6 miles per day when the river was right, but on smaller streams like the Piney, the rafts were smaller, and the river slower, so to go from the upper reaches of the river all the way to Arlington may have covered fewer miles per day.

And then there were the log and tie drives, in which loose pine logs and oak ties were just floated down the river. On these drives, logs or ties were said to number in the hundreds of thousands, filling miles and miles of river.

When rains came which caused flooding, dangerous jams could develop. According to Cunningham's article, there was a jam of 35,000 ties in 1913 at a place known as Cardareva bluff on the Current.

He wrote...."Drives might average a little more than 1 mile per day. A crew of 12 drivers followed on horseback or in john-boats. It was the drivers perilous duty to break up any log jams. Equipped with pike poles and cant hooks, they climbed onto entangled timbers and careful picked the jam apart. Jams created dams across the river that held back volumes of water. When these jams broke, without warning, an explosive rush of water and timbers went down the river, sometimes taking the drivers lives with it."

At the end of the log or tie drive, timber companies stretched cable booms across the river to hold the logs until a steam operated tie puller winched them out. But if there was a rise, or more log jams at the take-out points, the booms could break and send thousands of timbers down the river. In 1902, 5,000 hewn oak ties broke free at a Van Buren loading yard and floated all the way down the river to Doniphan and further.

Cecil Murray's great uncle John, living on the river, made much of his income rounding up lost ties and pine logs and selling them back to the companies.

The number of logs and ties which came down the Current

Giggers and Tie Rafters

NPS Photo
Ozark National Scenic Riverways

river between 1900 and 1930 is unbelievable. The Smalley Tie Company average 200,000 ties taken via the river for several years, and in 1912, Ripley county accounted for 808,000 railroad ties. In 1915, railroad tie drives were limited to 50,000 by state law, and log drives were limited to 2,000 at a time. By 1919, the drives became illegal because of all the problems created by the free floating logs and ties which blocked fords and jammed the river, flooding property and becoming a hazard to those who crossed the river via wagon or horseback. After that time, all ties and logs had to be floated in connected rafts.

But public opposition to the rafts of logs and ties each summer was growing. In 1925, there was intense pressure from

Giggers and Tie Rafters

sportsmen who believed the tie rafts were destroying fish spawn. Indeed, the records kept by the Carter County Sportsman's club bore that out. According to their fishermen's accounts, there was an average of 14 fish per angler taken in 1890, 13 fish per day from '91 through '99, 9 per day between 1910 and 1920 and only 6 per day between 1920 and 1925.

Bowing to that pressure, fifteen major timber companies agreed to suspend all rafting between April 15 and June 1. But by that time, the timber along the Current river valley, was disappearing. There were no sizable stands of oaks and pines left. Steam powered sawmills which were becoming common in the Ozarks put an end to the tie-hacking by individuals. The ties could be cut faster and smoother at those mills.

And so, by 1930, the great drives of floating logs was pretty much over. The river began to recover, and the scalped hills of the Current river valley began to regrow trees. But still today, you can see scars down steep hillsides and bluffs where thousands of logs and ties were slid to the river, and there are old ruts where logging roads accommodated mules, horses and wagons bringing loads to the river.

On the Big Piney, there is a swift shoal where old ties have sunk, and the tips stick up to ruffle the surface. You must float between them when the river is low. They have been there for 85 years. In his article in the Missouri Conservationist, Robert Cunningham writes a suitable ending for this chapter......

"As a matter of fact," he wrote, "in the bottom of every deep hole on the Current River, sunken timbers, ('deadheads') still remain, as do stories of the perils of the log drives"

Giggers and Tie Rafters

An old Current River johnboat 25 - 30 foot long from the 1930's. NPS - photo

9
BUFFALO RIVER COUNTRY

In the early part of the twentieth century, Joe raised a family on a small tributary of the Buffalo. His folks moved here from Tennessee to a log cabin overlooking the creek. Joe was born in that cabin, and so were all his children.

They were his stomping grounds, the hills and creeks of the Buffalo River country. Joe built a johnboat or two, and he trapped the river and creeks when the winter was hard. He sold catfish and redhorse and buffalo and bass in local settlements. He hunted turkey and deer and bear to feed his family and to feed others who had better gardens and produce to trade. He saw fur prices drop to near nothing. He endured the coming of laws that closed commercial fishing on the streams. When the first city folks came to float and fish, he paddled his johnboat for them and overlooked their strange ways and contraptions.

Joe saw his children educated in a one-room school and, with pangs of resentment and helplessness, watched them leave one by one for jobs and money in the cities, and for husbands that could make more money than a wife confined to the hills could ever know. Eventually, he buried his wife on a little knoll overlooking the creek. Then he lived alone in the land he loved,

Buffalo River Country

the only life he knew. He was kin to the wild creatures which made the river home. Joe was a happy man. Life didn't give him much, but then "it didn't owe him nothin' in the first place." He wasn't one to mingle in other folks' affairs, or ask for help. If you came to see him, Joe was a hospitable neighbor. He'd serve venison or squirrel and fresh greens with coffee made from creek water, and he'd talk of the river and its ways and his experiences.

If Joe gave his word, you needn't doubt it. If a neighbor needed help, he'd be there. Uneducated and simple, he represented some things modern men have lost, or traded away.

Today his weathered cabin has collapsed, the shake shingle roof on the ground, covering the rubble. He is buried beside his wife on the timbered hill that overlooks the creek, and the graves are grown over, the headstones crooked and weathered. But the spirit of Old Joe will never leave the Buffalo. On cold winter nights, when there is stillness and solitude, one can imagine little has changed. But Joe would know it has.

Buffalo River Country

He would shake his head as hundreds of shiny canoes bang along, passing in erratic course beneath the sunny skies of each new day. He'd notice that more floaters leave litter, and that hamburgers are in the evening skillet much more often than fish.

But few people wander from the river, canoes don't leave tracks, and it's a sight better than summer homes and wave-washed lake shores. Joe would tell you that.

He would echo the feelings of a handful of hill people scattered along the Buffalo watershed who would side with no faction. Of the river he would advise, "Let 'er be fellers, she don't need no improvin' . . . just let 'er be, an' let 'er run free."

Joe's ancestors began building homes and clearing land along the Buffalo River during the early 1820's. They came from Tennessee, Kentucky, North Carolina, and Virginia for the most part, and they thought that no place they had seen or would see could equal the Buffalo River country.

J.V. Waters, was one of those kind of people. I interviewed him back in the early 80's for a newspaper article I was writing, and he was one of the nicest people I ever had the opportunity to write about. It was no wonder all of his neighbors spoke so highly of him. Mr. Waters told me he had always lived "within a stone's throw of the river." He was born not far from the banks of the Buffalo in 1906.

When the battle to save the Buffalo began back in the 1960's, many local people believed that a dam would be the best thing for the river. The newspaper editors and businessmen in the local communities of Marshall and Harrison didn't dwell much upon the issues. If a dam meant more money, and more jobs, they were for it.

"We didn't know back then that the good fishing on Norfork and Bull Shoals would go downhill so much," J.V. told me that evening at his home twenty-five years ago. "Those lakes were fairly new and fishing pressure wasn't too heavy then. We thought everything would be better with a lake, especially the

131

Buffalo River Country

fishing. Now I'm glad the Buffalo wasn't dammed."

Waters worked for the government (Soil Conservation Service) for eighteen years, so he was a little worried about what the National Park Service (NPS) could do to the river. He says there's quite a difference between the Buffalo of today and

Buffalo River Country

the one he knew as a boy.

"There were almost no deer, no turkey, and no coons, but we had more fish and lots of quail and rabbits. But the biggest change is in the people."

Waters could remember when the Buffalo supported everyone that lived along it. In the earlier part of the century, zinc and lead mines were common along the Buffalo, and during the 20's, thousands of cedar trees were cut and floated down the river to Gilbert during times of high water; where they were carried by train to the Eagle Pencil Company. The river was the center of commerce.

But the river also provided recreation, just as it does today. Even so, with more visitors and more floaters, the emphasis isn't as much on fishing now as it once was. And the fishing has changed. For instance, when J.V. Waters was a youngster, 1915 through 1930, largemouth were not common in the Buffalo.

"We called smallmouth 'trout' back then," he said, "and largemouths were bass. A local boy would have told you back then that the river was full of trout, but had very few bass in it." He said also that channel cat were rarely seen, if ever. Flathead were common, and you occasionally saw a blue cat in the river, which came up from the white.

Today largemouth bass are common, though smallmouth still outnumber them ten-to-one. And the Game and Fish Commission regularly stocked channel cat until the National Park Service asked them to stop in the 1980's, because they weren't sure if channel cat were a native fish. Waters told me that 60 years ago, the Buffalo had many times more fish than it does today.

"My father, when I was a boy, would get bass with his old muzzleloader by standing up on a small bluff and shooting them. You didn't have to hit the fish to kill it. Sometimes I'd throw small sticks or something onto the water, and fish would come up to see if it was something to eat, and-bang!"

Buffalo River Country

In those days, people living along the river did whatever they could do to catch fish. That included filling small eddies with walnut hulls, which poisoned them, and using traps of various kinds. One such trap, built by Waters' grandfather, was an elaborate affair so large that the remains could still be seen a few years ago, near Swindell Ford on the upper Buffalo, near Hasty.

Waters explained that his grandfather had built a dam out of huge boulders pulled into the water by oxen. Assisted by several men in the community, the dam was created at the head of a shoal to make a spillway. A large wooden basket was supported with timbers below the spillway, and the river poured through it. Fish came through the spillway and were trapped in the basket. The larger rocks of the dam are still intact today and probably always will be.

As with most streams, the Buffalo's eddies, shoals, and fords were named after local events or people. In years past, everyone along the river knew each spot by name. Swindell Ford was so named because a man named Swindell had tried to cross there during high water on horseback and was swept away and drowned. Nearby Lost Hill eddy was named because two children had been lost overnight on a hill overlooking the eddy. Most of the other places were given names according to the families who lived there.

Waters pointed out that in his boyhood days, more people lived along the river than at any time since. Families were close, coming to the aid of one another during hard times.

"At one time, almost every hole had one or two old, wooden boats tied to a tree somewhere," Waters said. "You had to keep them in the water so they'd stay soaked up. If they dried out, they'd leak. No one floated them very far. You would use them along a stretch of the river close to home."

Waters remembered, too, when the first reels and artificial lures came to the Buffalo. "Dad got a reel sometime in the 1920s from a Sears and Roebuck catalog. It wasn't much of a

134

reel. You couldn't cast with it. All you could do was play out line and sort of throw bait by hand," Waters said. "My brother made a cedar rod for it, with wire guides. The rod was pretty big around, and stiff. I was with dad when he first used it, throwing out a big fathead minnow and letting it drift down in by a big rock. The first fish he landed that way was a bass about four or five pounds."

While Waters believed that there were ten times more fish in the river when he was young, he told me that in the late 80's when I conducted the interview with him, there were as many big smallmouth then as there ever was. But certainly there were much fewer small ones, and fewer suckers, and rock bass and sunfish.

Rock Bass or Goggle-eye

Buffalo River Country

Waters began guiding on the White and the Buffalo during the early 1940's. His experiences taught him that most city folks, whether from St. Louis, Kansas City, or Dallas, were great people even though they were so much different than locals. So Waters lost much of the distrust that other Buffalo River people had for northerners.

Friendships often developed when northerners or "city folks" and Buffalo River people actually got to know one another. They gradually learned to accept that in the environment of the other, each was like a fish out of water. Too many times, outsiders came to Buffalo River country expecting the people to be ignorant and backward.

But in the ways of the hills and the river, Buffalo river natives were very wise. You had to get to know them to appreciate how efficient and capable they were. There are many ways to be smart and when a city sportsman spent some time on the Buffalo, he gained a great deal of appreciation for what the local people knew. Both sides began to see the wisdom in Will Rogers' statement: "We are all ignorant, only on different subjects."

It took some of the National Park Service people awhile to learn that. Much of the early friction between the National Park Service and the local people took place because the two sides didn't have much common ground. And when the Park Service sent in all it's new personnel to take over management of the newly formed Buffalo National River in the early 70's, they were a little bit belligerent. Even though J.V. Waters knew the name of every eddy on the Buffalo, and could have told them so much, no one even thought to talk with him.

When I interviewed him, he laughed about the time the Arkansas Game and Fish Commission magazine used a picture of him wading the Buffalo with a string of big smallmouth over his back. A National Park Service Ranger, not knowing who the fisherman was, told J.V. that he didn't think those fish came from the Buffalo. J.V. assured him that they did, and told him

Buffalo River Country

why he would know, much to the embarrassment of the ranger.

I worked a short time as a seasonal naturalist with the National Park Service just after they took over the management of the Buffalo. Their strengths and weaknesses were easy to see. When it came to planning and financing and managing a campground, they were ahead of everyone. The administrators with the NPS were intelligent and hard working, getting as much accomplished as anyone could ask for. But NPS people came to the Buffalo from all over the nation.

Coming from Pennsylvania, New York, Texas, and California, they understood little or nothing about the river and the people of the Ozarks, and didn't make much effort to learn. There was an elderly Ranger there at that time by the name of Chuck Brooks, who was great at doing his job. There was another who gave no thought to anything but chain of command and his chances of advancement, and he was more of a politician than anything else. Because of regulations, Chuck could never rise higher than he was, and the other fellow couldn't be replaced regardless of how poorly he did his job.

Because of Park Service policy, which moves personnel every few years, nobody stayed anywhere long enough to get to know much about a region. Chuck Brooks would soon be off to another park. Naturalists, whether full-time employees or summer students, knew little about the river, the fish, wildlife, and plant life. A visitor to a Buffalo River Park back then might have embarked on a nature hike with a math student from Cincinnati who didn't have the slightest idea what a persimmon tree was.

Local people, considered to be ignorant, were amused by that, and a little disgusted by how they were treated. In time, it would smooth over somewhat, as the NPS began to become aware of the treasure local people like J.V. Waters were. But maybe it wasn't important that the parks people knew much about the river or even that they love it down deep inside as the old timers did. The National Park Service, after all, was the best

137

Buffalo River Country

chance the Buffalo had to remain wild and free and natural forever. With newfound popularity, it became crowded and cluttered at times, but still wild and free, as God made it. No dams, no summer cottages, no obvious pollution.

The native settlers wouldn't have destroyed it willingly. But the developers who come to get rich quick surely would have ruined it. Plans in the 1970's called for making an amusement park on the banks of the river where the old ghost town of Rush was located.

Buffalo River bluffs, among the most beautiful in the world, overlook valleys where panther and bear once lurked. Those creatures were gone for awhile but they are back now, at least a few, here and there. If those hills had not been set aside, they no doubt would have been dotted with the summer homes of people who couldn't care less where their septic systems drain.

In all probability, as the visitors to the Buffalo mushroom in number there will be restrictions imposed which J.V. Waters once feared would be hard to live with....favorite put-in points closed forever, live bait fishing banned perhaps, and length limits and reduced creel limits a certainty. The invasion of outsiders will continue, and the NPS will continue to clean up after them, because there are some of those city people who leave gravel bars littered, and throw beer cans in the water. But it isn't a problem in which outsiders can always be blamed.

There are those small numbers of local people who leave every can and bottle, every mess they make, for someone else to take care of. And the dumping of old furniture and appliances and household trash on back roads above the river does not come from park visitors, it comes from local folks. And even if it's only a few, it is a mess that destroys the very thing which made the river valley something special.

Places will remain in remote areas of the Buffalo watershed, where log cabins once stood and spring jonquils grow around centuries-old graves, which are visited only by those few who knew....Deep in those woodlands, far up Richland Creek, or in

Buffalo River Country

the drainage of the Leatherwoods or Big Creek, or at the Buffalo headwaters, there will be solitude for those who crave it.

There are places along the Buffalo where ruffed grouse will drum in the spring, and elk will bugle in the fall. Both these species have been restocked in the last 25 years. There are remote areas high in the hills above the Buffalo where a wandering mountain lion will stalk a doe at the dawn of a winter morning, just like it was 200 years ago. And at those times in mid-winter there will be no banging canoes, no multitude of visitors.

There will be times when you can fish the river without hearing or seeing another soul. And there will be days when a

Buffalo River Country

flock of wood ducks tip-up for acorns in the sloughs without interruption from man. And there will be days when it's so quiet and still that you can hear the snowflakes hitting the oak leaves that remain in the dead of winter. Old Joe and J.V. would have liked knowing that.

The Buffalo doesn't get the credit it deserves as a fishing stream. As much as a fisherman hates to see a caravan of canoes, a very small percentage of these floaters are fishermen. And of those who try to fish, only a small percentage are effective anglers. The canoeists are there to ride the current and see the bluffs, and they do it as quickly as possible.

A few of the river's fishermen have a theory. It's expressed best by a wader who likes to fish the water below the shoals where the current slows and brownies move to feed in the well-oxygenated water around rocks and weeds. This type of area is particularly good in the summer as the water begins to drop a little.

He was in such a spot catching bass when two or three canoes came by banging away with paddles and glancing off both banks and every rock in sight. Within fifteen or 20 minutes after the canoeists were gone, smallmouth were back, feeding as if nothing had happened. This fisherman believes that smallmouth in the Buffalo have grown accustomed to the canoe traffic.

Another angler who floats the Buffalo early in June before the water drops as much as it will in late summer, fishes topwater lures in some of the heaviest traveled waters. He likes to start at 5:30 a.m., long before most canoeists push off. In the big bluff swimming hole right at the park, he once fought and landed a 21-inch smallmouth. He catches and releases good-sized smallmouth and largemouth bass well up into the morning, and says that until canoe traffic gets really heavy, the topwater fishing is as good on the Buffalo in June as any other stream.

Fishermen who are serious about the fishing the Buffalo should make a two-day trip in the middle of the week. Before

Buffalo River Country

school is out in the spring or after school begins in late summer and early fall, canoe traffic in midweek is much more tolerable. An angler who finds inaccessible areas between put-in points can camp and enjoy some solitude.

When the water is low and often too clear to suit me from late June until the September rains, the fish are very inactive during the heat of the day. But very late and very early, bass will leave deep, quiet eddies and protective bluffs or rocks and move to the lower portions of the shoals to feed. After dark, bass become aggressive, cruising around and feeding in the shallows of the big eddies, especially near any incoming flowing water. That's the time to fish with a jitterbug or some other noisy topwater lure.

Fly fishermen can have a ball in the river during July and August. They can wrestle smaller bass, and hand-sized green sunfish all day. These scrappy panfish are everywhere, and are made for fly fishing. In the early and late hours, smallmouth below the shoals can keep a fly fisherman excited. There are some big, deep holes in the Buffalo that have flathead catfish up to 40 pounds, but trotline fishermen aren't very common.

Trotlines are dangerous, however, and the only way I'd set one on the Buffalo is to stay with it and take it up in the morning after running it. Because trotlines are set deep water, and weighted to put them on the bottom, they aren't a great danger to a canoeist. But with the kind of traffic the Buffalo gets, trotlines shouldn't be left out during the day, because there's always the chance that a swimmer can jump in right on top of one. Flatheads feed at night, anyway.

Tributaries of the Buffalo, on the other hand, are seldom floated. The Little Buffalo is the largest, and receives some canoe traffic. But the others (Richland Creek, Big Creek, Water Creek, to name a few) have small holes where fishing is fine, canoes never pass, and you can wade and fish with lots of action. But I have found cottonmouths on those small tributaries, so fishermen should be aware of that.

141

10
A BIG SMALLMOUTH

I was about twelve years old when I took Joe and Kate Richardson float-fishing from Mineral Springs to Boiling Springs on the Big Piney river. Joe loved to fish the river for smallmouth and he hired me not so much because I was the best guide, but because I was available and eager and economical. Joe was a top-notch river fishermen and it was easy to guide for him because he seldom made a poor cast. Mrs. Richardson was a good fisherman too, but you'd never expect her to outfish her husband. Joe got the best seat up front and his wife fished behind him. Somehow or another that day in mid-summer, Joe missed one and Mrs. Richardson took advantage of it.

Below Mineral Springs back then there was a stretch of flowing, shaded water beneath a high, long ridge. Dark and deep and studded with big rocks, it was known as the Ink Stand. I never knew why it got that name but I knew it had produced its share of nice smallmouth over the years. Mrs. Richardson was casting a black and white Heddon River Runt and it fooled one of the biggest bass I ever saw in the Big Piney. Her line was strong, her rod with plenty of strength as well. And she

143

A Big Smallmouth

fought the bass well, with me and her husband both yelling advice.

Kate Richardson and I with her big smallmouth from the Piney about 1961. I wasn't the best guide and she wasn't the best fisherman but you can't argue with the results... Larry Dablemont

The big smallmouth used the current, worked hard to throw the hook and then finally tired out. I got the old johnboat over in slack water off a sand bar and landed the fish by hand since

A Big Smallmouth

I had forgotten a net. Of course, back then no one ever released a big bass and I think Joe and his wife took it home and ate it. But we took pictures of it, and I believe it was a bona-fide six pounder or close to it, long and hefty and deep dark brown. I never saw a bigger smallmouth from the Big Piney when I was a kid and I doubt the river ever produces any of that size in this day and time or the future.

On the Gasconade river back in the early 1980's, my mother, Jessie Dablemont, hooked and landed a 23-inch smallmouth which was just as big. She caught that bass on July 5, and it had already spawned. If it had been filled with eggs, it would have easily weighed six pounds. Dad had it mounted for her and I think when he was talking to a visitor to our home and she wasn't around, or in the kitchen where she couldn't hear, he may have claimed he caught it himself.

Poor dad fished a hundred times more than mom did and never did land a bass that size. He always said she wouldn't have caught one either if it hadn't been for his expert paddling and advice and skill with a landing net. The bass was taken during the middle of a hot afternoon and hit a small pig-and-jig combination that my mom liked to use for rock bass. It just doesn't seem fitting that a pair of the biggest smallmouth I ever saw were taken by a pair of fisherwomen with so very little experience.

Everyone whom I ever took float-fishing on a river was after one thing, a big smallmouth. If it wasn't for big smallmouth, Ozark river guides would have had a hard time making a living. But any smallmouth is worth catching even if it is only twelve or fourteen inches long, because the brownie, or bronzeback or whatever else he is called, will put up a fight comparable to anything, pound for pound. And when there's a good current, he wins a lot of those fights.

Actually, most big smallmouth aren't 'he's', they are 'she's'. Females get to be four or five pounds in midwest rivers at times and six or seven pounds occasionally in reservoirs.

145

A Big Smallmouth

Few males ever tip the scales within a pound of a big female, even if they are both eight or ten years old, which is probably about as old as most smallmouth will get. Biologists who check scales to find the age of bass say that occasionally a smallmouth will live upwards of fifteen years, but that's really a rarity.

A five pound smallmouth could be that old, but it could also reach that size in only seven or eight years if it lives in the right waters and the right conditions. To tell the truth, I don't know if there has ever been a smallmouth reaching ten pounds in weight.

The supposed world record, which was reported to be 11 pounds, 15 ounces, has been exposed as a hoax. That fish was reportedly caught in 1955 from Dale Hollow Lake in Kentucky. A few years back, someone began to investigate that fish and the world record walleye, reportedly caught in 1960 from Old Hickory Lake in Tennessee. It was conclusively proven that both records were false and some of the participants in those two events, growing old and feeling guilty, admitted that the fish involved were smaller than reported.

I seriously doubt that any old records are reliable, and therefore expect that there has never been a ten pound smallmouth taken anywhere. North Carolina claims a 10-2 smallmouth as it's state record taken in 1953, and Alabama's record smallmouth is reported at 10-8, taken in 1950. I'm skeptical of those too, just because they were reported in that early 50's era when so many fish were filled with lead between the catching and the weighing, and so much of the record keeping was bogus.

California claims a 9-1 smallmouth, taken in 76, but I don't know that anyone should accept anything which comes from California unless it comes from Hollywood!!. West Virginia's record is set at 9-12, a fish taken in 1971. Again, I am skeptical. Wisconsin, Michigan, California, and New York have records in the nine pound range and most other states have record fish in the seven to eight pound range. But there are none of these

A Big Smallmouth

huge smallmouth reportedly taken from small streams, they are all lake brownies.

A female smallmouth which has spawned, may have reduced her weight by a half pound or so. If you catch one full of eggs, you will have landed a braggin' sized smallmouth, even if it is only fifteen or sixteen inches long. But the real lunkers are those in excess of 20 inches, most of which will weigh better than four pounds, eggs or no eggs. And seldom will male smallmouth reach that length. Most of those bigger fish are females.

In Canada or one of the northern states, if you catch a 20-inch smallmouth it will weigh a pound more than one from the waters of a lower midwestern stream or reservoir. Canada smallmouth are shorter and rounder and wider and they will look different, especially the coloration. But a smallmouth will fight much the same, regardless of where it comes from. In still waters, a smallmouth is a tiger.....in a current he is a sabertooth tiger.

Since this book is concerned with rivers, there's no reason to get into the particulars of fishing for smallmouth in Canada, or a Tennessee or Kentucky reservoir, or even the reservoirs of the Ozarks. What we are talking about is stream smallmouth, and if you ever get a six-pounder out of one of our streams, you have a real prize, a one-in-a-million fish. And if you land a five-pound smallmouth, that's akin to catching a ten pound largemouth.

I have caught an abundance of three-pound smallmouth, how many I can't say for sure, and if I estimated the number someone might think I was bragging. Come to think of it, I would be! Three pounders are worth bragging about.

Lots of good fishermen who float the rivers often brag long and loud when they catch a four-pound smallmouth. I think that in my lifetime I've caught about 20 or so four-pound-plus smallmouth. Some of those were very close to five pounds. But I have never caught a bona-fide five-pound smallmouth

A Big Smallmouth

from the rivers of the Ozarks. I have caught a couple in Canada, but none from the Ozarks.

When I was a boy, I used to ride my bicycle down to a place on the Big Piney river owned by a lady by the name of Myrtle Kelly. Mrs. Kelly was a friend of my grandparents, and her husband, who was dead by the time I came along, had fished with my grandfather. So they had one of Grandpa's johnboats tied up at the Ginseng eddy, a big deep hole of water that was a hangout for hefty smallmouth back then, little more than a gravel filled memory today. She had a nephew by the name of Larry Whitehair who would visit from Oklahoma in the summer, and he and I tried our best to catch a lunker smallmouth in the late evenings of July and August.

I knew that big bass was there because in the spring of the year I was fishing that eddy by myself for goggle-eye when an old mother wood-duck came down to river with a newly hatched brood of ducklings and swam down along the bluff with the whole bunch behind her. The last one, a little behind the others and making an unusual disturbance on the surface, was bound to attract attention, and as he followed around a bed

A Big Smallmouth

of weeds that began just below the bluff, where there was just the remnant of a current, the water erupted beneath him and he disappeared.

I was watching that duckling, I saw the big brown bass which nailed him, and I know it was a genuine five pound smallmouth. I wrote about that bass in an article for Outdoor Life magazine years later entitled, "Old Fighter, King of the Ginseng Eddy", and that article is included in my book "Ain't No Such Animal".

That very year, in the early winter, that big bass was gigged. And I knew then, as I know now, that the fate of most big bass in the Big Piney and other rivers where night gigging is allowed, was to be something similar to that. Some two- and three-pound bass may escape the giggers, but four- and five-pound bass do not. They are easy to find in this day and time because the streams have become shallower, and the best cover lies buried under sand and silt and gravel. Big bass don't make very difficult targets, they just lay there beneath the bright lights to become an easy mark.

One thing that little duckling's disappearance taught me was how tempting a noisy topwater lure could be to a small-mouth. Larry Whitehair and I didn't have much tackle. We fished with hooks and nightcrawlers, or minnows or crawdads, and we had old Shakespeare reels with fiberglass rods and braided nylon line. But we caught the heck out of goggle-eye (rock bass) and black perch (green sunfish) and punkinseeds (longear sunfish), and every now and then we would catch a twelve- to fourteen-inch brownie that would tickle us to death. What I remember best was the look and the smell and the cool-ness of the river there in the evenings, sitting in that old john-boat over deep, dark swirling water beneath the bluff, knowing Old Fighter was down there, and any minute I might have him.

Remembering the duckling and getting some old topwater lures from my Uncle Norten every now and then (when he'd pass through coming or going from Bull Shoals or Tablerock or

A Big Smallmouth

Norfork or Greers Ferry), had me paddling a johnboat up and down the Big Piney as I got older, learning to catch bigger smallmouth. Jitterbugs and Lucky Thirteens and Bass--Orenos and Hula-Poppers were all effective early and late in the day, but in that time, dad and I used Shimmy-flies to catch most of the rock bass and smallmouth we took.

A Shimmy-fly was just a small off-line spinner with a hairy body, made by a Salem, Missouri lure-maker by the name of Art Varner. He gave the body a bumble-bee appearance, and we would add a strip of thin, white, split pork-rind. That lure really tore 'em up, as did a similar lure which came out a few years later called a Beetle-spin, almost the same as a Shimmy-fly except with a plastic body. Beetle-spins may have been developed from a lure maker seeing Varner's shimmy fly, and they came along about the time that I was graduating from high school.

Despite my allegiance to the Shimmy-fly, the Beetle-spin caught a lot of goggle-eye and smallmouth and still does today in small streams all over the midwest. But then, you can take away the spinner and just use a plastic grub today and do as well, fishing it slower and hopping it along.

Dad learned, in the late 60's and 70's that one of the most effective bass producers in the Piney and the Gasconade, was a little quarter-ounce rubber skirted brown or black jig with a short pork jig attached. It was my mom's favorite lure, the one she caught her big bass on, and they just always referred to it as a 'pig and jig'. You could see why it caught so many fish, it was so similar to a crawfish in feel and color. That version was much smaller than a similar combination my uncle used for big bass in Ozark reservoirs and he always maintained that larger jigs would produce bigger bass.

In 1970, while working my first year as the Outdoor Editor for the Arkansas Democrat in Little Rock, I learned about Crooked Creek. It was a smallmouth heaven up in the Ozarks of North Arkansas, between Harrison and Yellville. Uncle

A Big Smallmouth

Norten had fished it as early as the mid-1950's and he always said no river could match it for numbers of brownies, and for size.

My dad and I floated it for the first time in June of 1970 and used our Shimmy-flies. It was a day to remember. Smallmouth in that little stream liked our old favorites from the Piney, and we must have caught 40 or 50 that day. Most of them were twelve- to fifteen-inch fish, but there were a half dozen from eighteen to twenty inches long and Crooked Creek, which was full that day, had so much current it gave the fish extra fighting power. Crooked Creek then and for years to come was a stream which indeed had five-pound-and-up smallmouth.

One of the greatest fishing stories I ever heard concerned an old fisherman by the name of Carl Emmick, whom my uncle had guided for over a 30-year period beginning in the 1940's. Mr. Emmick had fished a large number of Ozark rivers over that stretch of time, with Norten paddling for him each and every trip. He had eagerly fished for a five-pound smallmouth, and never caught one. Indeed he had come close before, within six or eight ounces of such a brownie, and many largemouth above five pounds from lakes and rivers they fished. But he had never landed a five-pound smallmouth until his very last fish, his very last trip, and that was on Crooked Creek.

It so wore him out that he had to stop fishing that day. He had made that last fishing trip with a weakened heart and within a day or so of landing that big bass he had waited a lifetime to catch, he passed away in a St. Louis hospital. That story is related in my uncle's life story, the book "Ridge-Runner...from the Big Piney to the Battle of the Bulge".

Crooked Creek was to give me some of my biggest smallmouth, because I left Little Rock in 1973 and moved back to the Ozarks near Harrison, Arkansas, hoping to work as a Naturalist for the National Park Service on the newly organized Buffalo National River. I did work there for a couple of years, then became a full-time outdoor writer. To help make ends meet, I

151

A Big Smallmouth

began to guide fishermen again, with my Uncle Norten who lived about one hour west, where the War Eagle river joined Beaver lake.

Norten caused me to re-examine the way I fished for smallmouth. We took an early summer float trip on Crooked Creek

Gloria Dablemont with a Crooked Creek smallmouth.

A Big Smallmouth

about 1974 and he was using one of the biggest spinners I have ever seen. It was red and black with a huge gold spinner and an eel on it that made the whole thing look a foot long. The spinner-bait itself was bigger than some of the bass I caught that day. The water was a little colored, and the smallmouth were hungry. I caught twice as many bass as he did by using smaller crankbaits and smaller Beetle-spin type spinners, but most of my fish were only twelve to fifteen inches long.

My uncle landed four bass between three and one-half to four pounds that day, and half dozen from fifteen to eighteen inches in length. I started using those big spinners on that day, and continue to fish them today. In all my years of fishing, I have never seen any lure produce more good-sized smallmouth than those big spinner-baits which cover most of your hand. The only time I don't use them is in very clear low water.

From 1975 until well into the late 80's my uncle and I guided fishermen on whatever river someone wanted to float, the Buffalo, the Kings, the War Eagle, the Illinois and Crooked Creek. We often took parties of four fishermen on two-day trips, and occasionally a three-day trip, with two nights of camping. But we never stayed out longer than that, and all the gear went with us in those two boats, we never used a commissary boat like they had in the good old days. Norten would guide in his 19-foot square-sterned Grumman, and I would use my 19-foot Grumman or a 17-foot Lowe aluminum river boat.

I particularly recall a big smallmouth on the Kings River in 1982. I was guiding a fisherman who wanted to catch brownies on light tackle and at the same time he wanted to land that big one he could put on his office wall, something three and one-half pounds or better. We put in that day at a crossing known as Old Alabam, east of Huntsville, Arkansas.

I remember telling him that he could catch lots more smallmouth, and have a great deal more fun perhaps, with his light action spinning outfit and small Rebels and Rooster Tails and Mepps spinners. That is indeed the way to catch a boatful of

153

A Big Smallmouth

ten- to fifteen-inch bass. But I told him that day that if he wanted to catch that a trophy smallmouth (and I hate that word 'trophy' applied to fish and wildlife) he would be better served with a casting reel and eight- to twelve-pound line, a rod with a little more backbone, and larger lures, preferably a half-ounce spinner-bait, pork-rind combination. He said he was an experienced fisherman, and he could land anything on his light tackle with six pound line.

A Big Smallmouth

Truth of the matter was, he could catch a lot of fish, because he was an efficient caster and knew how to work the lure. But he couldn't even land all the fourteen- and fifteen-inch brownies he hooked. Some of them outbattled him, because his hooks were small and his rod too light and whippy to set them well.

About an hour before sunset that evening in May, only a mile or so above our take-out point, he found what he was after. Just above a shoal, along a shaded bank where some big rocks and a log made a good place to look for crawdads, a dandy smallmouth was on the prowl. It engulfed the small Mepps spinner and bent that light rod double. The angler never did really set the hooks, the fish just took it and went with it. And in short order, she went down into the shoal below us, probably where she came from.

The brownie didn't give that fisherman much room for error, she was stripping line against the drag, and too strong to turn without risking snapping the line. We followed in the 19-foot, square-sterned canoe, but the smallmouth just came back upstream, flashing past us and creating five feet of slack line. She came out of the water at the head of the shoal just behind us, tail-walking on the surface and shaking her big brown head, throwing that little Mepps treble hook with ease.

The fisherman got to look at a bona-fide four pound smallmouth and he got to feel what kind of strength the fish had in the current. And he figured out quickly what I had been trying to tell him...he wasn't using the right gear for that kind of smallmouth.

And that's one thing that needs to be emphasized, if you want to catch big smallmouth, you need the bait-casting reel with ten to twelve pound line, a rod to set the hook and handle the job, and larger lures with hooks which handle a big fish.

I know that sometimes a big smallmouth is landed on light spinning tackle, and I have done it myself, but it is the exception rather than the rule if there is current and obstacles like rocks and logs for the fish to use. Smallmouth will use that cur-

155

A Big Smallmouth

rent, and any obstacle it can find.

One of the types of fishing I enjoy the most is finding a shoal in the mid and late summer when the river is low, and wading out up to my waist with a light spinning outfit and a little topwater Rapala or Rebel or Redfin minnow, casting for smallmouth which come up and take the lure off the surface. Most of those bass aren't lunkers, but they put up a lunker of a fight and there aren't many things you can do which provides more fishing enjoyment.

Sometimes you can catch ten or fifteen smallmouth in such a spot, but you know that if a three or four pounder comes along, you are likely to lose him, and perhaps your lure as well. If it's big bass I am after, it is with bigger gear and different types of lures.

The same topwater lures catch and land big bass, but with the casting gear and heavier line, use the bigger ones, six to eight inches long. I'll never forget a trip on Crooked Creek back in August of 1980, when I took my sister's husband, Jerry Wood, on a day long float.

Jerry was born and raised at Cushman, Arkansas, a Viet-Nam veteran who had done a lot of bass, catfish and trout fishing on the lower White, enough so that he wouldn't listen to all the good advice I was giving him. I wanted him to fish with a Wiggle-wart, because the river was up and murky colored just after a summer storm that had dropped a couple of inches of rain. When water is high and colored, fishing can be great. On such days there seems to be no particular time when bass feed best. You may catch as many fish at noon as you'll catch during late evening hours.

But just after we started that summer day, my brother-in-law found a big gold topwater Rapala lure hanging from a tree, and decided that was an omen. He tied it on and began to fish with it, and within an hour I was offering him all the money in my billfold, which never was much back in those days, for that eight-inch lure. Jerry would twitch that thing around in swift

156

A Big Smallmouth

water and some big brownie would engulf it and there'd be a five-minute battle while I tried to hold the boat. That day he probably caught six or seven bass above three pounds, one of them a largemouth. A couple of the smallmouth were right at four pounds, and he lost one that was even bigger. I caught some smaller fish on the Wiggle-wart, but I did one whale of a job handling the boat for him while he fought the lunkers.

I fish those big topwater minnows often, and other topwater lures which catch big smallmouth. The old poppers and chuggers like the Lucky 13, the Hula-popper and many others which

A Big Smallmouth

make a similar commotion on the surface, all catch black bass of both species on streams. They need to be the bigger lures with adequate hooks if you want to hold the bigger bass, and if there's some type of skirt on them, it seems to improve your chances.

But those topwater minnows, and other finesse type lures like the Zara Spook which don't produce lots of disturbance but give the appearance of a dying baitfish, are lures I love to use. And not everyone can fish them, because they have to be made to come to life, and if the rod tip isn't worked properly, that doesn't happen. Then there's the Jitterbug, which I'll get to later.

The Storm Wiggle-wart is one of my favorite lures for smallmouth, I use it often, and catch all three bass species on it, in every Ozark stream I fish. There are lots of crank-baits which imitate a crayfish, Rebel lures made a crayfish look-alike which some people catch lots of fish on, and I like it too. Bomber's Model A lure is a good one, I have caught lots of bass from the Pomme de Terre river in February and March on a chartreuse and orange Model A Bomber.

And I remember catching two, four-pound smallmouth from one shoal once on an Arbogast Mud-Bug. But my affection for the Wiggle-wart comes from seeing so many smallmouth fall to it's somewhat imperfect imitation of a crawdad. Most anglers fish it too fast...in fact, most anglers fish all crankbaits a little too fast.

In September of 1969, I came home from college to hunt blue-winged teal on the Big Piney River with my dad, who always told me that if you wanted to do something right, do one thing and one thing only.

I think that's why we only took one fishing rod that day, and one Wiggle-wart. We were hunting teal, with our blind on the old wooden johnboat, and we needed to concentrate on that. But there had been lots of rain the week before and the Piney was up and a little colored and so from the back of the boat,

158

A Big Smallmouth

while dad sat behind the blind with his shotgun watching for teal, I made a cast or two here and there and landed three or four two-pound smallmouth in a half hour or so.

Dad put down the shotgun and I gave him the fishing rod and he did the same thing. By mid morning we were taking turns fishing. Every four bass landed, we switched places. Somehow or another, we killed a limit of blue-winged teal that day and brought in a limit of smallmouth, most of them two to three pounds. There were no real lunkers, but almost no brownies under two pounds, and I guess we must have landed twenty or more taking turns with the only lure we brought along. I don't ever recall any trip on the Piney producing that many smallmouth over two pounds, it was just one of those days.

And I reminded dad that he always said you can only do one thing at a time. His response was that we should have done one thing that day, and that was fish for smallmouth.

The crank-baits will always produce big smallmouth, but again, use big ones if it is big smallmouth you are after. As long as you have colored or murky water, and streams which have some depth and habitat, the large lures and heavier line work for big bass. It's different when you have very clear water of course. It is tough to use big lures effectively in crystal clear streams, and when faced with those situations, I use the spinning gear and much smaller lures. Any kind of fish is more difficult to catch in low, clear water where you can read a newspaper in five feet of water. That is fly-fishing water, ultra-lite water, but seldom the place to catch an old wary smallmouth. You can do it by leaving the boat beached above the shoals at times and wading slowly and quietly, fishing the flowing water and swirling eddies below you.

When you float through low clear water where bass are feeding, you'll spook them, and find fishing to be tough. In such situations, I like to leave my boat and sneak up on them like a trout fisherman might do.

When fishing rivers where there's lots of brush and logs,

A Big Smallmouth

one of my favorite lures is an old-time Heddon Tadpoly. It's a slow-wobbling floater that runs down as it's retrieved. Years ago, my uncle showed me how to use a fly-strip pork rind to make a Tadpoly almost irresistible over logs or root wads, or any other type of cover. He took a small, thin white pork strip and cut a short piece about the size of a tooth pick, placing the wide end on a back hook.

Author with a Niangua River smallmouth - spotted bass hybrid taken in 2004.

A Big Smallmouth

There are other crank baits of course that can be dressed up similarly and produce fish when dragged across submerged logs but the Tadpoly will always be my favorite. Trouble is, some of those lures are collectors items now and often too valuable to fish. The old ones were just better fish producers than the new ones they are making. The paint and patterns of old lures were different. But any crank bait is a better lure when that thin, toothpick-like whip of a pork strip is attached to a back treble hook. It doesn't have to be white, but that's about all I use. A wider piece, with the back half split to give the appearance of a pair of whipping, kicking legs, also is enticing. The addition of that pork rind to a Tadpoly or Wiggle-Wart is something I hesitate to tell people about because it makes the baits irresistible. So go ahead and use it, but don't tell anyone about it.

Of course, they still make the little spoon-like lures to which you add pork eels or split fly-strips and they too are killers. We seldom use any spinner without some type of pork frog or eel attached, and usually a trailer hook added before the pork rind goes on. A trailer hook of course, needs a pork trailer of some kind to keep it on, and the trailer hook will catch lots of bass which hit short which you wouldn't catch without it.

A trailer hook and pork rind is of utmost importance if you fish a buzz-bait, which is basically a surface-riding spinnerbait which kicks up a disturbance on a steady retrieve, leaving bubbles in it's wake much like a jitterbug. It can be one of the most deadly smallmouth lures from July until the cold weather of the late fall drives bass to deep water dormancy. It is not used much in the spring because it is a lure best suited for lower water conditions. But it can catch bass in muddy water, and I have seen it fished in swift shoals to produce brownies. A buzz-spin doesn't make for so many small bass and you may fish it for hours and only catch a few fish. Chances are the fish it produces will be hefty ones.

It probably will catch more largemouth than smallmouth,

A Big Smallmouth

but the bigger brown bass in a stream will smash a sputterbug and do it at all hours of the day. It is an adventure to fish one, because so many bass slash at it and miss it, and there are so many explosions on the surface where the bass misses it completely. In mid-summer and late summer, I like to fish a buzzbait until dark, and the jitterbug after dark.

A Big Smallmouth

I suppose, if my life depended on catching a big small-mouth, I'd go after it after dark with a jitterbug in July or August, and perhaps late June and early September should be included. Jitterbug fishing seems best to me on dark nights, when the river is low, the water clearer than usual, the weather settled and still.

One night on Crooked Creek in the mid '80s a friend and I caught three four-pound smallmouth, seven or eight between 2-1/2 and 3-1/2, and a six pound largemouth, and we only fished three or four holes in a half mile stretch of water.

One of those big smallmouth I will never forget, because we were drifting slowly in deep water just below a shoal and a beaver decided to try to scare us off. He smacked the water about six feet from the boat, and it was such a racket and com-motion that I figured he would have spooked every fish in the eddy. I had cast the Jitterbug a distance beyond him, and when I reeled it along, retrieving it, the water exploded in almost the exact spot where the beaver had just been, maybe a matter of only a minute or so before. And I thought for sure I had hooked that beaver.

It was a big smallmouth, which stripped line against my drag because he was so close to the boat, but I sat there for awhile holding on, wondering how I was going to land a beaver and get my lure back.

Fishing a Jitterbug on a dark night is a challenge because you adversely affect the fishing by turning on a light. You need good night vision and a knowledge of the river so that you can cast without hitting the logs and hanging limbs along the banks. And no matter how good you get at it, you still get into the limbs at times, and you still don't miss all the logs.

Jitterbugs of course, are fished at a slow steady retrieve, and will produce fish in the spring and fall as well as the dead of summer, and they will catch fish during the early hours of the day and late in the evenings. But they are bass killers when fished in the heat of the summer on low to normal water, clear

A Big Smallmouth

164

A Big Smallmouth

to normal color, in the darkness of the night. Use the bigger ones, especially at night. My favorite is the jointed model.

And I guess that pretty much tells you everything I can tell you about catching a big smallmouth. Of course there's the plastic worm and the plastic grubs of various types which are also effective. My dad always loved a plastic worm in October, and my uncle fishes a hula-grub slowly in deep water with great results all times of the year especially when bass are deeper and when the water is a little colder in the early spring and fall.

You will catch more smallmouth perhaps on nightcrawlers, minnows and crayfish, if you know how and where to fish natural bait, but I hate to see a novice fish natural bait because fish are so often deep-hooked and killed.

And no doubt, there are those who will read this and say, "Oh, but you left out this lure or that technique." If you hear that, just tell them that this chapter is the last word in catching a big smallmouth and anything I have left out isn't worth doing!!! Just joking, of course. There are lots of ways to catch a big smallmouth, and too many lures to use them all.

It would be fun sometime to float the river again and use the Flatfish and the Midget Didget and the River Runt, and the Hula-Popper and the Shannon Twin-Spin. But you know what I'd rather do. I'd rather go back to the rivers we had then, when those lures were the lures we used, and find the smallmouth we had then, in the days when old time river guides paddled wooden johnboats.

11
OVERNIGHT ON A GRAVEL BAR

There's only one way to be there at dawn, when vapors rise and drift across the surface of the water and the jagged pine tops along the ridge are buried in low patches of fog. At dawn when the splashing of feeding fish along a weedy bank below the shoal tells you where the smallmouth are, when every sycamore leaf is dripping wet and the heavy dew makes spider webs between the limbs look like they were made of cotton yarn. There at dawn on the big eddy miles away from the access points, hours from the closest bridge or farm road, where there just has to be a five pound smallmouth, and no other fishermen.

There's only one way to be there at dawn, and that's by being there at dusk. Being there with your tent set, a campfire cracking and beans bubbling on one side of the pan, sitting on a rock next to the flame.

You get there at dawn by staying there all night. You know that if you can just force yourself out of that warm sleeping bag when its barely light enough to see, and cast a top water minnow alongside the weeds just below the shoal, a big, black-bellied frog-eater of a smallmouth might jump all over it.

I'm not going to tell anyone where that spot is. I'm not

167

Overnight on a Gravel Bar

even going to tell anyone the name of the river. There are many such remote eddies and many rivers where you can find them. But you only get there by exploring and investigating and looking for such places. By loading up a canoe or johnboat with a minimum of gear and heading downstream, moved along by a boat paddle and motivated by the desire to get away from everything for awhile.

The greatest fishing memories I have, come not from the wilderness lakes of Canada nor the wave-lashed shores of Ozark reservoirs where I've fished with pro's, lunker-busters and bass-masters. Give me a choice between a largemouth from a bass rig and a smallmouth from a johnboat and you know which I'll pick.

Rivers of course, are not easy to fish. You can't unload at a paved ramp, turn a switch key, lean back in a padded seat and find the fish on a graph. Fishing a river can be work at times, its a challenge, and it takes more time than money. If you aren't very good with a boat paddle, its tough to fish many streams.

For someone who seeks solitude and a back-to-nature basic approach to fishing, Ozark streams are worth more than gold, but many are packed with people.

Heavy canoe traffic can be found on many of our midwest rivers, where canoe rental businesses are situated side by side. These streams are not places to get away from the crowd, because canoe traffic is so heavy. But most of those canoes hold sight-seers and not fishermen.

Over the Ozark region, there are still some top-notch float streams that get very little fishing pressure, and if they do see fishermen it is on weekends. On many of these streams, the upper reaches are seldom floated because the water is smaller and shoals more difficult to run.

There's no doubt that May is absolutely one of the best months to float them, the water is higher and the bass more aggressive. Years of float fishing has convinced me that May is also the best time to get blown completely away by a storm. If

168

Overnight on a Gravel Bar

you intend to find a remote gravel bar to camp on in the spring and early summer, the first thing you need to remember is the possibility of a toad-stranglin', stump floatin', limb-wrenchin', fire-in-the-sky thunderstorm.

Back in the early 1970's, we found a real gold mine in Arkansas' Kings river, which flows north from the Boston Mountains to the Missouri border emptying into Table Rock Lake. There was a stretch of the Kings that covered 15 miles or so with no public access. Too many miles for one day, it was perfect for a two or three day trip. And there was that "spot", about five or six miles downstream, where two big beautiful eddies teemed with fish, a perfect campsite, and the opportunity to fish the early morning hours where few anglers had been.

Just out of college at the time, there were four of us, looking for adventure. We found it! We put in about mid-morning, with two wooden johnboats, camping gear and fishing equipment.

The fishing was good, with the water just right. We caught smallmouth, Kentuckies, rock bass and even a nice channel cat that hit a small spinner. I'll never forget the green sunfish that tackled my lure in a spot below a shoal, mostly because a four pound smallmouth followed him to the boat, trying to take the lure away. That type of thing happens often on float trips. Usually you hook a 10 inch smallmouth and a 15-incher chases him. That bass was the biggest one I've had follow a hooked fish. Sometimes if you are using a long lure with two sets of hooks, you'll hook two fish at once. Occasionally a follower will hit your fishing partners' lure if it's dropped in close to the hooked fish.

We had quite a fish fry that night, on a gravel bar above the big hole where we would catch a trophy smallmouth during the early hours of the next day. Visions of top water lures disappearing in a bronze swirl, helped me drift off to sleep that night, but it was something else that brought me to full alert at first light. Thunder! Way off in the distance. I lay there looking at

169

Overnight on a Gravel Bar

the roof of the tent, aware that it was too still. No birds singing, no breeze, no sound but that of flowing water from the river. Then again, the distant thunder.

I dug out a small radio and almost immediately picked up the tornado warning. The good news was, the tornado sighted and the severe storm behind it, were in another county to the southwest. The bad news was the whole thing was bearing down on us. We didn't have long to get ready.

Years of float fishing and years of guiding others on float trips had taught me that a river can rise rapidly and cover a gravel bar. Usually, on streams I know very well, there are nearby caves or bluff overhangs that represent shelter and safety in the worst storm. But that day, the bluff was across the river and it faced the oncoming storm. There wasn't enough time to go looking for a cave.

Behind us, a small draw approached the gravel bar. The dirt bank, held by a small group of trees, was about six feet high. We carried the heavy johnboats to that draw, turned them upside down. We packed all our gear beneath one, and then situated ourselves under the other one. Water coming down the draw would miss us, but we'd have the protection of the high bank behind us. Donning rain gear, and tying a tarp in place beneath the boats, we were ready when the storm hit, and I don't remember ever enduring one quite like it. The lightning was intense, one bolt splintered a big oak on the hillside across the river. The wind roared, snapping limbs and driving sheets of rain mixed with leaves and debris.

For an hour, we sat there under the shelter of those old johnboats wondering if we'd ever cast another lure. Finally, even though rain continued, the lightning and wind slacked up a bit.

Two hours after it began, the storm was over and we ventured forth to see patches of blue sky to the west.

The river was six inches higher, rising and dingy colored. I figured we'd see it downright muddy by mid-afternoon, maybe rising another foot or more. So we set forth to ride the current

170

Overnight on a Gravel Bar

and get in a cast or two when we could. With big spinner baits and the largest, brightest crank baits we had, we caught bass fast and furious. Between the four of us, we landed better than twenty bass that day between three and four pounds, smallmouth and Kentuckies and a few largemouth. There were five bass caught exceeding four pounds, but none were smallmouth. It was a trip to remember, but I was still disappointed. I wanted to fish that eddy at dawn with a top water lure. The storm had ruined it!

A year or so afterward, I camped at that same spot, a little later in the summer. There were no storms, and hadn't been any for awhile. We spent much of our afternoon before getting to the campsite, dragging over shoals and trying to lure a fish from the clear, low water with not much success. I was so worn out that night, and it was so hot and muggy, that we didn't even go out to fish the jitterbug as we usually did. Instead, we set two lawn chairs out in the gentle current before our campsite, and sat there in waist deep water, relaxed and cool, casting nightcrawlers down into the slowing, deeper water below the shoal.

Overnight on a Gravel Bar

Channel catfish were there, and we filled a cooler with hard-fighters from 1 to 3 pounds.

I did get the chance to fish the big eddy at dawn, and caught some good bass on topwater lures. There were no big ones that morning, and we broke camp knowing we had a long day ahead of us floating the Kings at late summer stage, and that was one of those trips when the fishing was tough.

Float-fishing isn't always great, of course. There have been lots of trips when I would have sworn all the fish had migrated. Those of us who write about the outdoors seldom write about the times when you can't coax a strike with anything. There are lots of reasons for that, usually some kind of front, or spawning activity, or somebody in the boat isn't holding their mouth right. But you forget the dry runs and remember the days when the bass were tearing it up.

Two and three day trips should only be embarked upon by float fishermen with some experience. You gain that experience, you learn how to handle a boat and fish efficiently by going and doing. Chances are there's a good fishing stream not far away from you. Most midwestern states have a few of them. The only way you'll learn how good the fishing might be on any stream is to give it a test.

When you get to the point where you have made some day-trips and figured out what floating and fishing is all about, you'll start thinking about an overnight river camping trip, or maybe two or three days on the river.

Preparation is essential! Poor preparation can lead to misery on trips of a few days. So start with a checklist. The checklist for a 3- or 4-day spring fishing trip for two men might look like this:

--FIRST AMMO BOX
camera and lenses
--SECOND AMMO BOX
matches
vial of carbide or lighter fluid (for starting fires

172

Overnight on a Gravel Bar

in rain) first-aid kit--snake bite kit
　roll of nylon cord--300 lb. test
　heavy hunting knife
　pen and note pad
　maps
　transistor radio (for weather warnings)
　extra mantles for lantern
　handful of 3- or 4-inch nails
　--container with drinking water, two to three gallons
　--small belt axe
　--cook set
　--extra skillet
　--two-man tent, lightweight
　--sleeping bags in doubled garbage-can plastic liners
　--extra clothing in doubled garbage-can plastic liners:
　this bundle should include personal effects such as
　toothbrush, razor and so on,
　several pairs of dry socks and underwear and a pair
　of hiking boots or shoes.
　--Camp stove and or campfire grill
　--Camp lantern and fuel-or batteries
　--pair of small strong flashlights
　--ultralight fishing tackle and small tackle box
　--casting gear and small tackle box
　--pair of folding camp stools
　--one or two plywood rectangles, 2' x 3' up to 3' x 4'
　(used for camp tables)
　--three or four paddles
　--two 8 x 10 sheets of heavy gauge plastic
　--one small plastic bucket

The following are suggestions for groceries. Naturally I
don't mean to suggest you take all of this on one trip.
　--FIRST COOLER (with ice blocks):
　butter

Overnight on a Gravel Bar

eggs
quarts or pints of milk
sausage
cheese and lunch meats
hamburger
sandwich spread
lettuce
tomatoes
soft drinks (not many)

-- DRY COOLER:
small roll of paper towels
aluminum foil
garbage-can plastic liners (use for trash)
pot holder
egg turner and fish fork
can opener and silverware
soap pads--small container of dish soap
bar of hand soap
bread or crackers
coffee, salt, pepper sugar in small containers
canned goods: beans, stew, potatoes, chili,
peaches, pears, etc.
cooking oil
raw potatoes
apples, oranges, bananas
cookies
corn meal or flour
instant packets: hot cocoa, oatmeal, etc.

Food is a matter of choice of course, but there are some things that make grocery storage easier. For instance, rather than packing a couple dozen eggs, subject to breaking, you can crack the shells and empty raw eggs into a small Tupperware container with a pour hole. The eggs, when needed, will pour

174

Overnight on a Gravel Bar

out one at a time without breaking. They're easier to use in this form and take up half the space of eggs in shells.

On float trips, it's unwise to take cubed or crushed ice. Blocks of ice last much longer. You can make your own by freezing water in three or four one-gallon plastic milk cartons, then drink the water produced as the ice melts.

It's not practical to take along food that occupies lots of space and really doesn't provide much benefit. Marshmallows and potato chips fall into this category. Cartons of beverages are nice to have on hot trips in midsummer, but they take up a great deal of space and may not be worth carrying. Ice-tea mix or tang is much better than large quantities of soda. Carrying a few cans of soft drinks are okay, but they make too much weight, and take up too much space.

Midday meals on the river are usually light: sandwiches, fruit and cookies. Breakfasts are also usually simple. But evening meals on the river may be more complicated. Canned stew and chili make good, easy hot meals and take up little space. Some floaters like to go all out and have steak and salad. Others like hamburgers and beans.

I was once partial to fresh fish on float trips. But at this stage in my life I've eaten so much fish I'm tired of eating it. Still, we have fish when people I'm floating with have a choice. It's something you can catch along the way and all that's necessary for a good meal is some luck, corn meal and cooking oil. However, it's good to have something to fall back on, just in case the fish aren't hitting, or in case you are an inexperienced fisherman.

Camps on the river are more comfortable at mealtime if you have a small table or two. This is why I carry a couple of plywood rectangles with me. With a hole in each corner of the plywood, all I have to do is attach legs of any kind, or you can set them on logs or rocks. When I'm floating, the legs are removed and the plywood rests on those wooden legs or some small wooden blocks, a couple of inches off the bottom of my boat.

175

Overnight on a Gravel Bar

This arrangement keeps my gear off the boat floor and dry.

I don't believe I've ever floated a river anywhere in a john-boat or any other craft, without getting some water in the boat before the end of the trip. Usually there's water in the boat early and often. Water runs off the blade of a paddle when you lay it down for a moment to fish. And water splashes in on rough shoals. In winter, moisture can condense inside an aluminum boat or canoe.

On many streams, it's necessary to do quite a bit of wading. You may want to fish a shoal or stretch of swift water by wading before you float through it. Or you may have to pull around an impassable stretch of water.

If you float without getting a drop of water in a boat, you've really done something. Chances are you won't be that fortunate. I recommend that you take steps to keep articles you want to keep dry off the floor of the boat. And have a couple of big sponges you can use to remove water, the sponges beat dipping water with a can

From fall through early summer, a floater must wear hip boots or waders. But in the summer, tennis shoes (or other wading shoes with good gripping soft soles) are the ticket. Since many stream bottoms are solid rock or are made up of large rocks, wading can be tricky. Wet rock can be slicker than ice. Always remember that, because you can injure yourself by stepping out onto a slick rock and taking a quick fall.

Whatever the season, be sure to include heavier clothing for nights on the river. Even in summer, nighttime on a stream can become cool. You have to use your head about taking too much or too little clothing. Most everyone takes too much of everything on overnight trips, especially clothing.

When you prepare for a float trip of any length, about the wisest thing you can do is take the time to pack your boat properly. The way seating is arranged in boats and canoes, the weight of two passengers isn't distributed equally in front and back. Normally, the front of the craft sets up just a little, with

176

weight just slightly heavier toward the stern. This is as it should be, but don't get too much weight toward the back. Passengers will shift the balance even more toward the rear, so try to load equipment and cargo around the center of your boat. If anything, load these things a bit heavier toward the front.

Heavy items should go as low in the boat as possible, with lighter gear on top. It doesn't take much experience to load a boat properly. When you have it completely loaded, your cargo may rise six to eight inches above the boat or canoe sides. It shouldn't rise higher than that if you expect to float safely. If you are a beginner, set your boat or canoe out in the garage a day or so before you make your trip, and load it with all your gear, just to be sure you aren't overpacking, trying to take too much.

When your craft is loaded, it's not a bad idea to cover the load with a tarpaulin or a sheet of heavy gauge plastic. I like the plastic because its lighter. When it covers your gear and is tucked in on all sides, you can float in a heavy rain without much worry.

Overnight on a Gravel Bar

At night, a pair of these plastic sheets can come in handy. One protects my camp equipment in case of rain and I use the other to cover the small lightweight nylon tent. These small two-man tents are convenient for floating, but in heavy rains they leak a little--especially if you touch the sides at one place or another. So when rain threatens, use that second sheet of plastic to cover the tent and keep you dry inside. And if you expect rain, be sure your tent is set in an area where rain won't run beneath it. Digging a small trench around it to drain water away is a good idea.

A heavily loaded boat or canoe is, as you'd expect, harder for you and your partner to control and slower to respond than is an empty craft. Be a little more cautious. A shoal or rough stretch of water that you can easily navigate with an empty boat may become more of a problem when you're carrying equipment. To make up for the extra weight, decide as early as possible about course changes you want to take.

By contrast, a lone traveler finds it hard to navigate without some balancing weight. When I float alone, I put a couple or three heavy rocks in the left front of my boat to level it when I'm sitting to the right in the stern.

Many years ago, people in the Ozarks where I grew up would have laughed at the idea of carrying drinking water on a float trip. But the use of agricultural chemicals and the inadequate sewage plants from small rural towns today have polluted all our streams and even much spring water is contaminated. Stream water, no matter how pure it looks, shouldn't be used in preparing food or drinking water. If it's boiled, perhaps there's little danger in using stream water for coffee or tea or washing dishes, but even the clearest, cleanest looking water can be impure. Boil the heck out of it, and if you have water filters use them too.

Spring water today is usually impure but it can have harsh effects even if it's pure. Many a time it has happened that canoeists from large cities in other regions get ill in the Ozarks

Overnight on a Gravel Bar

from drinking spring water known to be pure. Such spring water, often high in mineral content, can be so different from what a person is accustomed to that it causes minor stomach problems and diarrhea. If you run out of water, boil stream water each night and let it cool overnight for use the following day. But whatever you might forget, don't ever forget to take a good anti-diarrhea medicine, it's just as important as sunscreen.

By wisely choosing your supplies and supplementing them with fish and wild meat in season, you can float for many days at a time without having to replenish your supplies. For most people, three or four days of floating is a real experience.

The key to successful floating, whether for one day or several, is good planning and preparation. With a topographic map, you can plan the distance you'll float each day and generally find camp sites that will most suit you. In spring and summer, for instance, severe storms in my part of the nation can develop in a matter of hours. Bluffs that face east or north can sometimes provide shallow shelters. I like to camp close to protective bluffs or caves just in case of a really bad storm.

A bad storm on the river is rough to endure. High winds or tornadoes aren't the only danger. Lightning and hail can be dangerous, too. If you seek shelter from hail beneath a tree, you are in danger of being killed or injured by lightning. In an aluminum craft of any kind, lightning is something to be concerned about as well.

It's customary to camp on gravel or sand bars. If a storm is imminent, seek higher ground. Rivers can rise several feet in a matter of hours. I know of many occasions when floaters have lost all their gear to a rising river. Occasionally someone will camp on a gravel bar on the river and ignore low ground or a dry channel behind them. A four or five foot rise in the river may not only take away the boat or canoe that was left pulled up to the gravel bar but may also make an island of the camp site by changing the low ground behind it into a flowing channel.

Overnight on a Gravel Bar

Be sure when you make camp that you're far enough away from the water to withstand a rise in the river and to give yourself enough time to get your equipment out. Be sure there's high ground behind you, so you don't get surrounded and trapped. And tie your boat!! I've known of storms upriver causing a rise which sleeping campers weren't even aware of, and they would wake up to find their boat or canoe gone with a few inches of rise in the river.

In the heat of summer, it's nice to camp on sand and gravel bars. The closer to the river, and the farther from vegetation, the less problem with mosquitoes. If you get around trees and bushes and the mosquito problem increases. But in the fall, winter, or early spring when insects aren't a problem, you might be more comfortable a little further away from the river in a clean wooded area or in a small grassy meadow. Dampness is less of a problem when you're slightly away from the river.

When you're floating, it's a good idea to stop and pitch camp a couple of hours before dusk. This schedule gives you time to check out the area, gather firewood and so on. If you expect a storm, find and check out a bluff shelter if possible or perhaps a high bank that can protect a tent from the wind. Because of lightning, stay away from trees and fences. And don't crawl under an aluminum craft for shelter. As I mentioned before, a small transistor radio is valuable during stormy weather for floaters who wish to receive area weather warnings.

A tent is poor shelter in a severe storm, but it can be made passable if bluff shelters aren't available. Be sure your tent is well staked and is set up in an area that best protects it from lightning, rising water and winds. If your stakes are set in gravel or sand, they may not hold. Set heavy rocks on top of them.

Don't try to float through a severe storm. Find the best protection you can and sit it out. And if a river rises drastically, don't float while it's flooded. You're best off to stow the equipment you can't carry, bundle and cover it with your plastic covers and walk out, returning later for the gear.

Overnight on a Gravel Bar

Some floaters, after enduring a storm on the river, choose never to make another float. It's a humbling experience, but something all men should experience. As you sit in a tent that's suddenly far too flimsy, listening to lightning crackle about you, followed by deafening roars of thunder and tree limbs cracking with the wind, you realize what a powerless insignificant creature man can be.

But you forget those hard times when you find one of those big beautiful eddies far from any access, where the water's deep and dark and lunker smallmouth lurk, a place where you need to spend all night just to be there at dawn. If you find one of those places, don't tell a soul!

12 SYCAMORES

Maybe the most beautiful thing the Creator placed along the rivers of the Midwest is the sycamore tree. I knew that the first time I saw the river, as a small boy only eight or nine years old. I looked at those giant white sycamores and my eyes got big and my jaw dropped. To me, the king sycamore is awe-inspiring yet today. There are fewer of them, by far, but they are no less spectacular, these great white giants of the valleys.

When I was eleven or twelve years old, I began to float the lower Piney river and hunt ducks with my dad. The old wooden johnboat we used had a frame affixed to the bow with woven wire for weaving oak and willow and sycamore boughs which hid the boat from whatever was downstream. Sycamore leaves didn't last long into the winter, but early in the fall, you could cut the limbs from a young sycamore and the leaves were so big they concealed the boat. On occasion, a big sycamore limb would have fallen into the river, wrenched away by a summer storm perhaps. Those limbs would be snowy white, and the leaves bright yellow. In such a spot, quite often, you could count on a flock of wood ducks taking refuge. Many times they'd be next to impossible to see but as you drifted close,

Sycamores

We floated the river in the fall with our johnboat hidden by bows of sycamore and oak.

184

Sycamores

there would be some movement in the water amongst the leaves and maybe you'd spy four or five of the beautiful little ducks sitting in a row well above the water on a white limb. I saw that often, and no two pictures were the same, but I never saw greater beauty in all of nature.

One year, there was a sycamore limb jutting out across the river about fifteen feet above the water and it was hollow. A hole in the limb about six or eight inches around, faced upriver and inside that hole there was a screech owl. In the course of an entire fall, we'd make that float four, five, maybe six times. And he was there every single time we floated beneath that limb, sitting back in the hollow, most likely asleep until we came along. But his eyes were always open when we got beneath him, and he'd set there stone still until we passed.

I think back to the things I saw then, and if I had owned a camera like the one I have now, I would have had some great pictures of sycamores and screech owls and woodies and all the other once-in-a-lifetime sights and wonders the river gave us to see behind that floating blind.

I have told the story often about the foggy, misty November morning only a half hour into a duck-hunt when a commotion along the bank revealed a red fox chasing something amongst the roots of a big sycamore. There was a flurry and a splash, and a chipmunk entered the river and headed across the current, turning upstream toward our floating blind. The red fox followed, only a few yards behind, and gaining on his would-be breakfast.

They were only a few feet before me when I lifted my Iver-Johnson sixteen gauge intent on blasting the fox and saving the chipmunk. Dad stopped me just in time, and the chipmunk gained the rocky bank a few feet ahead of the fox, disappearing into the rubble of football-sized limestone chunks. The fox followed him, shaking the water from his fur and then frantically digging at the rocks where his prey had disappeared.

I couldn't understand why I couldn't shoot the fox. He was,

185

Sycamores

as I argued to dad, trying to kill that little defenseless chipmunk. Dad didn't dispute that. He just pointed out that we were there to kill defenseless wood ducks and defenseless squirrels. We were just like the fox, looking for prey which we would eat, just as he would eat the chipmunk. And he took the time to explain to me that day how nature works, and how perfect it is in the workings of it. "Nothing out here on the river is good nor bad" dad told me when we pulled into a gravel bar where he lit his pipe. "That chipmunk has no greater or lesser value than the fox, and some of them will end up being eaten by predators because God made them for that purpose. If any predator is evil or bad than we are the same, because we are predators too."

As we floated the rivers during all seasons, I grew and learned. From my dad and grandpa I saw it firsthand and experienced it. With the hours upon hours, being there and absorbing it, seeing and smelling and hearing nature's secrets revealed, I learned. The experiences gave me a simple, down to earth knowledge, but there was more than just the learning of how things worked. There was the feeling, the understanding, the perceiving of things. It was a perception which took place with the slowness of the sun's travel across the sky, the gradualness of leaves changing in the fall, the inevitability of a fallen log becoming decaying wood, and eventually becoming soil again, from whence it had first begun to grow. I loved the river so much that I thought of little else when I was young. I never attended football games or basketball games or parties. All my time was devoted to the river, to the outdoors that I loved. I didn't understand much about anything else in life, my grades were unimpressive, and I didn't get along well with people. But when I was on that river, in my old johnboat, or slipping through the bottoms hunting squirrels, I was in my element and I knew it. I also knew that the Creator had made me for this, and He had made this for me. I never had the problem of not knowing who or what I was. I never felt the need to go in search of myself as other young people did in those days. The river and

186

Sycamores

the woods around me taught all that at a very early age. My roots were there with the roots of those sycamore trees.

Somehow, years later, I wound up at the University of Missouri studying wildlife management, thinking I'd someday be a biologist, or a forest ranger or game warden. And I was fortunate enough to begin to see the outdoors through the eyes of professors who believed that all knowledge came from books, and all learning was a result of books. I learned all the scientific names, the anatomy of wild creatures, the way various species and families of plants and animals were constructed.... the nuts and bolts of nature.

Combining that with what I knew from being so close to it as a youngster, I gained a unique insight into nature and the great outdoors. My professors thought I was crazy when I would argue that at times that the books weren't exactly right. But very often, they were not. One of those professors told me I was a true product of the Ozarks. He didn't mean it as a compliment, but I took it that way. Another one refused to believe my grandfather had trapped a pair of 90 pound beavers, and when I showed him the photos, old black and white newspaper pictures from the early 50's, he still wouldn't believe it. He said the photos must have been doctored, no beavers ever got that big in the Ozarks. He knew all about beavers, but he never had trapped one, or skinned one, or stretched the pelt of one. He and the other professors at the University looked at the old-timers from the Ozarks as ignorant. And I have to admit, no one ever looked upon a college professor with more disdain than my grandfather and the old rivermen at the local pool hall whom I had learned so much from as a boy. But I did not share that disdain. I learned from those professors, and admired much about them.

But I began to realize that there were lots of ways to be intelligent. The old-time rural people in the Ozarks weren't ignorant at all. They had a great deal of intelligence, and abilities that were exceptional. My grandpa didn't know a thing

187

Sycamores

about scientific names, gestation periods, or osmosis and enzymes. But then, those college people couldn't find a sassafras tree big enough to make a boat paddle, nor set a trotline, nor paddle a boat down the river in a straight line. I was quick to point that out to them, and my grades didn't get any better because of it. Back home in the hills, when I tried to tell those country people why it was important that a fox squirrel was also known as Sciurus nigra, and why noodling catfish would ultimately hurt the survival of the species, they all shook their heads and agreed that college had turned me into a dad-blamed book-learned nitwit. I figured out early that you'd never get the two sides together. There are lots of ways to be smart, and intelligence doesn't have a lot to do with wisdom. Both sides could have done a lot more with some of what the other side had.

With that kind of background, I can tell you that nutrient and water flows up and down the sycamore tree through xyleom and phloem tubes inside the cambium layer just beneath the bark and the green chlorophyll within the leaves manufactures food. I learned that in college. But I can also tell you that sycamores grow bigger, taller and faster than anything else in the Ozarks, but they won't survive on high rocky ridgetops because they like sinking their roots into waterlogged ground, and I can tell you the wood is brittle and light, it burns fast and doesn't give off as much heat as other woods. I learned that from the Ozark country people I grew up around. But that's not what's important about the sycamore. What's is important is it's role as a protector...the strongman of the river... the great guardian of the valley.

And then there's the strength of the willow. While the sycamore beautifies the river with it's greatness, the little willow tree is of no less importance. Young willows grow in mass, and though small, are powerful in their ability to hold the soil and the gravel bars in place. Where the willows gain a hold and begin to grow, there is stability, and the river may change it's

Sycamores

A stately sycamore supporting an annual rookery of Great Blue Heron

Sycamores

course because of it. The willow can become a giant tree itself, but it is the small thickets of young willows which are so important in holding the ground around flooding streams. Willow stands are sometimes too thick to walk through, but they prevent erosion, and grow quickly to put up a stand against the swift torrents.

River maples are also majestic, though not quite as showy as the sycamore. In the early half of the twentieth century, river families actually did tap the river maples in the spring and fall to catch buckets full of sap, which in turned was boiled away to create a sweet syrup used to sweeten pies and cakes, and other foods and drinks. One old timer told me that what he remembered most about the river maple sap was that a big tree would produce so much of it without harming the tree, and that it took so much of it to boil down to a quart of thick sweetener.

The oaks and the hickories and the redbuds and dogwoods and hackberries and so many other species provide food, so the sycamore isn't needed for that. A sycamore is a poor provider of food. It's seed balls are not a great source of sustenance for anything. The sycamore provides shelter, a home at one time or another for almost every wild thing you can imagine. There are few big mature sycamores which do not have hollows inside the bole of the tree, and others inside the large high branches. There's always more than one den in one tree, always a nursery somewhere. A small hole here and there for a woodpecker or flying squirrels or bats, a roomy cavern for a family of coons, an upper chamber for a wood duck nest. One biologist told of seeing a hen wood duck apparently looking to nest in April, stick her head into a hollow in a sycamore tree where a fox squirrel had already set up house-keeping. The squirrel, according to the biologist, bit the hen through the head and killed her. I remember seeing a hen and drake wood duck do an effective job of driving a fox squirrel from a hollow tree nest one spring. Always, there was competition for those cavities high above the ground for nurseries. But beneath the tree, in the network of sprawling twisting roots, there maybe a groundhog den, a hunting ground for a mink or weasel, a playground for a young otter. A fox may den in the earth beneath it's tangled roots, and may have her young there. Or if there's less space, ground mammals of various types may take shelter there.

The same can be said of other den trees along the streams, oaks and river maples become hollow and even in death, stand for years to provide places for birds and animals to take shelter, to hibernate, to raise young. A woodpecker can find everything in a dead tree, a shelter and nesting spot, and food as well in the various insects and insect larvae found invading the wood.

But there are den trees and there are den trees. The ridge tops need the oaks and the hickories and the pines, but the river has to have the sycamore, or it has no heart and soul. White, high and strong, eye to eye with the bluff-tops, the sycamore watches over the river, whether it is swelled with spring torrents or July dry. The river must have the sycamore, or it has no companion

13
RIVER BIRDS

I'd be hard pressed to think of a river bird I haven't seen in the branches of a sycamore. On one river just this past summer, there were dozens of great blue heron nests high in the top of two magnanimous sycamores along the river. From that rookery came a constant squawking and squealing and grunting from young herons just getting big enough to fly. It was a noise much like that of a pen full of hogs.

There's no more common bird along the rivers of the Midwest than the great blue heron. He is significant because he is a very efficient fish eater, and game fish are often his prey. The tall, slate gray-colored wading birds are also an alternate host to a little worm-like parasite known as the yellow grub, which spends part of it's life cycle in the small aquatic, "pennywinkle" snails, and then finally in the meat of black bass. Sometimes most of the great blue herons will migrate in the dead of the winter, but some will stay all year in lower parts of the Midwest. Ozark people never called them herons, they called them cranes. And the bird river people called Shikepokes, were little green herons, about a third of the size of a great blue heron. The real old-time Ozarkians called them

River Birds

'fly up the creeks'. The little green herons don't look green, they have a purple cast to the breast feathers and bluish crest and slate colored wings. The bill is black, the legs orange and the eyes bright yellow. They are stalking, wading birds which, as a rule, do not stay on the rivers of the upper Midwest very long into the winter because the small minnows and sunfish they prey on become hard to find in shallower water when the leaves are gone and the frost is heavy. And while the great blue heron can get out into some deeper water, the little green heron cannot. But when they are feeding, shikepokes move as slowly as the hands of the clock, sneaking up on a school of minnows or small fish. In fact, they have been known to use fish food to attract minnows. At those places where fish food is given to visitors at parks or hatcheries or marinas, little green herons have been seen placing the food in the water with their beaks, and waiting for the fish it will attract.

The great blue heron can be a problem at times because they reproduce well and overpopulate small waterways, and at certain times of the year, they take smallmouth bass. They are even greater nuisances when they find trout hatcheries or trout parks and develop a taste for trout, or when they concentrate at fish farms where they prey on young catfish or fish being raised and sold for bait.

The bird most typical of Midwestern rivers is the kingfisher, flashy and acrobatic, diving to the water to take small minnows and bragging to the whole world about his ability with stuttering raucous cry that can be heard from one eddy to another. Kingfishers dig back into vertical dirt banks along the river, actually constructing a small tunnel to nest in. They lay their eggs, an average number of a half dozen or so, at the end of that tunnel. Old rivermen use to insist that the kingfisher reinforced his tunnel with fish bones and made a nest from fish bones, but they don't. Kingfishers regurgitate the small bones of the fish they eat, and by the time the eggs hatch, there are quite a number of them in that tunnel. The babies are fed regurgitated min-

River Birds

River Birds

Pen and ink drawing by Max Thompson

River Birds

nows while they are very young, and I am sure that there are times in the spring when high water from heavy rains destroys kingfisher nests and baby birds in those nests, along the rivers. In my boyhood, when we floated the river in the fall hunting ducks behind that floating blind, kingfishers would come flying up the river and be right upon us before realizing there were eyes behind the brushpile. A few times, kingfishers actually landed on the blind.

Another fish eater is the hooded merganser. You seldom see any of the other mergansers along the rivers, but the beautiful white-hooded fish-eating migratory bird which is not a duck, but associated with them quite often, loves the streams, and stays throughout the winter along smaller rivers and creeks. They are divers, and are actually included in the game bag limits for duck hunters who want to hunt them, but if you eat one merganser, you won't want to eat another. The drakes are so beautiful, however, they are often taken to taxidermists to be mounted for display in a hunters den as part of a game bird collection. I've never seen a merganser nest in the Ozarks, but they nest like woodducks, in hollow trees not far from streams and sloughs and small waters.

Another fish eater seen along the Midwestern streams is the osprey, often known as a fish hawk. They are said to nest in some parts of the upper Midwest. I have seen pairs in the Ozarks in the spring, but never an osprey nest along one of our streams. Ospreys can dive on the water with considerable speed, and nail a fish of a couple pounds or so. The pads on the underside of the feet have tiny little sharp spikes which help them to hold onto the fish after they nab it. A year or so back in October, we were conducting an interpretive float trip down the Niangua river when an immature bald eagle and an osprey got into a short period of aerial combat about 150 feet above our caravan of floaters. There were about 20 people along, and most of them had never seen an eagle or an osprey. For some reason the eagle was mad at the osprey and was chasing him

197

River Birds

down the river screaming in rage. The osprey was giving forth his high pitched chirping noise and eluding the eagle easily, almost as if taunting him. I imagine the whole thing was over a fish.

Eagles have been on Ozark rivers since I was a boy in the 60's, but there are many times more of them now than there were then. They are fish eaters too, but also are very partial to the coots which pass through in the fall, and they prey on sick or crippled ducks of all species. I have had eagles dive down and pick up a duck I had just dropped while duck hunting. Several years ago, one took a crippled mallard drake right out from in front of my Labrador which was in hot pursuit of the floundering duck. In Canada, I lost two ringneck ducks in one afternoon to a pair of eagles, and a third one to an otter. Eagles do nest in the Ozarks now, but most of their nests are on reservoirs. In 1962, dad paddled our johnboat up on a mature bald eagle which was taking a bath just above a Piney river shoal. I

River Birds

sat there behind the blind and watched him throw water all over himself and ruffle his feathers and shake. He had his feet in about 6 inches of water and seemed to be enjoying it, despite the fact that it was December, and that water had to be terribly cold. When we got to within about 25 or 30 feet, he flew up on a dead snag not 15 feet above the water and watched us pass as if he weren't sure what we were. It was one of the most thrilling moments of all those years of floating the river. Now eagles are as common as herons in places during the winter. You might see 15 or 20 on one full day's float, or half that many in one area of one of our big reservoirs.

Hawks and ospreys and eagles make similar nests, but they are considerably different in size of course. For some reason, a river itself isn't the prime habitat of our Midwestern hawks, but owls really do seem drawn to small waterways. Great horned owls and barred owls and screech owls are seen often in the early dawn or dusk on a river. Barred owls are the most vociferous, and many many times I have called them down to the trees above a river camp on a summer night. Sometimes you can get two or three of them hooting and laughing in a tree right above your tent and campfire. They certainly aren't the wisest of the owls. Their call is easy to imitate and they are easy to fool. If you have never heard barred owls get excited and begin to laugh back and forth in a frenzied calling contest, you have missed something. Spend much time on the river at night between April and August, and you will hear it.

Screech owls give forth a wavering, spooky wail, which is harder to imitate, but they too are not hard to call right in to the branches above your camp at night on the river. You won't do that as easily with the warier of the three, the great horned owl, which gives forth a soft and subdued call nothing like it's cousins. Few people realize that an owl does not build a nest, he can't use his beak in such a manner as other birds can. Owls may nest in hollows in large trees, or they may use the abandoned nest of a hawk or osprey or other raptore.

River Birds

Other fish-eating birds visit the river of course, pie-billed grebes pass through in the fall, migrating with the waterfowl species. On the rivers of the Ozarks, I have seen almost every species of waterfowl found in the Mississippi and Central flyways except canvasbacks. In order, from most abundant to least abundant, there are woodducks, mallards, blue-winged teal, green-winged teal, gadwalls, scaup and ringnecks, widgeons, pintails, redheads, blondes and brunettes (Just joking about the blondes and brunettes). Occasionally Canada Geese stop along the rivers and a few snows and blues and white-fronts. But Ozark rivers aren't made for geese. They were once attractive to passing geese when there were bottomlands planted in corn, but that all ended in the '50's and early '60's. Only once did I ever see a ruddy duck on an Ozark river and that was many many years ago. On a couple of occasions, also many years ago, we found a small flock of black ducks. They have become increasingly rare in the middle flyways.

Only one species of waterfowl nests along our lower Midwest streams in any number, and that of course is the woodduck. They too were attracted by cornfields, but lacking that, they are very fond of acorns. The acorn-bearing oaks along the river in the fall may attract huge flocks of woodies, up to 50 or 60 in one area of a small stream. They will not tolerate extreme cold, and if you get some nights in the twenties, Fahrenheit, they pick up and head south. We always got woodducks in November, and usually by Thanksgiving, when the big flocks of mallards began to come in, the woodduck hunting was over. They come back in April, right behind the first spring migrators, the blue-winged teal. The teal pass on to the north, as do many of the woodies, but many woodducks stay along Ozark streams to nest.

So they too occasionally seek out the big hollow trees along the river where they fill a nest with eggs and wait for the ducklings to hatch. If you float the rivers in the early summer and come across an old hen woodduck flopping along the surface and shrieking as if she is badly hurt, be confident she is not. She just has some little duckling close by, and she uses the broken wing act just as good as the killdeer to draw the attention of a potential predator.

In the 1950's, woodducks were considered to be a very endangered species and there were some naturalists who expected them to become extinct. But throughout the upper Midwest, nature lovers began to build woodduck nesting boxes and put them up around waterways and marshes, and the little ducks began to respond. By the time I started hunting ducks, they were coming back a little, and hunters were allowed to have one per day in the bag limit. Around 1961, my dad pad-

dled me up unto a big flock of 30 or so on the lower Piney, and when they flushed, I dropped a nice drake. When I retrieved him, he had a band on his leg. I sent the information in and learned that he had been banded a few months earlier in Onalaska, Wisconsin. I carried that band for years, my only connection with the great northern country that I read about in outdoor magazines but never dreamed I'd ever see. Woodies and mallards that pitched in to the Piney river in the fall fascinated me more than all the other river creatures because they came from the far north, from Canada where there were moose

River Birds

and bear and loons, from the country where my ancestors had lived.

The woodies we hunted in November were seldom the ones which nested there in the early summer. I always wondered about that in June when we'd see a bunch of young woodducks along the river, dashing madly into the vegetation along the river bank when I'd paddle close. They just disappeared somehow, and when I was young I'd take a dipnet and try like crazy to catch one. Those summer ducks would leave the river before the first heavy frost and go south, and new flocks of woodies would come in from Iowa and Wisconsin, Minnesota and the Dakotas and Canada.

While there are many birds typical of the Midwest riverways, the woodduck has always been my favorite. When you see a drake woodduck in the wild, it's beauty is beyond description. I remember times when dad and I would float up close to a big flock behind our blind and I would be so spellbound watching them I actually would forget to shoot. I remember many occasions when I would be on the river and two or three or even a dozen woodies would come in to settle on a slough or eddy, and they'd whiz through those branches as if they were acrobats. The shrill cry of the old hens could be heard hundreds of yards away, and there was no sound more a part of the river than that.

A woodduck might nest quite aways from the water at times, which is a little surprising to me. I've actually seen them nest in trees a quarter of a mile from the stream, even partway up the side of a wooded ridge. Those little woodducks come out of the hollow just a little while after they hatch and they may fall 30 feet or so to the ground. I mean they fall head over heels, with no semblance of flight. But they are never hurt by the fall, because they are so light and fluffy it's like tossing out a pile of feathers. I don't think they'd leave an imprint in a bowl of whip cream when they meet the earth below them. And then they follow the hen in a quick march to the river or slough

202

River Birds

where they will seldom leave the water again. I remember once many years ago seeing a mother woodduck and her young stop traffic on a busy city street, as they headed to the safety of the Arkansas river backwaters. A few years after that, I watched a comparable sight as a woodduck hen and 7 or 8 little ones waddled down the middle of a remote gravel road toward the Buffalo river a quarter mile away.

Maybe there are other birds less conspicuous which are just as typical of the river. When you camp on the streams in the summer, there are the whipporwills and their cousins, the chuck-wills-widow. Both are fascinating and seldom seen close-up. They don't have legs for walking, but ornithologists say they will occasionally move their eggs by holding them between their thighs and flying them to a safer spot. They can do that because they don't build nests, they just pick a spot in the leaf litter. They feed in flight, on a variety of insects, and nothing but insects, in the faint light at the end of day, and before dawn.

Along a summer river, there are dozens of bird species, all the common ones, and some not so common. I am fascinated by the rain-crows, also known as the yellow-billed cuckoo. They are large and slender, brown, white and black with curved dark beaks. They give off that weird clucking call, that sounds like a sound created by striking bamboo canes together. And when you hear them, according to the old timers, it is soon to rain. I can say without reservation that every time I have ever heard a rain-crow, it has rained somewhere within 24 hours.

There are also the colonies of cliff swallows which nest beneath the bluffs close to the water, making nests of mud, raising hundreds of tiny fledglings in those groups of close nests sometimes hanging out over the water. You would think that quite a few of them would wind up in the water, but if they do I have never seen it. The swallows also feed in flight on insects, and they are swift and streamlined, yet can flutter in one place as if they are light as feathers.

River Birds

But when it is all said and done, most of the birds flee the Ozarks and the surrounding regions come winter. Ah what a woodchuck would give to be a bird. He has to waste half his life asleep in a deep hole, while the woodduck and all the other birds can wisk away to warmer climates.

The real Ozark birds are the ones tough enough to stay through the winter, to tough it out when the snow gets deep and the temperature takes a nose dive. The owls and the red-tailed hawk, the cardinals and the woodpeckers, the wild turkey and the bob-white quail. The big pileated woodpecker, who splits the air with a call even more raucous than that of the kingfisher, is known as a woods-hen to the old time Ozarkians. He is typically a bird of river and ridge-top alike. Maybe none of the others are typically river birds.

But the wild turkey finds the river a good place to roost, especially where there are steep hillsides above the water, and high trees like the sycamores growing from the very edge of the stream. It isn't easy for a heavy bodied turkey to fly from the ground straight up into the branches where they want to roost, so they like to walk up the hillsides, even to the tops of some of the bluffs, so that they may pitch off a higher point to roost-branches below. Streams which flow through hills afford great roosting areas for wild turkeys. If the roosts along the river are in the right places, they shelter the wild turkey from strong, cold winter winds which are usually out of the north or west. Instinct helps them know that.

No matter the season, the river has birds to add a great variety of sound, whether from melodic notes or just a loud cheerful noise. There's the scream of a hawk, the squawking of a great blue heron, even a woodpecker hammering at a hollow tree, But birds add more than sound, they add color, and to fill the branches and the thickets and the waters edge with life. If indeed the river is a living thing, it seems most alive with birds, and flowing water isn't really a river without them.

River Birds

Pileated Woodpecker

14
FURBEARERS

Many years ago I was floating a river in the fall when I became aware of a commotion in shallow water close to the bank. I glanced toward it and saw a young mink, probably one born in the previous spring, in a mock battle with a big yellow sycamore leaf. As I watched, he actually rolled over on his back, batting at that leaf as it lay on his belly.

It made me smile, but I knew there was another side to the comical-looking little furbearer playfully attacking a floating leaf. I remembered once, years before, watching a mink in mortal combat with a muskrat, which was as big as he was. The mink had ahold of the muskrats throat and was wrapping his long wiry body around that of the shorter, wider muskrat, turning him around and around in the water, trying to subdue his prey. It was a violent but short battle. You could see blood in the water as the muskrat finally died and the mink pulled him into the pocket beneath some logs and limbs.

Darrell Hamby, a good friend of mine and a great outdoorsman who grew up in the Black River country of east Missouri, told me of an experience he once had, hunting cottontails in the snow. He kicked a brushpile and a mink came bouncing out, its

207

Furbearers

head and neck red with blood. It headed down the hillside toward a small stream, folding its front legs every few bounds and gliding over the snow like a sled, leaving smudges and specks of red in the snow as he went.

Darrell said he first thought the mink was injured, but a close examination of the brushpile revealed the true story. The mink had followed a cottontail into the thick covert. There was blood and rabbit fur everywhere. He was apparently just finishing his meal when Hamby came along.

I have always been thankful that God created the mink and weasel so small. If either of those creatures were the size of a fox, nothing would be safe. A lot has been written about the ferocity of the wolverine, but there's nothing more vicious than the mink. He's not cruel or bloodthirsty, he's just always hungry. He has a high metabolism, burns energy as a high level, and never sees anything he won't eat if he can catch it and kill it.

His small size, a long but slender body, serves him well. Wherever a muskrat or rabbit can go, he can go. And he can even go quite a distance up a tree after a squirrel if he is so inclined.

In addition, he can swim like nothing you've ever seen. He can't catch every fish he gets after, but he'll outswim most of them, if fish is his choice for dinner.

And then there are his two cousins. One of them is the weasel which almost no one ever sees. He's about one-third the size of a mink. The other is the otter, which is commonly seen and four or five times the size of a mink.

Weasels are very nocturnal in habits, but in truth any 100 acres of river bottom watershed in the Midwest probably shelters more weasels than mink or otters combined. The weasel is no less aggressive as a predator. He'll tackle small mammals and birds that are larger than he is.

In the lower Midwest the weasel stays brown all year but from Iowa and Nebraska northward, he begins to change over

208

Furbearers

to a white coat in the winter. Northern weasels are known as "ermine", and their pelts have been extremely valuable in years past. Southern weasels as well as all other southern furbearers are not as valuable as northern members of the same species.

I've always thought what an oddity north and south creates among fish and wildlife species. Mammals grow larger and furs more prime the farther north you go. The bigger deer antlers are found in the northern states and into Canada.

And yet, the bigger, heavier individual fish are found in the south. Walleye in the Ozarks, as well as brown trout and large-mouth bass and other sunfish family members, grow much larger than the same species in the north.

That's good for the bigger cousin of the mink, the otter. Otters love fish. They were almost completely gone from the Ozarks until the early 1990's when the Missouri Department of Conservation decided to restock them throughout the state.

There was no uproar when the restocking program began. Missouri traded wild turkey for the otters and they were beautiful, playful creatures. But even more than the mink, the otter loves-- and is even better at outswimming and catching--- fish.

It was like sowing seed on fertile ground. The otter thrived, repopulated and repopulated again. Soon there were a hundred in a region where only 10 or 20 had been stocked. And they found stream fishing to be much better than they left it.

Midwest streams as they were 100 years ago were fuller, deeper and ran a great deal more volume of water. Shoals which are today two feet deep were three or four feet deep years back. Eddies were sometimes fifteen feet deep beneath the high bluffs and filled with big rocks and ledges. Otters found fish to eat because there were so many more fish back then, and there were plenty left. It was the way nature meant it to be.

In the '90s they were introduced to heavily fished streams where gravel and silt and filled in deep eddies and covered the rocks and ledges. Those 10- and 15-feet deep pools of water became four- or five- foot pools with little cover for a 12-inch

209

Furbearers

bass to hide beneath. The public began to see the otter as a fish-killing machine. Fishing went from not-all-that-good to gosh-awful when a family of otters moved through.

But they were more deadly in farm ponds and hatcheries than anywhere. Some farm ponds lost half their catfish in only a few days when a family of otters moved in. And they were obnoxious enough to leave the skeletons right there in a pile on the pond bank. The Conservation Department biologists knew they had a problem when they experienced first-hand the otter's ability as a fish catcher. Three of them moved into Bennett Springs trout park and liked trout so well they had to be given special attention.

Only the trappers became the otter's friend. The slick sleek furbearers were worth more than anything else in the river. So the besieged and exasperated M.D.C. biologists opened the trapping season on otters, hoping to take away some of the heat they were getting. Then a group of city folks from St. Louis and Kansas City blasted them for not protecting the otter.

It is likely that the otter is back to stay because trappers are fewer now. But even so, they will shrink in population from the booming numbers seen just after they were stocked. The otter is a convenient scapegoat. We can blame him for the poor fishing, instead of blaming the pollution, the clearing, the filling and the overfishing, which we have caused. Sure, he'll make an easy meal of a two pound smallmouth when he can, but 100 years ago the rivers were havens for the same-sized small-mouth.

Back then, the rivers protected the fish from the otter too. Now, we have less water, more fishermen, hordes of giggers in the winter and less place for fish to hide. The otter wasn't the straw that broke the camels back, but they were perceived to be.

My good friend and Corps of Engineers Ranger, Rich Abdoler, who works at the Truman Lake in west central Missouri, told me quite a story about seeing an otter trying to kill a small fawn. Rich was floating the Little Niangua in early

Furbearers

summer when he heard the fawn bleating and saw the otter, holding onto the fawn's nose with its body wrapped around its neck much as the mink had attacked the muskrat.

Rich took a swing at the villain with a paddle and the otter let go of the fawn, retreating to the river and disappearing as the fawn struggled back up the steep bank to it's mother. Rich acknowledges he probably shouldn't have interfered but it's sort of an instinctive reaction. Like most of us, he eats deer and fish and he'd just as soon the otter didn't.

The mink and otter were the prize furbearers for river trappers of a by-gone era. It probably was the high price of fur which caused the otters to become nearly extinct in the Ozark region. When I was a small boy, there were very few mink in the lower Midwest and no otter at all.

For awhile, there were very few beaver in the greater Ozarks region, but a healthy Midwest river system of 150 or 200 years back supported good numbers of beaver and muskrat- - the herbivores, and otter and mink-- the carnivores. The raccoon was no less a part of the river. He was omnivorous, feasting on frogs and fish and crawdads, or berries and corn when he had the chance. Those five species were the river trappers main objective.

When the depression began, fur prices dropped so dramatically, that many trappers quit for good. That was the beginning of a comeback for all furbearers, including the gray and red fox and the bobcat.

My grandfather and river trappers like him used "drown sets" which meant that the furbearer was drowned quickly after being caught in a steel trap. Muskrats were easy to catch, farm kids throughout the Midwest made spending money catching muskrats. It was easy to find their feeding platforms on logs or rocks, and dens and runs back in beneath the creek or river banks. Pond owners hated muskrats because they tunneled back into pond dams and caused the ponds to leak. Their pelts weren't worth a great deal, but they brought more money than

211

Furbearers

possums and skunks.

It was the mink which brought the most money and mink were so smart you didn't catch one without a great deal of effort and experience. My grandfather burned his traps, eliminating all scent, and placed them while wearing leather gloves. He liked to put mink traps in shallow water next to rock outcroppings down at the rivers edge, which would channel the mink into the water at that point. But even then he would carefully cover the trap with leaves or river debris, so that the trap nor trap chain showed. He was so good at it, that when he finished, you couldn't tell the river hadn't washed the leaves in on top of the trap. Nothing about it looked manipulated.

My uncle told me that as smart as mink were, you could just about take away his wariness by hanging a bright red cardinal over the trap with a string. He said mink just loved cardinals for some reason, and if you shot one and hung it from a string above a trap at the edge of the water, you would attract a mink. Back then, no songbird laws protected the cardinal.

Raccoons were caught at the edge of the water too, but they weren't as hard to fool as a mink. My grandfather used bright objects like tinfoil on a trap pan occasionally which aroused the raccoons curiosity. He also would carve little fish out of potatoes and attach them to trap pans if he couldn't find minnows in the winter.

Beaver weren't hard to find or trap, you just set the trap at the end of a slide they were using, or at the entrance to a den back under the bank. Along many Ozark streams they didn't have to build dams and lodges because hollows back in the banks gave them the protection needed. Such dens were always marked with shoots and bark from small trees they dragged back into the opening. But it took a big strong trap to hold a beaver. They had big, tapered feet, nothing like the feet of other furbearers, and the trap had nothing to hold. If it wasn't a powerful set of jaws, the beaver would just pull free.

Drown sets for river furbearers insured a quick death.

212

Furbearers

Coons, mink, muskrat and beaver would swim out into the river when trapped, and trappers would attach the trap chain to a wire which ran down into deeper water and secured to a heavy rock. Sometimes the trap chain had at it's end a small piece of L-shaped angle-iron with a hole in it. The chain could then slide down all the way to the rock, but wouldn't slide back.

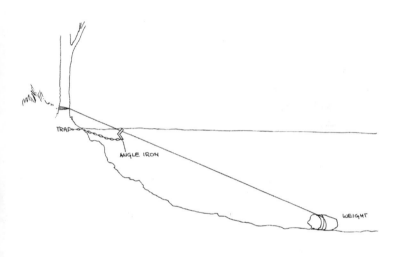

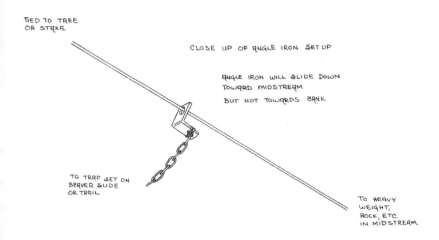

Furbearers

If it seems a cruel way to do things, it is because in the world men today live in, most people have little knowledge of nature's ways. Natural death in the outdoors for those furbearers might be a disease which takes days, or starvation, or predation which is often so brutal that modern man can't accept it when they see it. That muskrat I saw killed by the mink was no more comfortable in death than he would have been had he drowned at the end of a trap chain.

Raccoons which die of distemper over a matter of days, or beavers which age and die naturally, are not more kindly treated than they would be if they were trapped. There are no hospitals in the wild for the creatures of woods and rivers. Nothing dies an easy death. But it is the way of nature, and the old time trappers accepted that. They were predators themselves, just like the mink and the bobcat, and they made their living taking furs.

It is a fact that many times, the species declined because of their efficiency. The raccoon was evidence of that, but in the early part of the last century, night-time coon hunters who use hounds and sold pelts and even ate the raccoon at times, would stop at nothing to get all the raccoons they could get. If that meant chopping down an occasional tree, so be it. About that time, there was heavy logging in the Ozarks and all through the Midwest. Entire counties were nearly stripped of timber. Some parts of the southeast Ozarks looked as if it had been destroyed. So raccoons also suffered from a loss of den trees.

Outdoorsmen who were around in the 1930's say raccoons were as rare as deer and turkeys. But they began to come back as a result of something you might call evolution. They evolved into a creature of caves and ledges, began using holes in the bluffs for escape and for birth of their young.

Now raccoons are overpopulating their habitat in much of the Midwest, and at the time of this writing, with few coon hunters and trappers and rock-bottom low prices for fur, the raccoon can be a problem. It is thought by some that the

214

Furbearers

ground-nesting bobwhite quail's biggest problem is the raccoon and skunks which are constantly hunting for nests in the spring, and love to eat the eggs. But with those numbers come a different problem. Nature finds ways to cut back exploding populations of anything.

Furbearers

With raccoons, it is distemper, and it does an effective job. And then there's the automobile. In the past few years I have seen so many possums, skunks and raccoons killed on the highways you'd think they had dens in the ditches. One old trapper said that if furs were worth anything anymore he'd make a good living traveling the highways at first light in the fall.

Beavers were as hard to find as other furbearers in the thirties and forties along rivers of the Midwest. Conservation Departments restocked them in the early fifties, and they released a pair of Wisconsin beavers near the mouth of Arthur's Creek on the Big Piney which became somewhat notorious. Nowadays, you never see a cornfield on the Piney, it's all pasture and cattle. But in the ten or fifteen years after World War II, bottomlands were planted in row crops, most often corn. The reason we found so many ducks on the river when I was a boy was because of all the cornfields.

About 1950, a landowner just below the mouth of Arthur's creek told my grandfather that he was having problems with beavers wrecking his cornfield. Grandpa and his trapping partner, Bill Stalder, decided it would be a good place to get some beaver pelts, so they set traps along that part of the river in the fall, and caught several. But they were really surprised when they found some of the large beaver traps sprang, pulled out into the river and empty.

As stated before, a beavers foot is tapered, and beaver traps have to be large and strong to hold one, but Grandpa had never seen a beaver too big to hold, and neither had Bill. The landowner told them why. He said he had seen one of those two original beavers stocked there years before and his corn had fattened them to twice the size of ordinary beavers.

Bill Stalder came up with some bear traps, and they set them at the bottom of a well-used run. The next day, when they lifted the trap chain they could hardly lift the drowned beaver into the boat. In another trap, they caught it's mate. Neither

216

Bill nor my Grandfather could believe what they had, two beavers almost twice the size of a normal beaver. They took them to the feed mill and had them weighed. They weighed 90 and 94 pounds, probably the biggest beavers ever taken in the Ozarks.

Author's Grandfather, Fred Dablemont with Ozarks biggest beavers.

But they were not the biggest beavers ever taken, because beaver of that size and even larger ones had been trapped in Wisconsin and other northern states.

Until that time, and years after, Grandpa never saw another beaver above 70 pounds. And there are few beaver trappers

Furbearers

now. The fur isn't in demand as it was, and beaver in the Ozarks and lower Midwest isn't worth enough to get most trappers to skin one. The beaver pelt has to be cut from the meat, rather than pulled, as other skins are removed from the carcass. You can skin muskrats, minks, raccoons, and skunks, pulling the pelt off from incisions down the back legs, like pulling off a sock. Then you stretch those pelts inside out over boards fashioned like small ironing boards, where they can be scraped and dried. Most trappers stretch raccoon pelts flat.

Beaver pelts are cut off in a manner to produce a flat round pelt, and river trappers use to cut saplings which they made big circular frames out of by tieing one end to the other. Then the beaver hides were stretched inside the circle by lacing the edges of the pelt back to the sapling. The value of the pelt, when it came time to sell it, was determined mostly by it's prime, or pelt quality, but to some extent, it depended on how well the fur was skinned stretched, scraped, and dried. When it came to skin-

Furbearers

ning, you could easily tell experienced outdoorsmen from the beginners.

Maybe the most important furbearers are the little ones, dozens of little mice and voles and which live by the thousands along the rivers. In the bluffs and ledges above the river there are the woodrats as well. Field mice and woodrats are nothing like the house mouse and Norway rats which are filthy in habit and capable of spreading disease. Wild mice and rats and voles are not dirty, they do in fact have beautiful pelts.

But they are so important because they supply food for birds of prey and an assortment of predatorial furbearers. Along most Midwest streams, there are about 10 or 12 species of voles, harvest mice and deer mice. This is something else which you could write a book on, the little mammals no one thinks about, teeming along the rivers. I won't do that, other people already have. In your local library, you can find mammal books that give all the particulars on each species, right down to how many toes and teeth they have and how many eggs they lay. Well maybe they don't lay eggs, but some mammals do fly...the bats that live in caves and trees along the streams. There are also about eight or ten species of those, and they are some of the most fascinating creatures in nature.

Along our streams as well you will find shrews and moles, groundhogs and gray squirrels, fox squirrels, chipmunks and flying squirrels. Occasionally there's a wandering mountain lion or a black bear, depending on what river you are on.

The only other species with hair which I haven't mentioned is the white-tailed deer I suppose. Oh I almost forgot, there's the grizzled, fuzz-faced river trapper. But they are rare now. Time was, there were a whole handful of them.

219

15
UNDERWATER CREATURES

One spring weekend in the late 1960's, Darrell Hamby and I left School of the Ozarks College and headed for the Big Piney to recover from another week of pretending like we had been studying. Darrell loved the outdoors as much as I did, he had grown up on the Black and St. Francis rivers at the eastern edge of the Ozarks, and he was a very good outdoorsman.

We loaded our gear and floated the river, camping that evening at the mouth of Hog Creek just below the Catfish Rock Eddy. That spot on the upper Piney was one of my favorites, a place where I caught flathead catfish in the 30 pound range, and boatloads of bass and goggle-eye....well, bucketfuls anyway.

When our camp was set up, and darkness had settled, we sat on the gravel bar and cast nightcrawlers out into the deep hole of water where Hog Creek flowed in. Goggle-eye, or rock bass, are nearly nocturnal as summer comes on. I think during the summer they feed more at night than they do in the daytime, and that night Darrell and I were catching them faster than we could count them, turning back most of them, keeping the big ones. Darrell was tossing the keepers in a bucket behind him, rebaiting and hooking another one, having the time of his life.

221

Underwater Creatures

In the darkness, we just reeled in the fish, grabbed them, estimated their size and tossed them back or in the bucket.

I heard Darrell say something about having a hard fighter, and then the splashing of another hefty goggle-eye as he pulled it from the water. Except that one wasn't a goggle-eye! Darrell threw his rod and reel down just after he grabbed it and hollered for a light. In fact he hollered several things, some of it unprintable. Whatever Darrell had grabbed, he didn't feel like he needed to hold it long.

When we got the lights on, we could see what it was...a big ugly Ozark hellbender, the only one of ten or twelve I ever caught or saw in all my days on the river. They are one of the most mysterious, homely creatures I have ever encountered. But they are unique and special to the rivers of the Ozarks. Hellbenders are creatures of flowing water.

I saw a picture of a common waterdog in an Ozark newspaper many years ago, mistakenly identified as a hellbender. While hellbenders live in fairly good-sized streams and rivers, waterdogs, commonly called mudpuppies in the Ozarks, are found in ponds, rivers, lakes and sloughs. Both are large salamanders, and both are night-dwelling creatures. But the mudpuppy, or waterdog, has bright red gills showing. Hellbenders have internal gills which do not show after they mature.

Waterdogs are fairly common, and can live in a varied environment. When they are in well-oxygenated cool water, the gills shrink. In warmer, poorly oxygenated water, their gills seem to grow, becoming bushy and bright. These salamanders are found over a large area of the Midwest from north Alabama into Canada and east to the Appalachians.

Hellbenders are heftier in size than mudpuppies, the latter usually only eight to twelve inches long and more slender, with a smaller head. Old timers say that the mudpuppy, or waterdog, got its name from a barking sound it makes when out of water. None ever barked at me, but I wouldn't swear they don't!

The hellbender is the gosh-awfullest looking creature that

Underwater Creatures

ever came out of the water, or anywhere else for that matter. I caught several from the Big Piney river as a boy, most around 15 to 20 inches long. My grandpa said he had seen them better than two feet long, but I never did. It's head is large and shovel-like, rounded, flat and wider than the body, and the hellbender feels like nothing you have ever touched. The skin is loose, and wrinkled and a notch or two beyond what we ordinarily call "slick and slimy". It is nearly gelatinous, and when you handle a hellbender, your hands will feel dry and somewhat irritated for some time afterward. Still, there is nothing poisonous about them, as Ozark hill people once believed. That belief persists, and there are many who are afraid of these giant salamanders.

As ugly as they are, hellbenders are fascinating creatures which are rarely seen by today's Ozark outdoorsmen. They are yellowish to dark brown in color, with mottled dark splotches. The Ozark hellbender is a subspecies found most numerous in the drainage system of the Black river, but there are some in all the streams of the Ozarks, or at least there were once. The main hellbender species is found from southeast Kansas to St. Louis, mostly in the Osage river drainage system.

I'm not sure which of the two we were catching in the Big Piney, as the differences are subtle, but since the Big Piney is in the heart of the Ozarks, I'll call the ones I saw

223

Underwater Creatures

Ozark Hellbenders too. Hellbenders are also found in a band from north Alabama to New York, and in the lake Erie drainage. The largest specimen ever found in that region was 29 inches long. There's an Asian hellbender that grows to a length of five feet, and was once eaten in Japan and China. Probably the hellbenders and mudpuppies found in our area would he edible too, but I don't know how you'd ever hold one securely enough to clean it, and I'd have to be awful hungry to eat one.

I'm not sure how you'd go about finding a hellbender. They are attracted to blood, and eat liver in captivity. In the wild, they feed on dead fish, crayfish, worms and other aquatic organisms. Mudpuppies have the same diet, essentially. Of course, there are dozens of salamanders in the U.S. and there are five species which are found only in the Ozark highlands of Missouri, Arkansas and a small area in Oklahoma. One is the cirotto salamander, a four inch blind cave species found in total darkness, nearly white or pink and sometimes referred to as a "ghost lizard.'

Ozark hellbenders are found only in small region of the Ozarks, and in my opinion, should have been given a similar eerie name. Surely they are ancient creatures, and for me they bring back memories of johnboats resting on gravel bars, low-burning campfires, and trotlines to run at midnight. I don't particularly want to catch another one, but I hope there are some left..I doubt if there are many in the Piney, if any, because it is no longer the clean Ozark river I knew so many years ago.

Not long ago I received this information from Jessica Caplinger, a biologist with the National Park Service, working on the Current River...

"Hellbenders have flattened bodies which helps them slide under rocks for cover and remain stationary in fast moving water. Part of what makes them look so peculiar is the fleshy folds of skin along their sides. These skin folds actually provide surface area so they can breathe underwater. Hellbenders like cool water with high oxygen levels, especially spring fed rivers

Underwater Creatures

like the Current and Jacks Fork. They are nocturnal animals, only coming out at night to feed primarily on crayfish. Hellbenders have a long life span compared to most salamanders, sometimes up to 30 years, and they don't even start reproducing until around age 7.

The Ozark Hellbender is listed as a candidate species for the federal endangered species list because populations are declining throughout its range in the Ozarks, particularly over the last twenty years. The hellbender population is also getting older with little indication of consistent reproduction. There is a lack of juveniles in the population which indicates that reproduction may have been limited for some time. Scientists are working to understand why the population is declining and what is causing this lack of reproduction. Hellbenders have very specific habitat requirements which makes the species extremely vulnerable to habitat disturbance and changes in water quality."

There aren't many things living beneath the surface of our rivers which that could not be said of. The quality of the water at certain times of the summer and fall is so poor I wouldn't want to wade in streams Ozarkians once drank from, a century ago.

The suckers make up a large number of the fish found in a healthy, clean Ozark stream. I can vaguely remember seeing big redhorse suckers when I was a boy. My grandfather did a lot of gigging, and my uncle talks about how he remembers redhorse suckers of 15 to 18 pounds in weight. In his book, "The Fishes of Missouri," the renowned fisheries biologist William Pflieger identifies those big suckers as "River Redhorse" and he says that they seldom exceed 8 pounds, but acknowledges that he had witnessed a 17 pounder. The giant suckers are rare now in some waters where they were once common, and there are a variety of factors affecting their decline. The loss of deep eddies, the influx of silt and mud, and the tremendous pressure on them from ever-increasing numbers of giggers, all are factors. If you find river redhorse today, they will be small.

Underwater Creatures

In addition to the river redhorse, there are several other species commonly linked together and known by local fishermen as "yaller suckers". There is no yellow sucker listed by Pflieger....that fish is referred to as a golden redhorse. The black redhorse is the fish commonly called a "white sucker" in the Ozarks.

These are the two most common fish found in the take of Ozark giggers and snaggers. There is also a shorthead redhorse which also falls into the "yaller sucker" category. The shorthead reaches a size of one or two pounds commonly, and is found throughout more Midwestern waters than any other sucker. The golden redhorse is a little smaller, but either of these species could get to 4 or 5 pounds if they were allowed to reach the old age of 10 or 12 years. Pflieger finds the Black Redhorse to be the largest of the three, one specimen reaching 7 pounds in the Eleven Point. In our heavily gigged streams today finding any of these species reaching three pounds is a real rarity.

Not as common, found in larger north Ozark rivers like the Piney and Gasconade, is the Silver Redhorse, which grows faster and larger than the other species mentioned. In a long ago time, they were gigged in weights exceeding 10 pounds. William Pflieger lists the largest one known as 9 pounds.

But then there is another species known as a white sucker. So if you catch a fish a local riverman calls a white sucker, it might be a white sucker or it might be a black redhorse.

And then there is the blue sucker, not common in smaller waters, but seen often in the Missouri and Mississippi. Last but not least there is the spotted sucker.

The average fisherman would have a difficult time looking at one of these species in the 1 to 2 pound range and knowing for sure what he has. The characteristics which separate them isn't color so much because the colors of suckers change according to the waters where they are found and the time of year. Spawning fish are never colored as they are seen in the fall of course. I'll bet Pflieger himself had to count the rays of fins, and figure the size of scales to be absolutely sure what he had.

My favorite sucker, the one that makes me think of the Big Piney when it was deep and clean, and the creeks which fed it, is the Hog-mollie sucker, scientifically known as the Northern Hog Sucker. Hog-mollies fascinated me when I was rummaging around on the river as a boy. They too were great bait for flathead catfish, and one sucker which you couldn't confuse with another. Boy were they ugly. Maybe that's another reason they fascinated me. It was nice to know something not all that attractive had a place in the scheme of things. That gave me some hope as a youngster, I was a little bit on the ugly side myself.

In a boatload of gigged yellow suckers the fish at the bottom with a large head is a hog-molly sucker.

Hog-mollies have really declined in Ozark rivers, they are easy to gig, and they can't tolerate much silt and pollution. They once could be found in the 2 to 3 pound size, and were as good to eat as any sucker except the large head allowed less

Underwater Creatures

meat. Nowadays, a 1 pound Hog-mollie is a big one.

There aren't many forms of fish-harvesting from 100 to 150 years ago which have increased in popularity, but gigging has indeed. Today, even some of the giggers who are the most devoted to their sport question whether or not there are enough suckers left to be gigging them as intensely as they do.

But it became a sort of social event, as giggers would gather in the middle of the night on a gravel bar and build up a big fire to heat a cauldron of grease to deep fry the nights catch. Suckers are full of fine bones, but they are delicious if you score the meat and cut those bones up so they aren't noticeable. What you do is....you lay the sucker out on a boat paddle, scale it, gut it and remove the head and fins, then use a razor sharp knife to cut across the body down to the backbone, making cuts about 1/4 inch apart, but leaving the backbone intact. Just writing about it makes me hungry, because those sucker-fries in the middle of a cold night produced some delicious fresh fish.

I did quite a bit of sucker grabbing in the spring, with old casting reels and big treble hooks. That too was very popular, though not done as much today because there are smaller schools, smaller fish than ever before. All the species of suckers move to the shoals of the streams in April and May to spawn, and there use to be hundreds of them on some of the shoals. The water was so clear you could tie a small white rag on your line a foot or two in front of one or two treble hooks, and when a fish swam over the white rag, you jerked. And when you hooked a two or three pound sucker in that current, you had a fight on your hands.

Suckers were also grabbed in the winter months when they were found in deep quiet, clear pools where there were overhanging trees. You just climbed out on a limb over the water, lowered a treble hook and grabbed suckers.

I remember too that on the Big Piney after a summer rain, suckers were easy to catch in a rising, murky current in eddies just below a strong shoal. We'd catch goggle-eyes, sunfish and

The author grabbing yellow suckers from a tributary to the Buffalo.

suckers together on night-crawlers as the water rose and became murky. All seemed to be drawn to the swirling eddies just below the shoals, and there were always bass and catfish in the mix as well.

Underwater Creatures

There were no 'sunfish' in the Piney when I was a boy. You never heard that term. Everything that wasn't a bass or catfish or sucker was some kind of 'perch'. There were sun perch, shade perch, black perch, and punkinseeds. Punkinseeds were long-eared sunfish and black perch were the common green sunfish. Shade perch and sun perch were the various- colored bluegills found in the river, which probably came in as ponds were stocked with that species.

I'm not sure you would have found the bluegill in the Ozark Rivers 200 years ago. I think maybe longears and green sunfish would have been all that were there. And I can't say for sure, but I wonder if there were any largemouth in the highlands of the Ozark rivers 200 years ago. Certainly there were no spotted bass, they were introduced well before World War II, and I wonder if there was a time when smallmouth were the only bass found in the Big Piney and it's tributaries, or rivers like the upper Current, the Eleven Point, the Buffalo or the Niangua.

The old farmers you saw fishing along the river with cane poles when I was a boy were happy to catch a stringer of 'perch', a mix of green sunfish, longears and bluegill. Some of them, especially the longears, were not very big, but you could scale them, gut them and fry them whole, with head and fins removed, and have a bite or two of the tastiest fish in the creek.

Long-ear sunfish

If there is a more beautiful fish in the Midwest than the spawning season version of the longear sunfish, known to Ozarkians as the 'punkinseed', I have to be convinced of it. Some small minnows are beautifully colored in the spring, but a longear has every color you can find in the rainbow and some that you can't.

They had tiny little mouths, so they were seldom caught on anything but worms, and they almost never got any larger than your hand.

The green sunfish were plentiful and grew to respectable sizes. We caught them in the 50's and 60's up to a pound in weight, as hefty as the rock bass. But there were more green sunfish than goggle-eye, and you could catch enough of the smaller ones to bait a trotline. A big flathead might favor small suckers or horny-head chubs, but close behind was the green sunfish.

Green sunfish were also great fish for the fly-fisherman, because they eagerly took surface flies or small surface lures.

Green sunfish

Underwater Creatures

And they fought hard, had a mouth large enough to tackle a pretty good sized lure. They seem to be the hardiest sunfish in the river, capable of living in polluted water, with very low oxygen levels. But I remember the time when we considered green sunfish to be beautifully marked, hard fighting little versions of gamefish found in abundance in every river and creek of the Ozarks.

There were catfish of course, but the only catfish I cared about was the flathead, found in the deep eddies, and the biggest fish of the Midwestern streams. Flathead catfish in the Missouri and Mississippi rivers grow to weights exceeding 100 pounds on rare occasions. In larger Ozark streams, and Midwest streams which feed the Missouri, Mississippi and Arkansas, flatheads grow to 70 or 80 pounds. In smaller Ozark rivers and small streams on the periphery of the Ozarks, flatheads were seldom found in excess of 50 pounds, but a 30 to 40 pounder was always something you could figure on if you set trotlines well and had good bait.

There were channel catfish in most Midwestern rivers, but there were fewer in the Ozark highland streams than those in outlying flatter regions. As a boy, I never saw a channel catfish in the upper half of the Piney, nor were there any walleye.

Walleye, known as jack salmon to some, were common in the southeast Ozark streams, but not in the Piney. Local folks always blamed the dam on the lower Piney at Ft. Leonard Wood for the lack of walleye and channel catfish. But I have heard some fisheries biologists say they think the channel catfish, like the blue catfish may not have inhabited the higher, clearer, colder streams 200 years ago. They seem to prefer more turbid, slower streams of flatter regions of the Midwest. Blue catfish were found in the larger Ozark rivers, like the Gasconade, and the White and the Current, but in the lower sections.

Bullheads were always abundant in Ozark ponds and some of the slow, turbid streams, but I never found them to any degree in rivers like the Buffalo, Big Piney, Niangua or Current.

Underwater Creatures

Then there are mad-tom catfish, several subspecies of little miniature catfish which never exceed 6 or 7 inches in length. The smaller Ozark streams, some too small to float, sheltered those little catfish, and for awhile when I was young I was sure they were baby flatheads.

It was the flathead catfish which caused me to become aware of all the small minnows and fishes found in the rivers. We would seine bait for trotlines, always trying to get small sunfish, horny-head chubs or what my grandpa referred to as "dough-guts".

I didn't know, until I got to college, that "dough-guts" were stone-roller minnows, abundant in the Big Piney, growing to 6 or 8 inches in length, and easily-obtained-catfish-bait because of the schools found in shallow shoals, where it was easy to seine them. With them were creek chub minnows and shiner minnows. The bleeding shiners had bright red-trimmed fins and black stripes to accent it. They were beautiful minnows in the spring when they were spawning, then lost much of the bright red coloration as summer advanced to fall. But always, they were great bait for goggle-eye and bass. They were hard to keep alive on a trotline, so almost never used for that.

Then there were other kinds of shiners, and the top-floater minnows, known as studfish, with every color you can imagine, and the red-bellied dace minnows, both so brightly colored in the spring you just couldn't stop looking at them, fascinated with the beauty of those little underwater creatures.

The Big Piney had three varieties of sculpins, which were ugly and beautiful at the same time. They lay motionless much of the time on the bottom of the stream, nearly invisible, but capable of darting away in a flash. You have to see the sculpins to believe them, they look like something from prehistoric times.

Similar to the sculpins are the darter minnows, spending their life on the bottom, brightly colored in their spawning phases, indescribable in their beauty. Rainbow darters were

Underwater Creatures

something to see, but there is a little darter called a "saddle darter" found in the Big Piney and other Ozark rivers which can't be equaled in spectacular spawning color. Of course there are the rare Niangua darters, found only in the Niangua river system. There are about 3 dozen different darter minnows, many of them similar, but none exactly the same in color. There are about a dozen of the different darter minnows found in Ozark streams, and if you had them all in an aquarium at once in breeding colors you'd think you were looking at tropical fish.

In the western Ozark rivers, there were red shiner minnows which I never saw in the Piney. I kept some of them in a small aquarium in my office, and in the spring they were spectacular in their beauty, a blue body with fins bright pink.

That's something that seems very strange, certain minnows and darters found in one river system, completely absent in another system not all that far away. But it would take an entire book to talk about all the different small fish and minnows found in the rivers of the Midwest. There are hundreds of them. Should you become interested in seining them, and becoming something of an aquatic "bird-watcher", you need to find the book by William Pflieger, "Fishes of Missouri". It is a great work on all the fish found in rivers, and how to identify them, how they live and survive. Anyone interested in fish in our Midwest streams should acquire his book.

Then you'd need several books on aquatic insects, if you really want to get into learning about life beneath the surface. Ozark fishermen knew one aquatic insect well, the larval stage of the Dobson fly, called a hellgrammite. Hellgrammites live in the river for more than two years before maturing into mature insects. They are found in river shoals beneath rocks, and used to catch panfish, and bass. The Dobson fly, seen on the rivers in the summer, has big long pinchers which can really hurt if they get ahold of you. I've seen some with mandibles longer than two inches, almost as big as the insect itself. The wings are large and prominent, and when spread, they exceed four

Underwater Creatures

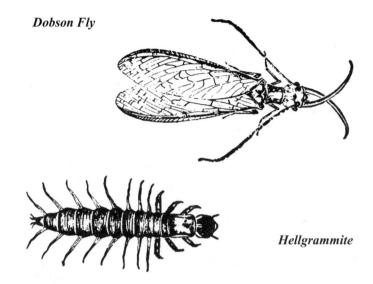

Dobson Fly

Hellgrammite

inches.

Mayfly nymphs are not used for bait, but doubtless are a valuable foodsource for small fish, and if you have been on the rivers at night in the early summer, you have seen the unbelievable Mayfly hatches which sometimes resemble a snowstorm. Sometimes they become "June-flies".

Insect hatches occur on the river all through the summer, and there are dozens upon dozens of insect larvae species found in the rivers throughout the Midwest. When you fish the river at night, or try to catch frogs or run trotlines, you quite often have those nights when you can't turn on a light because of the swarms of insects. You could write an entire book about the aquatic insects, but the only one of much significance to the fisherman is the hellgrammite.

Of significance too are the mosquito larvae and the problems they will eventually create for anyone on the river at night. While the mosquito larvae of course thrive in brackish water and still water, the hellgrammite thrives in swift shoals and they will live there for nearly three years before crawling out onto a gravel bar and becoming a Dobson fly in only three or four

Underwater Creatures

weeks.

That Dobson fly will only live a few weeks itself, and then the female will lay a couple of thousand eggs on leaves or limbs over the water which will hatch, fall into the water and presto, more hellgrammites. Similar insect species living in the water as larvae and on the land as adults are the damsel flies, dragon flies and stone flies.

The most aggravating of the aquatic insects in late summer is the horsefly, which never gave me much trouble on the Big Piney but is a menace on the Niangua. They bite like the devil, and circle my boat at times like Indians around a wagon train, one or two or three at a time. Their larvae also lives in the water. Hornets are a big problem on our Midwestern streams because of those paper nests they build hanging from branches along and over the river. You have never been stung until you have been stung by a bald-faced hornet. They aim at your forehead, above and between the eyes, and they can nearly knock you down with their sting. Remember that the larvae develops inside that nest, and while many who float the river in the winter like to collect those big nests for their office or basement rec-room or school classroom, some of them will produce live hornets when they are warmed for awhile. I always figure that if the devil ever created anything it was hornets and horseflies.

Crayfish and bullfrogs are abundant in most clean Midwest rivers. In the deep eddies of the larger rivers, crayfish, or "crawdads" as we called them in the hills, were big enough to eat. So Ozarkians knew a little bit about how good Lobster is to eat. Crayfish are just as good, although it takes a few more to make a good meal. Smaller crayfish made good bait for smallmouth bass and largemouth bass of course, but they were so important to the river because they reproduce well and everything along and in the river would eat them, from bullfrogs to raccoons.

And I don't know for sure how many species and varieties of frogs were found on the river, but it wouldn't have mattered

236

Underwater Creatures

to me as long as we had bullfrogs. There was nothing better to eat, and we would catch them by hand at night, using a headlamp to blind them. Long before I was born, my grandfather depended on bullfrogs for much of his summer income, selling them by the dozens to a seafood company in St. Louis for 15 to 25 cents each.

We also ate quite a few turtles when I was a boy, the big wash-tub sized soft-shell turtles which had a long trumpet-like nose and didn't bite. There were several kinds of meat on those big turtles, and they were a job to clean, but I remember they were good eating. We only ate the big ones we would occasionally catch on a trotline.

The sliders seen all over the river, laying on logs in groups of 8 or 10 at a time, were never eaten, but the huge snappers which you occasional saw, and caught occasionally on a trotline, were said to be good eating.

I never tried one, grandpa hated those snappers, and wouldn't fool with them. But he never left one alive when he caught one, because he said they were fish-killers of the highest order.

Rumor had it that if one bit you, it wouldn't let go until it thundered. I know that when I was a youngster on the river, one of my biggest fears was those hard-shelled snappers. I always thought maybe a really big one might come up from the depths and get ahold of me somewhere while I was swimming. Thankfully, it never hap-

Underwater Creatures

pened, but it is still on my mind when I go swimming.

I caught a few eels on trotlines when I was young. I don't know how they got there in the upper Big Piney river because of the dam across the lower Piney at Fort Leonard Wood, which was small, still should have blocked their progress upstream. And eels do not reproduce in the Ozarks. they live in Ozark rivers for years, eventually migrating back to the Sargasso sea in the Atlantic Ocean east and south of Bermuda, where they spawn and die. The young eels, actually called elvers, are like little transparent pieces of ribbon about three inches long, and those biologists who have studied them say some of them wind up in the rivers of Europe, while others transcend the Mississippi and work their way up the smallest of tributaries into all Midwestern states. Experts say the adult may live and grow in rivers like the Big Piney and Gasconade for up to 10 or 20 years and grow to lengths of about five feet before beginning their migration to the sea. They bury themselves in the mud in the bottom of deep eddies in the winter, and it is said that old-time rivermen thought they sprang from the mud, because they never caught any with eggs in them.

I remember catching two eels on trotlines in the Piney which were every bit of five feet long. Back then it was about half scary to catch one, and my grandfather told me that if they got their body wrapped around your arm while they were still hooked, they had enough strength to break a bone. They looked a lot like a snake, but when you had one in the bottom of a boat, he whipped around like a catfish and could not crawl up over the side and out like a snake would be able to do. They had little mean-looking heads, but they actually had pectoral fins and a fin on the back half of the body that went completely around the tail and partway up the belly.

We ate several eels, as I remember, and I never thought they were that good, because the meat was stronger than catfish and a little oily. But Europeans prized eel meat, and it was something traditionally eaten at Christmas time in some European countries. Some people in the Ozarks were very afraid of them, back a half century or more ago, and when I was real young I was one of them, though I didn't want to admit it.

There are those who are much more afraid of water snakes....and I am one of them too. It isn't so much that I am afraid of snakes I can see....I just don't like being surprised by one. Once when I was a youngster catching bullfrogs, I was wading along a shallow weed bed, with a nice frog in my headlamp glare. I was reaching down to grab him when a two foot watersnake swam up on top of the bullfrog, both of them blinded by my light. I left that one...quickly, with a great deal of splashing and hurrying. I think whatever I had in the burlap sack that night before that incident was what I wound up with.

There are a number of harmless water-snakes along the rivers, the banded watersnake being the most common, and capable of getting several feet long, and fairly hefty.

Banded water snake

They will indeed bite, but their teeth, very sharp and numerous, are small. I have been bitten by them, and I am surprised how aggressive they can be. They have something in their saliva, or on their teeth, which keeps blood from clotting.

When I was a naturalist for the National Park Service on the

Underwater Creatures

Buffalo River, we kept 7 or 8 species of snakes in captivity and would have a daily program for park visitors showing them the different species. We had a cottonmouth and copperhead, and other common species. We would take out the hog-nosed snake and the green snake, and let park visitors touch them. I reached in the wrong cage one afternoon and the banded watersnake nailed me. It hurt a little, but not much, and I didn't want anyone to know how much I didn't like snakes, being a Naturalist and all, so I just pulled him out of the cage as he hung onto my hand for all he was worth.

When I finally got a hand behind his head and pried his mouth loose, blood began to ooze from the pin-prick bites, and drip off my fingers. It was hard to convince the park visitors that I really wasn't seriously injured, because it looked as if I would never quit bleeding.

Thankfully I have never been bitten by a cottonmouth, but I have had a couple of close calls. Once on Crooked Creek in Arkansas, I was wading through some weeds along a gravel bar in August when one struck at me and missed. It was a dumb thing to be doing, I recommend against walking in weeds or brush on a river where you can't see where you are about to step.

A cottonmouth is aggressive, much more so than a copperhead, and more so than a rattlesnake. Still, they do not come after people. They strike when they feel endangered, and their venom is lethal, much more so than a copperhead, whose bite likely will not kill a healthy adult. I don't know of anyone dying from a cottonmouth bite in the Ozarks, but if bitten by a cottonmouth, you'll be in danger of losing a foot or a hand, so get to a hospital, but don't panic.

A cottonmouth, also known as a water moccasin, is easy to discern from other watersnakes by a dark band from the nose beyond the eye, very drab coloration, a short, heavy body. Watersnakes develop big triangular heads, but they are longer, thinner snakes. When a banded watersnake gets large, he is

Underwater Creatures

Young Cottonmouth

very long. Cottonmouths seldom get longer than 30 inches on Ozark streams. I have only seen one longer than 36 inches, and that one was on Truman lake.

But if you use your head, you can spend a lifetime on the river and avoid contact with them. They do not bite underwater or attack people, as the tales go.

But let's don't end this chapter scared by the prospects of a snake. The old rivermen I grew up around never were afraid of them. There were other things to be afraid of, a hornet's nest on an overhanging limb, stinging nettle and poison-ivy and mosquitoes. And there were occasionally river monsters which were something like aquatic dragons. They'd just kind of rise up out of the river in the middle of the night! I heard a couple of the old-timers at the pool hall talk about one eddy where they loved to fish having one of those monsters in it, twelve foot long, with red and green eyes and teeth like a tiger. No one ever fished there but the two of them! Bravest two guys you ever met.

I never actually saw the monster, because I stayed clear of that stretch of river too. Luckily, there was only one of them, and it never did eat anyone that I know of.

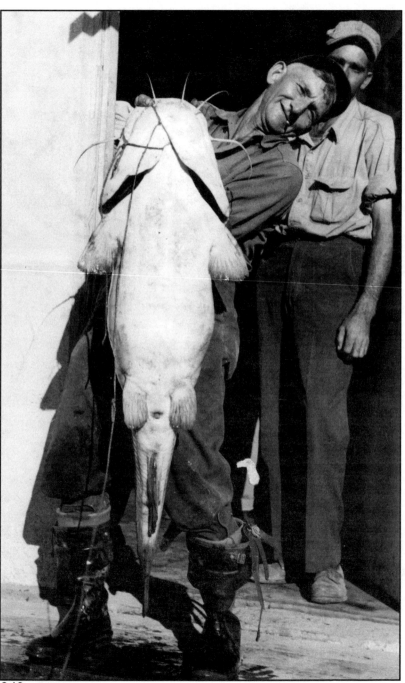

16
RIVER PEOPLE

    I was born right about the middle of the twentieth century, one of the late members of the baby boom. In my boyhood, the old days of the Ozarks were coming to an end, and technology was changing things rapidly. River families were getting electricity and appliances, running water inside the home, and telephones.

    But I can remember seeing and tasting the old life just a little, there along the Big Piney where some folks were slow to modernize. My grandfather wouldn't change much, he said 'no' to everything new, and lived all his life as he had lived as a youngster. What I didn't see of the old life, I was told about, but I can remember so well the smell of kerosene lanterns, and the smoke from wood cook stoves, traps and guns hanging on the walls, and doors with leather hinges.

    The people who first settled Ozark rivers were hard-working resourceful people who knew all about how necessity was the mother of invention. They built the johnboats and used the river for travel, and for food, and for a very meager income. They sold fish, waterfowl, bull-frogs, and furs. They sold mussel shells for buttons, and garden produce which grew in the

River People

rich bottomland soil. They smoked and canned wild meat, and likewise any stock which they raised.

Cattle and hogs ranged free in the woods, and were branded or marked by the owners. They raised their own chickens to eat and to produce eggs. Sometimes they had a milk cow, if they were lucky, and they of course canned vegetables they raised. They ate mushrooms, nuts, berries and wild greens which were found in the woodlands around them, and stored food for the winter in cellars they dug, and in the floors of caves along the river. Wild tubers, fruits, potatoes and sweet potatoes could be preserved wrapped in grasses and buried well back in the floors of a cave, as deep as possible. On the Big Piney, there is a cave still bearing the name, "Sweet 'tater cave".

Those river people also learned they could have ice in mid-summer by cutting blocks out of the river during the winter, and burying them deep into the floor of caves, covered with straw, and then soil. There would usually be a big Fourth of July picnic in which the ice would be used to make ice-cream.

Much of the time, they sweetened pies and cakes and ice cream with syrup from river maple trees. The Ozark maples which grew along the river did not produce syrup as sweet or as tasty as the northern maples, and it took a large amount of sap to make a pint of sweetener, but many a river family boiled down the maple sap in the spring and fall to derive the syrup.

And pies and jellies were made from wild berries and fruits of all kinds...some of them completely forgotten in this day and age, like paw paws and persimmons, and elderberries and gooseberries, mulberries, wild grapes, raspberries and blackberries and even wild strawberries. Backwoodsmen found bee trees, and retrieved honey from them at the appropriate time of the year, and honey was treasured.

Spring and summer and fall, there was food to be found, both wild and domestic. It was winter which produced the difficulty. Families had to know how to store food, how to can it, if you were lucky enough to have jars, or dry it, smoke it, pre-

244

River People

serve it for those times when the snow was deep and the winter winds howled.

Surviving the winter meant having enough wood cut and stored in September and October to get through until spring. Axes and cross cut saws did the job. Those same axes and saws cleared the ground for gardens and home sites, and cut poles an brush for fences to keep the varmints and free ranging stock out of them. Many times, homes in the river bottoms were built without floors, and sawdust from a local sawmill was used as a carpet, changed from time to time to keep it fresh.

Those old homeplaces were sometimes built in days, and a family of eight or ten might live in a small two or three room cabin, with beds in each room, including the kitchen, and beds in an attic where younger, lighter kids slept. Water was hauled from the creek or the river, or, if a family was lucky, from a nearby spring. There were few good springs along the river which didn't have a homeplace close. Of course, cisterns were often dug to store rainwater running from the shake-shingle roof of the cabin.

River families bathed in the creek or river most of the year...went without baths during the severe part of the winter, or used a wash tub if they were lucky enough to have one. The outhouse, of course, was a primitive place of necessity, and many had small stoves in them for heating in the winter.

I remember using those outdoor privies as a youngster. The homes I lived in until late in the 1950's had no indoor bath-rooms. It was tough to go use an outhouse late at night in January. Elderly people kept bed pans inside, under the bed. But summer outhouses could be a big problem too, because wasps built nests in them, and copperheads seemed to like the coolness they provided. Maybe the one thing which made out-door privies such a difficult experience was the harshness of old Montgomery Ward or Sears Roebuck catalogs, or local news-papers.

The river produced emergency food, and local people

River People

learned to make rock dams to block the river except for small passageways where fish traps could be placed. Smaller creeks were sometimes poisoned with walnut hulls or crushed legumes which contained a natural form of rotenone. River people understood the fish were safe to eat, even though they didn't know why the plant called 'Hoary Pea' killed them.

But the main method of collecting fish for the table, and to sell, was gigging. Gigs were forged by local blacksmiths, some became famous for the gigs they made. But there were smaller bow-gigs made and used in the Current River country. Regular gigs were large, with 16 or 18 foot handles. Bow gigs were only three or four feet long, slender arrow shafts with small, fine forged forking tips, sometimes kept in place only by the swelling of the wet wood. Bows were hand-made from ash or sassafras or osage orange, and strong enough to drive the arrow-type gigs deep into the water and through a bass or walleye or small catfish. They were soaked in water before using, to make them supple and less likely to break.

The best gigging was at night of course, when the winter produced clear water where you could sometimes see the bottom ten or twelve feet below the boat. Giggers built baskets, out of wire and old wagon rims bent to shape, which fit over the end or the sides of a wooden johnboat, and filled them with burning pine knots to light the river beneath them.

From some time after World War I, into the nineteen thirties, most of the rivers in the Ozarks were used to transport long processions of railroad ties, which had been hewn out on the hillsides and ridgetops above the streams. In Arkansas, the Buffalo and White rivers were used to float cedar logs downstream to cities where they were loaded on railroad cars and sent to pencil factories. Railroad ties were floated down the larger rivers, especially the Piney, the Gasconade and the Current.

Hacking out railroad ties from eight foot logs was difficult and dangerous. Backwoodsmen who lived along Ozark rivers

246

River People

learned to do it fairly well, using a broad-axe which they kept as sharp as a butchers blade. When they finished, they had a 7-inch by 9-inch, 8-foot long tie. My Uncle Norten, born in 1923, remembers a great deal about tie hacking and rafting. When he was a small boy he would go with my grandfather to the ridge-tops over the Big Piney where a group of a half dozen or more men would work together to cut oaks with cross cut saws.

When there were enough logs on the ground, they would go to work, hacking out the railroad ties. My uncle says he would watch his father stand on one of those oak logs and work on the right side of it until he had it carved flat, then turn around and do the same thing to the other side. With two sides chopped down he would then turn the log up and stand on the flattened edges and work down the other sides. He said that it seems my grandfather would sometimes hack out 20 to 30 per day, and would receive 33 cents for each one.

Each worker would mark his ties in a certain manner so they would be easily distinguished from the others, because when the final raft was put together to go down the river, there might be a thousand ties or so, and one man might have 200 or so. Norten said that it seemed, in his memory, that Grandpa once cut almost 250 ties over the winter about 1930.

"That was great money, just about the time the depression was coming on," he said. Six or eight dollars a day, almost 100 dollars over a period of a few months. Dad would rather be trapping or selling fish, but when the trapping season was over and before the spring trotlining was good, he could gig at night and cut ties during the day."

From the mid-Piney to Arlington, many miles downstream on the Gasconade river, it might take three days to reach the railroad crossing, where ties were counted, sorted and loaded on flat cars.

Norten had one interesting story from the late twenties, when he was very small, but remembered going into the woods with his father and watching the ties being made, formed into

247

River People

rafts and floated down the river. He said that often, the strong current would push some of the rafts up onto the gravel bars, and then they were carried back into the river from the pressure of the current and the rafts connected ahead and behind. He recalled that one tie rafter, uncle Buddy Adey, bounded out onto a gravel bar after a huge catfish that had been pushed out of the river by a surging raft of ties, and he killed it with a broad axe. Folks said it would have weighed about 75 pounds and no one had ever seen a bigger one in the river.

Some of the tie cutters were scarred for life by those broad axes. If you cut off a toe or two, you could keep going, but occasionally someone got careless and hit their foot or ankle with a broad-axe, and the injury could be disabling for weeks or months. The biggest fear was a heavy rain, and a river rising to flood stage while that tie raft was being moved downstream. There was much danger in a river which was too full. A man riding the raft, trying to keep it away from leaning trees and submerged logs and big rocks in the shoals, could be knocked into the water and crushed or drowned. And it was miserable spending a night on the river in a bad storm...unless you knew where the caves were. Caves on Ozark rivers were protection and shelter and early rivermen found them.

River caves were often homes for entire families. My grandfather would sometimes take his family to a big dry cave on the river during the intense heat of July and August, and take a vacation, living in it's cool temperatures, fishing and trotlining late and early in the day, spending the mid-day relaxing and resting inside a cave where the temperature was 30 degrees cooler.

Often, a cave provided a constant temperature in a period of intense cold, and the first settlers and explorers took advantage of that as well. Not only was it protection from rain or snow, dry caves were perhaps 30 to 40 degrees warmer. Sometimes they meant survival in the dead of winter.

I remember seeing a cave walled off with rocks and mud,

248

River People

down in northwest Arkansas, where a family had lived for several years. It had a door and two windows in that front wall, and one child had been born there while the family built their cabin.

But those caves had been permanent homes for families long before the first white settlers came to the Ozarks. Call them native Americans, Indians, Bluff Dwellers, whatever, they certainly used those caves along the Midwestern rivers, perhaps thousands and thousands of years ago. Maybe their life style was roaming and nomadic, and maybe they were born and raised and stayed in one small area of the river, where one big cave gave them shelter from the elements.

Painting by Steve Miller

I knew of such a cave. Perhaps a thousand years, two thousand, maybe ten thousand years before I was born, men and women and children lived there, and when I was thirteen years old I began to think about them in a way that has made it difficult to stop thinking about them.

My grandfather showed me caves along the river which he had lived in, and stayed in as a youngster, hunting and running

River People

traplines, staying out on the river in winter when caves were needed to keep him warm, or in the summer when a bad storm came up. Most of them had fairly dry dirt floors. In one of them, I found 15 to 20 arrowheads (or projectile points as the archaeologists called them) just sifting through the top inch so of loose dirt. It was a very well hidden cave back up a small spring branch a couple of hundred yards from the river, and it wasn't real large, maybe twelve feet wide and about seven feet high.

Back 15 feet or so, it narrowed to a small passageway that went back another 25 feet or so and ended. In that passageway, you couldn't stand up straight, it was only four or five feet high, five or six feet wide. But most of those projectile points were back in the beginning of that passageway. I figured there had been few people in that cave, or someone else would have found those arrowheads.

A few months later, my grandfather showed me a similar cave that was about 20 feet across, 30 feet deep, and maybe eight feet high, with a dry dirt floor and a small passageway in the back going into the hillside 40 feet or so where it ended in a room with a domed ceiling 25 feet high. Water dripped down from the ceiling, and flowed in a small stream back beneath one wall, then came out again toward the back of the large entrance room. In that little stream, and on some of the ledges back in the dark passageway, I found several more projectile points. The one in the shallow stream was amazing. It was about four inches long and almost three inches wide, sharp and beveled on both sides of the blade.

I looked at that cave and could almost see the families of early men living there. Amazingly, in the time they did live there, it must have been a much larger cave, because the dry floor out in the front was about 3 to 4 feet deep. What a home it must have been, facing the east, with the river down below and water flowing in the back of it.

My grandfather and I, along with several of my cousins,

250

River People

began to excavate the floor of the cave when I was about 14 or 15 years old. It was an awful thing to do, because we had no idea what we were doing, and may have destroyed evidence of how those early men and women lived. We used shovels, and moved lots of dirt in a hurry, sifting it through a seive about two feet long and wide. Immediately we found an abundance of broken pottery, bone tools, projectile points from the tiniest bird points to 6 or 7 inch blades.

The Cave on the Big Piney where generations of families had lived thousands of years before.

We were some of the most excited kids you have ever seen. But Grandpa wasn't. He had a dream that night, and in that dream he said he saw those people and watched them alive there in that cave. He said the bones we were finding were bones of many of them who had been buried there. He would never go back, and we never talked him into it again.

He was right about the bones. There were human bones in the back of the cave, along the sides of it. We never found a skull, but I took one of the teeth to a dentist who told me it was the molar of a 9 or 10 year old child, and was remarkable because though it had no cavities it was worn down to about the

River People

gum line.

There isn't much we didn't find there in that cave, beads and bones with intricate designs carved, fish hooks, bone awls and needles and a huge ground axe that must have weighed six or seven pounds. There were a hundred or more projectile points found in three visits, and as we dug down, we went through layers of ash from ancient campfires, some several inches thick, others very narrow, all the way down to four feet below the floor.

All the way down, we found pieces of pottery with various designs, and finally at the very bottom, off to the side and beneath a large rock which itself had been buried by dirt, I found a flat, but concave-convex adornment of some kind which had a hole in it at the upper edge. When I washed it off, it was polished and pearl colored, and at the time I assumed it must be some type of shell. For years I kept it with the other artifacts which had been my part of the bounty, and never thought much about it.

About four or five years later, while attending college at University of Missouri, I was assigned a job working for the Archaeology department, and I met the noted Archaeologist who was the head of that department, Dr. Carl Chapman. When Dr. Chapman saw the artifacts I found in the cave, he seemed amazed, but when he saw the polished 4 inch round pendant, his jaw dropped. For a long time he didn't believe me when I told me where I found it, and he asked lots of questions. Finally, he said he wanted to see the cave, so the next weekend I took him and his son on a float trip down the Piney and we camped out there.

The artifact I thought was a heavy chunk of shell, turned out to be ivory, from a tusk which would have been about twelve inches in diameter. I haven't got the slightest idea how if could have gotten there, but it was no doubt very very old. Dr. Chapman said it had to be 8 to 10 thousand years old, and was perhaps brought there from some other area, maybe traded cen-

252

River People

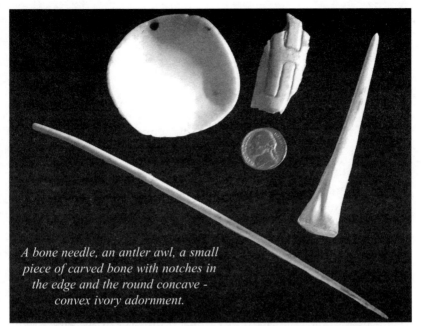

A bone needle, an antler awl, a small piece of carved bone with notches in the edge and the round concave - convex ivory adornment.

Below - a few of the projectile points including far left center an arrowhead beveled on both sides. The lower two points were found several feet deep while the upper two were found near the surface.

River People

turies ago between nomadic wandering people from the far north.

I think about that cave a lot, and about the people who lived there. I hold that little ivory pendant and think about other human hands which held it thousands of years ago and I wish I could meet them so bad I can hardly stand it. My imagination runs wild with me. Was it a man or woman who wore it, and how. Was it something which hung on a leather thong or was it worn in the hair. Was it an ear-ring, with a matching piece we never found. Did they communicate with a language of some sort, and how advanced was that communication. Did they live in fear of enemies of a different tribe or culture. What kind of family structure did they have, did they play with their children and love them as I loved mine.

I worked long enough with the Archaeological department at M. U. to know that no one really knows. Sometimes scientists convince themselves that their theories are fact. Sometimes theories are so ridiculous that I am sure if we actually could know the truth we would laugh at how silly our notions of those ancient cultures were.

There is no way to know them, we can only have the slightest glimpse, and it may be that there were several kinds of peoples who lived on the rivers of the M idwest. Some may have been there awhile, some there and gone with the passing of the seasons. Maybe some of the later ones were much like the Indians we knew, the Sioux and the Cherokee. But the earliest people who lived on the Ozark rivers....think about it. The very first people who arrived in the valley of the Big Piney or the Buffalo or the White or the Current. Where did they come from, when did they get there....and how did they dress and eat and live.

I remember how adamant my Grandfather was that he had seen those people in his dream. I can't say if it was just his imagination, but I often think I'd like to have that dream he had. As far as I know, Grandpa never went back to that cave. He felt

254

River People

he knew them, and didn't want to desecrate their graves.

Sometimes I think about putting that piece of ivory on a leather strand and wearing it for awhile. Maybe if I slept with it around my neck I'd have a vision, like the Indians use to have. But I am too much a realist. I don't smoke that stuff the Indians had and I'd probably just choke myself in my sleep. Still, given the opportunity to know the past, given the opportunity to climb in a time machine and go back...you'd find me on the Big Piney in front of that big cave, thousands of years ago.

But I feel fortunate to have known so many of the old-time river people who lived in a different day, with a different set of values than todays generations have. I saw the best of it, perhaps.

17
ALL ABOUT THE RIVERS

Until I began guiding fishermen in North Arkansas in the early '70's, I didn't realize how different each river was. The Big Piney and the Gasconade, where I had spent all my time as a kid, were very much alike, but the former was a tributary to the latter, so you would assume they'd be much alike. There were differences too, of course. A small dam built on the lower Big Piney at Fort Leonard Wood may have been the reason we never caught channel catfish out of the Big Piney while they were plentiful in the Gasconade.

But by and large, if you were floating the Big Piney or the upper two-thirds of the Gasconade river, you would have had a difficult time knowing which of the two rivers you were on. In my youth, these were smallmouth streams deluxe. The Gasconade, which has no impoundments built on it, has about 300 miles of fishing stream, the longest river of float-fishing quality in the entire midwest. It doesn't have tremendous drop, it is pretty much an arm-chair river with big deep slow eddies, scenic bluffs and clean gravel bars. If there was ever a river made for float fishing and two or three day camping trips, the Gasconade is it. Still today, it harbors as many or more big

257

All About the Rivers

smallmouth per acre than any river in the midwest region, as well as largemouth and rock bass, sunfish suckers and catfish.

The Big Piney and Gasconade flow in a northerly direction, as does the Niangua and Pomme de Terre and Sac rivers to the west. The latter three flow into the Osage and eventually join the Missouri. Just to the southeast, the Jacks Fork and Current, Eleven Point, the Spring and Strawberry rivers in Arkansas empty into the Black River and eventually the lower Mississippi. Up north, the Bourbeuse, Curtois and Meramec are the northernmost Ozark streams, flowing into the Missouri. Of these, the Meramec gets the most canoeing traffic, and was once known as a great stream for bass and walleye, with some stretches stocked with trout. The Bourbeuse is a much murkier stream, much less scenic, which, in recent years has become overcrowded with Kentucky bass, seeing a resulting decline in smallmouth.

Down in northwest Arkansas, the Kings and War Eagle, Crooked Creek and the Buffalo flow north or northeasterly into the magnificent White. Missouri's James and Finley, Bryant Creek and Norfork River flow southward into the White.

All About the Rivers

Amazingly, you can see a single small thunderstorm to the east of Springfield Missouri dumping raindrops into the watershed of the Black, the White and the Osage and Gasconade, into a small area which have drainages going in all directions.

Then in southwest Missouri and northwest Arkansas, there are west-flowing rivers like the Spring (two Spring Rivers emerge from southern Missouri) the Elk, and the Illinois, which eventually go through Oklahoma reservoirs and into the Arkansas River. Arkansas' Mulberry and Big Piney flow from the southern slopes of the Ozark mountains draining a region only a few miles and over the ridges to the south from the headwaters of the Buffalo, and they flow into the Arkansas River as well.

South of the Arkansas river in west and southwest Arkansas, there are streams of the Ouachita mountains, the Caddo, the Cossatot, the Saline, the Fourche La Fave. And Oklahoma has many miles of good floating streams as well, though most of Oklahoma's rivers flow into and then out of, manmade reservoirs. The Ouachita mountain range rivers are so different from Ozark streams that they could be a world apart. Yet they still have the smallmouth and the largemouth bass, rock bass, green sunfish and long-ear sunfish, flathead and channel catfish. Once on the Fourche la Fave, we caught a four-pound bowfin, a very strange, prehistoric sort of fish I never saw in the upland Ozarks of north Arkansas or southern Missouri.

The Fourche La Fave is a good representative of the Ouachita mountain rivers. It begins in the Ouachita mountains southeast of Ft. Smith, Arkansas and flows eastward into Nimrod Lake, and it is a beautiful stream in it's own right. Rock bars on the Fourche have some perfectly formed rectangular rocks of all kinds of sizes and dimensions which look like they were fashioned in a factory somewhere. Some are so precise they look to be cut out like whetstones. There aren't many gravel bars there of small gravel, the bars are rock bars, larger rocks than you would want to throw a sleeping bag on. And on

259

All About the Rivers

the flats above the river you'll find thickets of cane which are nearly impenetrable. That's something it has in common with north Arkansas rivers, but when I was a boy on the Piney, I never saw a cane patch, the streams of the northern Ozarks don't have any.

A float stream is a float stream, and there are many in other parts of the midwest besides the Ozarks. If there's current, and clean water and fish, I call it a river worth seeing, and there aren't many in Missouri and Arkansas I haven't seen at least once or twice. I only floated the Poteau river in west Arkansas once, and I didn't fish it. I always thought I'd go back and catch some fish there, but never did. We spent the night on that river in one of the most unbelievable thunderstorms I have ever endured. The river rose so much we couldn't finish our float the next day.

I floated the lower Eleven Point down in Arkansas, and watched it become something so different from the Missouri portion of the Eleven Point that I wasn't sure I hadn't taken a wrong turn and joined a different stream. The cold, clear rocky water of the Missouri section, which harbors an abundance of stocked trout, became a slower, more colored, warmer stream with an abundance of Kentucky and largemouth bass the farther downstream you went. And there were logs and root wads everywhere, a lot of current which made some places difficult to run. A landowner I talked to said the lower Eleven Point scares lots of floaters because there are so many logs in the swift current. The upper portion in Missouri gets beat to death by floaters, the lower portion pretty much ignored.

Missouri's Niangua river, which parallels the Gasconade to some extent, 30 miles to the west of the Gasconade, is one of the strangest streams I have ever seen. From it's beginning back to the south of Buffalo, Missouri, there's several miles of river which is floatable but small. There are no trout there, but largemouth and smallmouth bass and all the sunfish and catfish and suckers. The giant Bennett Springs pours about 180 mil-

All About the Rivers

lion gallons of icy water into the Niangua, three or four days float, and about 30 miles below Buffalo, Missouri. The river below the springs has an abundance of rainbow trout for quite some distance downstream, because they are raised in the park hatchery and stocked by the tens of thousands in the Bennett Springs trout park, for the elbow to elbow fishermen who come there.

Thousands of trout go from the trout park down into the river, especially in the spring, and they survive just fine. The river above Bennett Springs is too warm for trout in the summer. In the winter time, that upper section of the Niangua may get colder than the river below the Springs, but in the summer, it is much warmer. When you pass Bennett Springs, it does indeed feel as if you have gone from one river to another. For eight or ten miles below Bennett Springs there are trout to be found, and even farther in the winter. The Missouri Department of Conservation has been stocking brown trout in that section of the river to take advantage of the situation. The browns can reproduce in cold spring-fed waters, while the rainbows cannot. The browns are much warier, but grow rapidly. It was hoped that some of them might eventually reach sizes of 15 to 30 pounds. But some of the local guides say that too many of the browns are gigged in the winter to allow this program much success. Even so, there are a number of five to eight pound brown trout caught there each year.

The third portion of the Niangua is 36 miles below Bennett Springs, where a small dam known as Tunnel Dam backs water about four or five miles up the river. That lake, Lake Niangua, was formed in the early part of the last century, and water from the lake was channeled through a one mile tunnel cut in a mountain to a power plant about six river miles downstream. In doing this, there were years during the middle decades of the last century when there was almost no water in the river itself below the dam because it was all being diverted through the tunnel. The Niangua's flow was sent through that tunnel and

261

All About the Rivers

through the power plant and then on downstream to Lake of the Ozarks. Today, at least at the time of this writing, that is no longer the case. The power plant remains in operation, but the majority of the Niangua flows over the dam and the six miles of river between the dam and power plant has plenty of water. For ten miles between Tunnel dam and the upper reaches of Lake of the Ozarks, the Niangua is a different river than anywhere above. It harbors some big bass, but two thirds or better are largemouth and Kentuckies. There are quite a number of hybrid

Niangua Hybrid

All About the Rivers

Kentucky-smallmouth.

Not nearly as many rock bass and a respectable number of walleye which you almost never see above the dam, some of them quite large. Because of Lake of the Ozarks, that lower section also has an abundance of gar and carp which you won't see as much of in the upper river.

It is not unusual to see rivers change a great deal in only a few miles. I have floated the Saline River in central Arkansas a couple of times, and the upper part and lower part of that river is as different as night and day, with the upper part in the fading eastern area of the Ouachita mountains and the lower portion slowing, flowing into the cypress, lowland type of region southeast Arkansas. There are smallmouth on the upper saline, alligators on the lower part. If I ever go back, it will be only on the smallmouth end, way upstream.

I love the Fourche la Fave River, hunted turkeys in it's mountain forest watershed for many years and fished it many times. But I never had any great fishing trips on that river. Good trips, fair trips, but no great trips. My uncles, on trips I was never a part of, tell of days on the Fourche when they caught good numbers of big bass, both smallmouth and largemouth.

To the west of the Fourche, there aren't as many miles of the Caddo and Cossatot Rivers which you can float, but I have a friend, Dennis Whiteside, a fishing guide out of Dover Arkansas, who floats and fishes both of them and says they teem with smallmouth. Like most of my friends, he's honest about everything but the size of the fish he catches.

Arkansas' Big Piney and Mulberry are bayou-type rivers on the lower portions above the Arkansas river, and have some big slow holes where there's some good black bass fishing, mostly largemouth and Kentuckies. On the upper reaches of both rivers, there are smallmouth, but seldom any big ones in my experience, partly because the two rivers nearly cease to flow in the mid-summer. Those two rivers come out of the high moun-

263

All About the Rivers

tains, raging and wild in the spring when there's plenty of water. At those times, they are an exciting ride for a canoeist or kayaker looking for swift white water. The gradients of those two rivers on the upper end are extreme, but when the rain stops you can't have much fun because the big rock shoals which roar in April and May, become barriers between the eddies in July and August. Beginners shouldn't float those two. But I'll note this, the Big Piney and Mulberry probably look much like they did 100 years ago, as they drop down out of mountain forests still in the Ozark National Forest. They haven't filled in, they haven't become polluted or exposed to the livestock and agricultural chemicals and bank clearing that have so badly hurt rivers to the north. They are rivers for joy riders and naturalists more than fishing streams. But even so, you can catch a mess of fish for supper if you camp along them and run out of sandwiches. As long as you aren't looking for lunkers.

Crooked Creek and the Arkansas Spring River have a great deal of drop in feet per mile. The Spring has falls along its course which you have to portage around, but biologists say it has more walleye per mile than any stream in the state. When there's lots of rain in the spring, you can get a wild ride on Crooked Creek, which has some terrific spring shoals. From Harrison, Arkansas to Yellville, Arkansas, it is good floating until the summer heat and lack of rain drys it up. But even in the summer, when the water is low, it is a good place to find lots of smallmouth. Once upon a time, Crooked Creek had more big smallmouth per mile than any river I ever saw. It never had much scenery, but it still had it's own personality and beauty. Some local landowners liked to use it for their own personal dump at times. The water rose to carry away the trash a couple of times a year.

But Crooked Creek was unusual in that the lower part of the Creek wasn't floatable. Past Yellville, the water began to flow underground, and for miles, until it approached the White, Crooked Creek didn't have enough water to float a paper sail-

264

All About the Rivers

Author's daughter Christy Dablemont with a stringer of Crooked Creek smallmouth.

All About the Rivers

boat. That river has provided me with more memories than I have room to right about. It was a smallmouth heaven....back then.

My uncle, Bryce Dablemont moved to Springdale, Arkansas when I was just a teen-ager, and he began to fish all the rivers in northwest Arkansas, eventually introducing me to several of them. Uncle Bryce was quite a fan of rivers, and loved to fish them. He got a great kick out of floating some stretch he had never seen before and figuring out how to catch fish there. One of the funniest things I ever heard about was the time he and my Uncle Vaughn decided to float the Kings, and they left a pickup at one bridge and put in at another bridge upstream several miles. They would float and fish several miles downstream to the waiting pick-up and take out.

My Uncle didn't know much about the Kings, and he knew even less about the War Eagle, which closely paralleled the Kings. He left the pickup downstream alright, but at a bridge which crossed the War Eagle about ten miles from the Kings. He and Vaughn were so confused an hour or so before dark they

All About the Rivers

*Uncle Bryce with a nice largemouth from the War Eagle.
He may have had trouble with finding the take-out point
but he always was a great fisherman.*

All About the Rivers

stopped and found a local farmer who was willing to help them out by taking them to find their pick-up. First he had to stop rolling on the ground with laughter. To Uncle Bryce, it still ain't funny!

One of the first streams I floated in Northwest Arkansas was the Illinois, which flows westward into Oklahoma. It originates near Fayetteville, Arkansas not far from the creeks which flow eastward to form the mighty White River. We floated the Illinois often, jumpshooting ducks, and it was great duck hunting. But back then the Illinois was great fishing as well, though most of the bass were largemouth or Kentucky bass of pretty good size. Only about 1 out of 10 bass were smallmouth and they were seldom very large. I say 'was' because that fishing declined in the late 80's and 90's as the population of northwest Arkansas mushroomed and the cities which lay on the headwaters of that stream polluted it badly.

We fished the Illinois a lot in the 70's, and it wasn't typical of Ozark streams in that it didn't have many bluffs, and there wasn't the spectacular beauty found along better known rivers. But it had some deep water and lots of cover, and if you fished large spinnerbaits around those logs and rootwads, you caught bass. It was a particularly good winter stream, and we caught bass there in December and January on duck-hunting trips. That's something you just could not do on the Big Piney, and I couldn't believe what I was seeing. But again, while it was indeed a great river for three to five-pound largemouth bass and two-pound Kentuckies, it wasn't a place where you would go after big smallmouth. Every now and then on the upper portion of the river in the spring, summer and fall, you hooked a good-sized smallmouth, but they were few and far between.

The Kings River, 40 or 50 miles east of the Illinois was a smallmouth stream like few others. It flowed north into the White, now Beaver Lake, and it was a stream where you could catch a big largemouth and Kentuckies as well. But eight out of ten bass in the Kings was a smallmouth, and there were lots

All About the Rivers

Kings River 1978

All About the Rivers

Gloria Dablemont with a Kings River smallmouth

All About the Rivers

of three and four pounders if you could land one. The Kings was beautiful, with clean gravel bars and high scenic bluffs. The water was swift and deep and clean and the hills around it were high and green. It almost equalled Crooked Creek in the number of fish caught per trip, but it was my favorite Arkansas River because it was so beautiful and so wild. Most float fishermen concentrated on the lower Kings, but I spent most of my time on the upper part of the river, where it was smaller, and where few people ever floated. What a bass stream! It had those stretches of water where there were big submerged rocks and gently flowing water and it teemed with smallmouth. Then there were the deeper slower eddies with some logs along the shallower banks across from the bluffs and you might find a largemouth of five or six pounds. By mid June, the upper Kings would get very low, and by July you just couldn't float it. Unlike the Missouri east Ozark rivers which were fed by springs, most of the north Arkansas Ozark rivers, and those down in the Ouachita mountains as well, had few springs. I don't mean to say there were no springs, there were many, but they were small, and by summer, they just didn't contribute much to replenishing the river. The Kings, War-Eagle, Big Piney, Mulberry and even the Buffalo, are streams which rely mostly on rainfall for their flow. In the spring and fall, the Kings was a float fishing jewel because the rain kept it full. In the summer, there were still big, nice holes to fish, but the shoals were so shallow it was tough to get down the river.

I remember some of the best float fishing I have ever had taking place on the Kings River in the 1970's. We would float it often on two or three day trips, cover only a few miles a day and fish hard, catching 70 percent smallmouth, and Kentuckies and largemouth making up the rest of the catch. Usually, you could catch 20 or 30 smallmouth per day that were one to two pounds, but the river also gave up it's share of three to four pound brownies as well. It was full of channel catfish back then. During the low water period of late June one year, we

271

All About the Rivers

struggled to float it, but camped on a gravel bar above a big eddy about sunset. It was so hot and muggy my companion and I took a pair of folding lawn chairs we had brought along, set them out in the shoal and sat in them, fishing downstream where the water flowed. We were sitting there up to our chest in cool water, casting night crawlers down into the slowing current and catching two to three pound channel cat one after another.

The War-Eagle was so close to the Kings you would have thought they were just alike. But in the winter, the Kings, predominantly a smallmouth stream, wasn't a good stream to fish. The War Eagle, only about 20 miles to the east, was a good stream for winter fishing because of the abundance of largemouth and Kentuckies. There were more mud banks in the War Eagle, and more logs. It had it's share of bluffs and rocks, but not the spectacular beauty of the Kings. How could those two be so close and yet so different? To give you an idea of how strange it could get, there were a couple of years that we could cast little Hump-back Rebel lures in the upper War Eagle and just slay the rock bass, chunky little panfish we referred to as goggle-eye.

Rock bass seldom reach a pound but they are one of the Ozarks gamest fish.

All About the Rivers

In the Kings, the same lure seldom produced any. I could write a book on oddities like that I saw in my years floating the various rivers.

As much as they are alike in some ways, you have to remember that no two rivers are the same, and fishing techniques that work on one may not work on another. For instance there are Ozark rivers which have more logs, root wads and brush than rocks. Those rivers, like the War Eagle, the Illinois and the Fourche La Fave in Arkansas, may have more large-mouth and Kentuckies than smallmouth.

In smallmouth streams during the summer, I concentrate on those areas where the current enters an eddy and slows, especially where there's deep water around large boulders. Gently flowing stretches of current where there's three feet or so of water and boulders the size of bushel baskets are great spots for smallmouth until late fall, then they move to deeper quiet eddies as the cold comes on. You'll find largemouth bass on a different type of bank, sometimes over gravel, sand or mud substrate where there's log jams or fallen trees, in sloughs and around quiet waters where aquatic plants grow. Kentuckies may be found anywhere, but they are more fond of a little current than largemouth bass are, more tolerant of slower water than smallmouth.

Submerged logs and brushpiles are hard to fish but I like to fish a spinner bait in just such spots, dropping it into the holes between logs and then retrieving it rapidly over the logs. Kentuckies love to come up out of the brush to nail a lure in such cover. Bass in some rivers will begin to do that as early as mid February when there's a stretch of warm weather. On Arkansas' western and southern streams, largemouth and Kentucky bass will hit a slow spinner bait almost anytime of year. Smallmouth are not very active in winter streams anywhere. But in the Missouri Ozarks and other midwest streams, mid-winter fishing is tough. Bass in the Big Piney and Gasconade were next to impossible to catch in the dead of win-

273

All About the Rivers

ter when the river was very clear and cold. You could do it by fishing small lures or minnows in deep holes, so slowly it would put you to sleep. Years ago I read an article in an outdoor magazine by a Missouri writer touting the great winter fishing for smallmouth in the Ozarks. The writer talked about all the two and three pound fish that were caught on a trip in January, but the only picture shown was the author with a little 12-inch bass. In truth I suspect it may have been the only one caught. Winter bass fishing for brownies is very very tough. I catch them into early November and then they turn on again in late February and early March, If the weather is mild, and in some streams, not all. But the main part of the winter, I'm hunting the rivers, not fishing them. The ones I did fish in the winter with some success were the Pomme de Terre a few miles above the lake, the Illinois, the Fourche, and the War Eagle.

The War Eagle was a fantastic fishing stream in the 1970's. But the Kings and War Eagle are only a hint today of what they once were, perhaps because of the pollution caused by Northwest Arkansas' agricultural boom, and the powerful chicken industry that polluted and ruined wells across that region 20 years ago. In the same manner, Crooked Creek, once a fantastic smallmouth stream, was adversely affected by gravel dredgers and has lost much of the great smallmouth fishery it was known for.

The upper half of the Big Piney which I grew up on, is badly polluted and filled in. Year by year, that degradation moves downstream. Sometimes in the spring and fall, when the water is high and the streams have been flushed by more than adequate rains, you can pretend that they will shine forever. But they won't. The days of our rivers are numbered.

Float them now, run the rapids and ride the currents and catch a fish or two...because the earth has no greater treasure than these rivers which once flowed free and clean and alive... and gave the land its strength.

All About the Rivers

18
DIVERSE WATERS

It's not easy to compare the various craft that are used across the country today for floating, hunting and fishing.

One difficulty is the tremendous diversity of streams, marshes and lakes. Certain waters are not suitable for johnboats or canoes. Many rivers of the West fit into this category. And you must use your own judgment on large lakes. A calm body of water is never much of a problem. But during high winds, that same body of water becomes impossible. I often see someone out paddling a 17 foot double-end canoe on a major reservoir where there are bass boats and ski-boats roaring past. Northern rivers often require a good deal of portaging. Johnboats and larger canoes are impractical for such use.

Large rivers in the Midwest such as the Missouri, Ohio, Arkansas and Mississippi are not for small craft. Expert canoeists often float them, but these large streams will fool the inexperienced floater with whirlpools, undercurrents and unnoticed obstacles.

Dozens of drownings happen each year when people try to use small boats and canoes on major waterways and large lakes.

My grandfather used to tell me he could float the Big Piney

Diverse Waters

River at flood stage, if he had to do it. But he was quick to add that he wasn't fool enough to do it unless he had to. Most of today's floaters underestimate the relentless and unstoppable power of even a small stream.

Floaters who enjoy the thrill of bouncing over a white-water shoal envision similar thrills in riding the current of a flooded river. But no one should float a flooded stream unless he absolutely must. Only experienced, capable floaters should even tackle rain-swollen waters. And larger, major rivers are not for recreational floating.

Large lakes are hazardous to small craft because of wave action and the wakes thrown by larger motor-powered boats.

When Norfork Lake was constructed on the Missouri-Arkansas border in the 1940's, wooden johnboats were built for use in the rough water of the large lake. They were powered then by small outboards. The boat builders found that the same boats used so well on rivers could be modified and used equally well on lakes.

My grandfather used the same basic design, but for lake johnboats he lengthened the craft, gave them greater width and increased the height of the sides by adding a 4 or 6 inch board to increase the depth of the boat to 16 or 18 inches.

My grandfather was an avid trotliner. He made numerous trips each year to Norfork, either trotlining by himself or guiding large parties. Thus, in the 1940's he put together some 18- and 20-foot johnboats. On small streams, he stayed with 14- to 16-foot lengths. For larger rivers like the White, the Gasconade and the Osage, Grandpa built some slender 17- and 18-foot boats. For small farm ponds and creeks, he built several 12-foot boats; however, they were not as stable. They were o.k. for two people, but if you wanted three people and gear in a boat, you should have something 15 feet or longer. He used the same basic design for boats of any length by varying angles and dimensions. And it is a misconception to think he took out a set of plans everytime he made a boat. He used the same forming

278

Diverse Waters

Fred Dablemont with a little 12-foot johnboat he made for a small pond. Whether 12-foot or 20 the wooden johnboat was basically built with the same pattern.

braces, but he built the boats as he went, and there was never two exactly the same. My Dad did the same thing in building his boats, and I'm sure Charley Barnes did it the same way. In general, the boats looked alike, but if you took precise measurements and angles none would never be exactly the same. But they didn't need to be. In a wooden johnboat, there's plenty of room for some variation and change.

Diverse Waters

Johnboats are not suited for large motors. As a rule, any motor too large for a canoe is too large for a johnboat. Extra-large boats made for lakes are suitable for motors of 9 or 10 horsepower. But 14- to 16-foot boats should be powered by motors from 1.5 horsepower to 5 or 6 horsepower.

On small streams, such as the Buffalo in Arkansas, motors are neither necessary nor desirable. I can't imagine anyone taking a float on a scenic free-flowing stream and wanting a motor along. The peacefulness and quiet beauty of a stream are destroyed by the drone of a motor. A wild stream isn't a place for man's machinery. The river is slow at times, but it has much to offer those who will travel slowly and quietly.

Larger streams, especially those with little current, may be more appropriate for a motor, especially when upstream travel is necessary. But motors are more appropriate for small lakes.

Though I have seldom used outboards on our johnboats, I have often used the small battery-powered trolling motors, especially when I float to photograph wildlife. A trolling motor isn't much faster than a boat paddle, but it moves you along quietly and leaves your hands free to operate a camera.

When it's absolutely necessary to travel several miles in a hurry, it's good to know that a well-built johnboat can be powered by outboards. But I feel, as do many others, that most wild and scenic free-flowing streams should be off limits to motor-powered boats. It is a shame for the peace and solitude of nature's best work to be ruined by the drone of motors in the hands of someone too lazy to use a paddle.

In comparing the various small craft available for floating streams and small marshes and lakes, it is very difficult to make absolute statements about the advantages and disadvantages of each.

I can only give my own opinions, based on my own experiences. Other outdoor people with different experiences may arrive at different conclusions, and write their own book.

In the limited amount of guiding I did in my teens and years

Diverse Waters

since, I've had a opportunity to float in everything from wooden and aluminum johnboats to canoes of aluminum and fiberglass to the later models of plastic. I even floated in styrofoam canoes which were tried for awhile in the early 70's. There were years when I floated more than a thousand miles. Now, I probably average a few hundred miles a year. Many of those miles are interpretive float trips, during which we take along 10 to 30 people at a time and teach them about the river. Many of those miles, I'm by myself, hunting or fishing, and sometimes doing both on the same trip.

During the winter, when I'm hunting or photographing wildlife, I like to average 10 or 15 miles of river per day. During the summer, when I'm fishing or just enjoying the river, I average 5 to 8 miles a day. And on some rivers, when I want to fish slowly, I may spend most of a day on a mile or two of water.

Of course every river is different. On some small streams, five to six miles will take most of the day. When a stream is full, without a lot of obstacles and a good current, you may float five or six miles in a couple of hours. You'll shoot right on down the Current River, but you'll just ease along on the Gasconade.

I learned the most about canoes and the people who use them while I was working as a canoeing instructor at a summer camp in southern Missouri and at the Buffalo National River where I worked as a naturalist in the early '70s. During several summers, I tried to teach canoeing to park visitors. Some people would pick it up fairly quickly, and others couldn't ever get the hang of it.

I could never understand why most canoeists seem to figure that the more miles you travel each day, the better. I think the key to enjoying a float trip is a leisurely pace, stopping from time to time on a gravel bar or exploring a cave in a nearby bluff.

By traveling quietly and even slowly, the river traveler gets

Diverse Waters

to see the stream and many of the wildlife species that live along it. But if you make a mad dash for a take-out point with paddles banging against aluminum, you drive wild things--fish included-into secluded hiding places.

The johnboat was built years ago for a river traveler not too concerned with speed. He was a man with work to do. The ability of those early guides and trappers and commercial fishermen was a thing of wonder. Toughened hard-working men, they could run a johnboat upstream over a shoal so strong you couldn't stand up in it. They could put the miles behind them when it was necessary, or paddle slowly with one hand.

If he knew what he was doing, he never switched sides with a paddle. Rivermen paddled all day from one side and they could maneuver a boat for any distance without a splash or other sound. Many of them would slip along for long periods and never take the blade out of the water.

Outdoorsmen of that generation thought little about the weight of a johnboat. Most boats never left the river. Generally they were chained and locked to a tree where they were last used and where they would be needed again. Usually they weren't carried any distance overland.

That weight is the wooden johnboat's great disadvantage, especially now that floaters load and unload boats at a variety of access points. But the advantages of the wooden johnboat are many. It has tremendous stability and it will hold a greater load than any other craft of comparable length. You can walk down the side of a johnboat like a tightrope and fall out of it without capsizing.

The wooden johnboat will make little noise as it slides over an object. If you hit a rock, you slide over it. Aluminum tends to hold as it grates against solid rock and if it does slide, the noise can be heard a half mile away.

I would not try to evaluate each type of boat without using each for considerable amounts of time.

One of my favorite craft is a 19-foot Grumman square-stern

282

Diverse Waters

canoe. I use it in the spring on many Ozark rivers because it floats high and is stable and easy to handle. It is noisy on shallow shoals, but then it is light and easy to carry when I want to reach rivers with poor access.

On windy days it is a challenge to float in the longer square-sterned canoes. If you have a headwind or crosswind, the long light canoe is harder to control. That's another good thing about the short and heavy johnboat, it holds a course much better in a strong wind.

The 15-foot johnboat is easy to camouflage by attaching a blind to the bow. A longer craft is harder to hunt or photograph from. But the greatest advantage of a wooden boat for some sportsmen might be its low price. It can be built for about $200 and two days of work. When I wrote the first book on johnboats, that cost was about $50. Who knows what the future will bring. You may read this someday when lumber costs twice as much. When I got my first 19-foot Grumman square-stern it sold for about $500. As I write this, the cost of one of those canoes is about $1200. and the cost of an aluminum johnboat is near that. But....I obtained my Grumman in 1970 and it has taken unimaginable abuse on a hundred different waters and I am convinced my grandson could still be using it when he is an old man. The aluminum johnboats won't last as long without welding up some holes, but they will give you a lifetime of use if you know what you are doing. So wouldn't that make the cost worth it?

The 19-foot square-stern is hard to get, but I'm convinced that in most respects it is far superior to small canoes. The 17-foot canoe has few advantages. It is light and fast, but it is also relatively unstable and will go over easily. It doesn't float any higher than the 19-footer and it is used primarily by those who want to float fast and light, or those who float northern streams where portaging is necessary. It is the only craft, of course, for those canoe rental places which figure on having some of their canoes bent up and ruined by greenhorn floaters during the

283

Diverse Waters

course of a year. They are cheaper than anything else.

The double-ended 17-foot canoe is a craft I use only when I don't mind the possibility of getting wet. I never fill it with expensive equipment. This craft is unforgiving: make a mistake in it and you're wet. Lose your balance, turn sideways in a rough shoal or start horse playing and you will go over in a hurry. I've seen beginning canoeists on average streams turn over half a dozen times on one trip. But an experienced canoeist may load the canoe fairly heavy and take a two-day trip without incident. No matter how good you are, however, the 17-foot canoe can throw you. Expect it and let that be your guide in determining what (and how much) you put in it.

Almost anyone who's done much floating in the 17-foot canoe can tell you about the times they've gone over. Where portaging is necessary, however, as in the north, the 17-foot canoe enjoys clear superiority to all others because of its light weight.

Square-stern canoes have an advantage over the double-enders in that they are easier to turn. A double-end canoe has 18 inches of aluminum behind the paddler that creates resistance in turning. When the stern paddler is closer to the absolute rear point of the craft, as in the square-stern models, it is much easier to turn quickly. In a johnboat or square-stern canoe, I can backpaddle right up to an object on the bank. But in any double-end canoe, the space behind me prevents this maneuver. A 17-foot square-stern, which has three or four inches more width than the double-end, has more stability.

The 19-foot canoe has not been used on most streams. It's more expensive than the shorter double-ender or the shorter square-stern and rental places can't afford them. But they hold heavy loads and float high. I've used 19-foot square-sterns on the smallest of streams.

The fiberglass canoes I've seen are not suitable for use on any rocky shallow water, because the fiberglass is easily broken. New plastic canoes seem to be fairly effective, but they

Diverse Waters

won't take the heavy blows aluminum or wood will and they seem to me less stable than aluminum canoes of the same size.

Aluminum johnboats began appearing in the 1950's. Aluminum johnboats are best in lengths of 16- to 18-feet.

Diverse Waters

Shorter lengths give less stability, so I recommend the 17-foot length. Heavy-gauge aluminum is an absolute necessity. Boats made of light aluminum are tipsy and easily punctured.

The old Lowe-paddle-jons used .051 gauge aluminum in their boats, a 17-footer painted a drab green. The Voyageur johnboats I mentioned in earlier chapter can be purchased today in .51 gauge or .63 gauge, and are painted gray.

The boats travel very well, handle easily, and are stable with exceptionally heavy loads. Three people can float and fish from a 17-foot aluminum johnboat quite easily in small streams. For two fishermen and a good load, the 17-foot boat is easy to handle. It weighs 110 pounds, with 14-inch sides and a 33-inch width.

When aluminum boats are built so much like the original wooden johnboats, they are extremely good river craft. In choosing a boat for floating, the prospective buyer must decide for himself which craft offers the advantages he needs for the type of floating he will be doing. While it's true that wooden johnboats are a great deal cheaper, not everyone can build one. He must also consider that a $1200 craft that may last 20 years may be a better buy that a $500 boat that will last about 10 years depending on how it is used.

I would recommend that serious floaters, especially those carrying equipment in all seasons, choose the wooden or aluminum johnboat or the 19-foot square-stern aluminum canoe.

When a floater has become very proficient with a paddle, he will find that a well-built 15-foot wooden boat is easy to handle in most streams and tends to hold course better than other boats. But a wooden johnboat usually is not the best choice for a beginner. You shouldn't try to build and use one until you've at least gained some experience in aluminum johnboats or canoes.

A johnboat is valuable to you if you spend several days at a time on the river with large loads or expensive equipment. If you're a serious river fisherman, if you're interested in gigging or trotlining, if you wish to hunt or photograph from a boat, the

Diverse Waters

johnboat will be useful to you. If you're interested in traveling in a hurry or doing summertime sight-seeing with a light load, you'd be better off with your choice of canoe.

14 - foot wooden johnboat with plywood bottom built for two people.

19
SWIFT WATERS

If you're a beginning floater, start out easy. Take your johnboat to a quiet stretch of water and practice until you get the hang of things. While you're learning, be sure to wear that personal flotation device and clothes that you don't mind getting soaked. In fact, don't take anything with you that you can't afford to get wet.

Get accustomed to paddling your craft in quiet water. Learn how to make it turn quickly, how to back it up, and how to go forward in a straight line. You're beginning to learn the fundamentals when you have developed the ability to paddle in a straight course from one side of the boat, without switching. Until you learn that basic skill, you shouldn't be thinking of loading a boat or canoe and making a long trip.

As you learn to handle your boat better, make short trips with little or no load down streams that aren't difficult. Don't go out and tackle a stretch of white water somewhere that you aren't ready for. First learn to run some easy shoals and straight chutes of swift water. Take short empty trips until you feel comfortable in your boat and it responds quickly the way you want it to.

Swift Waters

I've seen people learn to master a johnboat or canoe in a matter of days, but I've observed others who never learned to paddle proficiently. For most people, two or three short trips down an average stream will go a long way toward teaching proper handling.

Another caution: when you're learning, stay away from high waters. Tackle streams that are normal, even a little low. Don't go to the swift, bank-full streams till later.

Looking at a shoal of swift water and knowing whether you can run it safely or not comes only with lots of experience. And no matter how skillful you become, there are some shoals and rapids that you just can't run. I've run the rivers for forty years now, and I still pull around an occasional shoal. I figure I can run most shoals if they aren't blocked, but I don't always try. especially when I have a heavily loaded boat. I don't take stupid chances with equipment that is worth a lot to me. A swollen stream has too much power to take chances with.

When you're paddling well, handling your boat proficiently and beginning to feel comfortable in it, you may begin to take longer trips and carry more equipment. I believe in personal flotation devices (PFD's) for those who can't swim well. Anyone in your boat who fits into that category should always be wearing one. I firmly believe that children, even if they can swim well, should have a flotation device on while they are floating. When I was growing up on a river, we never had PFD's. I don't wear one because it limits my movements and because of confidence in myself and the knowledge I have of the rivers I float. Most of these rivers are small and offer little threat to an experienced floater. But when there is danger, wear the life vest. Only experience allows a person to know which water represents a threat and which doesn't. If you don't have that experience, be safe and wear your PFD.

Wooden johnboat s (because of natural buoyancy) and most aluminum boats and canoes (because of factory-installed flotation) won't sink in calm water. But if any of these crafts lodge

Swift Waters

against an object in swift water, they will tip, fill with water and sometimes be forced down by the current.

This is one reason I don't recommend tieing anything in the boat. Sleeping bags, clothing and personal effects that will float should be sealed in two thicknesses of plastic bags used for lining garbage cans. This arrangement will keep them dry even if they go into the river.

If you have something valuable with you that will sink, you might want to try a method I've seen used, the cord-and-buoy. Camera equipment should be kept in a waterproof army ammo box. This will sink, but 10 or 12 feet of cord with one end tied to the handle and the other fastened to a small floating jug or piece of Styrofoam will help you recover it, should you turn over. The cord-and-buoy idea is good for camp stoves, lanterns and other gear that will sink.

In ammo boxes you might wish to carry matches and a small radio as well as topographic maps. I hate the noise of a radio on a float trip. But in the spring I carry a small one to check severe-weather warnings.

The topographic map is one of the most valuable things you can take on a river. It helps you keep track of how much river you're covering each hour and how much you need to cover before arriving at a take-out point. Your topo map shows the closest roads and farm houses or settlements (handy in case of emergency). The map will also show sheer bluffs or caves that can provide protection from high winds or heavy rains.

By examining your topo map closely, you may detect areas of extreme drop. The rate of fall can be calculated, helping you to predict the swiftest water or falls. It will also show potentially dangerous bends and rapids. If I don't know the river I'm floating, a topographic map is as important to me as a spare paddle. I guess this would be a good spot to mention the importance of good paddles. Have three or four on each trip, with the extras on top of any load and within easy reach.

Cheap paddles cause a lot of capsized craft. Buy good

291

Swift Waters

strong paddles. Next best to the sassafras paddles the old-time guides once made and used are probably today's laminated ones. If you don't care anything about tradition, the aluminum and plastic paddles are good too, but grizzled old veteran rivermen like me aren't about to use one.

There is no ironclad rule about paddle lengths, but usually you'll do best with one that reaches from the ground to just beneath your chin when you're standing. If you like a shorter paddle, try one that comes to your armpit. I use the shorter paddles only when photographing wildlife or hunting. The shorter length allows me to minimize arm movements, which might show over the blind that I attach to the front my boat.

As time goes on, you'll become efficient with a paddle. Only then should you consider serious fishing, hunting, or overnight floating.

I learned long ago that you can't teach people much about how to paddle a boat or canoe. You can show them the fundamental strokes, but then they must learn them through practice and experience.

Beginning floaters often get carried away with the exhilaration of the trip and make costly mental errors. For example, when they approach a shoal or rapid in which a tree or rock presents an obstacle, they are likely to forget that they must begin to maneuver around the obstacle even before they enter the shoal. When they wait too long, they're in trouble. That's when the life vests are important. Floating cushions can be carried away by the current and aren't of much help in a river.

When a boat or canoe capsizes in swift water, it is usually because it hits something broadside, tips and then fills with water. The craft is pinned to (and often wrapped around) the obstacle by the force of the current.

If you start to tip over in such a situation, do everything in your power to avoid being pinned between the boat and the obstacle. The current can be strong enough to keep you there. In these circumstance, your safest move is to exit from the craft

292

on the upstream side.

In calm water, any boat or canoe with proper flotation will float when overturned or filled. In such a case, it is wise to stay with the craft and get it to shore. But in a current where trees and rocks are prevalent, it is best to stay away from the boat or canoe, or at least try to stay upstream from it.

Current is relentless. It stops for nothing or nobody. As it forces a craft under, it can wrap an aluminum hull around the obstacle like a piece of foil.

A floater who gets between a boat or canoe and an obstacle is in extreme danger. He can be pinned, a leg or arm can be crushed and he can even be pulled under.

The wide, deep, quiet eddies of a river are of little threat to a floater. Trouble comes on fast shoals or stretches of curving rapids where you must avoid obstacles. The biggest problem in my region are logs or leaning trees jutting out from the bank at, or just above, the surface.

Swift Waters

When you can't go over or under such an obstacle, you're in trouble. A fallen or leaning tree that goes across the current at a 90-degree angle can even block the entire stream. When you see this situation in time, you portage around it. But when you're confronted with such a situation on a sharp bend without warning, your only recourse is to try to back paddle to slack water.

Of less danger to the floater are midstream obstacles such as large rocks or groups of small willows. Sometimes in high water a stream will split around clumps of trees or even a small island. I determine the best course by picking the side with the greatest flow but that's not a foolproof method. If both sides look dangerous it's best to stop and check them out from the bank.

Very often swift-water shoals make a sharp bend. You can't see what you're going into. It's usually wise to check these out on foot from the bank before floating through.

When you enter a bend in swift water, stay to the inside of the curve. Slack water usually occurs on the inside of such bends and it's easier to get to the inside bank if you meet an obstacle. Periods of high water usually stack logs and other obstacles against the outside edge of a bend. The inside course will normally help you escape them.

Where shoals bend, your ears can often be of help. If you hear a roar around the bend, there may be a rapid fall or drop, or it may be the sound of water piling against a rock or log. Don't proceed till you check out the situation.

In swift water, it's important to keep your craft straight. When it hits an obstacle head-on, you're in trouble, but when it hits an obstacle broadside, you're sunk.

When entering a swift and treacherous shoal, never let your craft get completely broadside. As an obstacle appears dead ahead, turn the bow rapidly and then pull the stern back around to straighten the craft. You may be angled nearly broadside for a few seconds in this maneuver, but you should never allow

Swift Waters

yourself to be swept completely broadside.

Entering such a shoal, worry about the bow first, then pull the stern around. For instance, move the bow into quiet water first, then move the stern into quiet water. Don't try to do things the other way around.

You can't run a shoal without some aggressiveness. When you must maneuver around obstacles, you'll do best by moving slightly faster than the current If the current is carrying you at its own speed, it's the boss. you're at its mercy. You may get wet or worse. In some instances, an extremely good paddler can back paddle and travel slower than the current to maneuver around obstacles, but this maneuver can be done only by skilled

Swift Waters

boat paddlers.

You'll stay out of trouble by reading an upcoming shoal properly, discussing your course ahead of time with our partner and running it aggressively. This can only be done after you've mastered, or at least become familiar with, the basic strokes. Describing those basic strokes is a difficult task. The illustrations give a basic idea of how they're done.

To turn a boat or canoe to the left, the bow paddler, working on the left side and the stern paddler, working the right, must essentially PULL the water toward him with the paddle blade. To make the craft turn to the right, the stern paddler basically digs the paddle blade in close, angles it and pushes it back and away, while the bow paddler does much the same from the opposite side.

To make a johnboat or canoe travel a straight line, the bow paddler uses a straight stroke and the stern paddler uses a J stroke, as shown in the illustration. If the sternman is the only paddler, he still uses the same stroke.

The J stroke (exaggerated in the illustration) enables you to paddle in a straight line. The first half of the stroke gives you the power necessary to push the boat forward. However, with most people, that portion of the stroke (if you paddle on the right side) will turn the boat slightly to the left. The last half of the stroke, in which the blade is turned away from you and the paddle is slightly rotated in your hand, compensates for the tendency for the boat to turn, and therefore makes the boat keep a straight course.

No two people paddle exactly alike, but as you exercise this J stroke, you'll begin to understand how a boat can be powered forward in a straight line by only one boat paddler, paddling from only one side.

I often see canoeists traveling down the river in a zig-zag course, paddling first on one side, then on the other. These people are inexperienced and asking for trouble. They underestimate the power of the current and can't maneuver well enough

Swift Waters

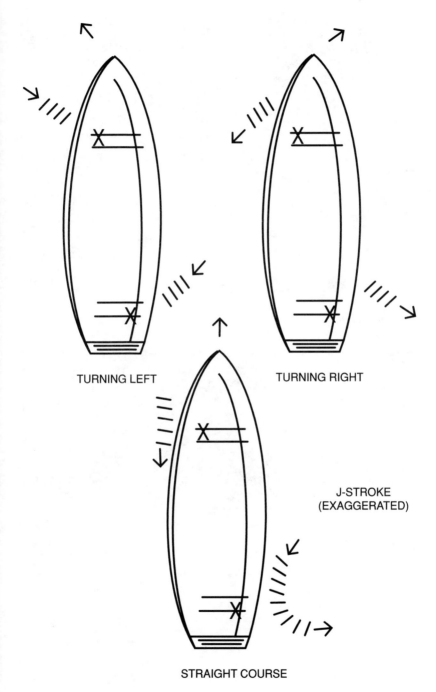

Swift Waters

You have to run rough rapids with some aggressiveness, traveling a little faster than the current. Always position the bow first where it needs to be and pull the stern to match it as you pass the obstacle.

If you don't have confidence in your ability to run rough waters where the current is strong, wade around it. A river's current is powerful and dangerous. Don't take a chance on becoming broadside against an obstacle.

Swift Waters

to avoid problems. Their difficulties begin when they are too impatient to learn the essentials before tackling a stream. Inexperienced paddlers lose thousands of dollars worth of equipment each year, and every now and then, one of them loses their life.

When you can handle your craft from one side without switching, you're a good boat paddler. You're even better when you can do the same thing with a load, a non-paddling passenger, or both. When you can paddle your craft for long periods of time without a sound and without taking the blade from the water, you're getting quite good. But being a good paddler is not enough. You must also learn to read the stream.

Reading the stream is something that cannot be taught. Only experience--with perhaps some help from instinct--gives a floater this knowledge.

In approaching shoals or rapids, the floater must often look ahead and choose the proper course. In scanning an upcoming shoal, he should be able to discern the deeper water, the strongest part of a current and whirlpools. He also needs to recognize submerged logs and rocks, which may be hard to detect.

The best riverman is not necessarily a guy who can run any shoal or rapid. Sometimes it's the guy who can look at a certain bad stretch and know he'd better portage around it. I've spent my life on rivers, from the Ozarks way up into Canada, and believe me, I don't float every shoal. No matter how good you get, you shouldn't either. Don't forget that!

299

The author building a wooden johnboat at Buffalo River National Park in 1973.

20
TECHNIQUES OF BUILDING JOHNBOATS

The johnboats my grandfather built in the 1920's and 1930's were crude. I was always amazed in later years at his ability to cut a seat to fit perfectly an unfinished boat by just looking at it.

Late in his life, Grandpa began to use measurements and more precise angles. But most of his boats were built from memory and were improved through trial and error.

Most of the rivermen were like that. They were interested in efficiency and not too concerned with appearance. Those early johnboats must have looked fairly ragged.

It was hard to get good lumber. Boards often had a layer of bark on one edge. But of course the builder was happy to get scraps at low cost to build seats and live wells out of.

When a side board had a loose knot, Grandpa would remove it, tar it heavily, then replace it and perhaps tack a leather patch over it to hold it securely in place. It didn't look too good maybe, but it worked, and what he worried about was efficiency, not looks.

The bottoms of those johnboats were made of pine boards. Usually the boards were four- to eight-inches wide. They were

Techniques of Building Johnboats

nailed on crossways, with a crack left between each board and the next one. This crack was about 1/8 inch, or the thickness of a pocket-knife blade. When the boat was soaked with water, the bottom boards would swell and seal tightly.

In the 1922 issue of Forest and Stream magazine I found plans for making what was known as a 12 foot fishing punt. The boat was so similar to my grandfathers johnboats it was amazing (see photo on page 24). But the bottom boards were not placed to be tightened by swelling when they were in the water. The author told how he sealed his boats.... "Before nailing the bottom, however, we must give some thought to making the boat water-tight, and we have a long joint or seam between sides and bottom. The easiest way to do this job is to lay a thread of twisted cotton caulking along the edge, daub it well with paint just before nailing on a board and see that some nails are driven so that the cotton can't get out. In the absence of regular caulking four or five strands of white string loosely twisted together will do, or even the ravelings from a gunnysack."

In the early part of the 1900's, boat bottoms were sealed with old rags and tar between the boards and made with three or four long boards running lengthwise of the boat, rather than across it. Later, some of the boat builders chose to tongue-and-groove those bottom boards and put some type of sealer between them. This idea emerged when power tools came on the scene but it wasn't really much of an improvement. If the bottom boards were placed too closely together, the subsequent swelling would cause them to buck and crack. And the sealer was only good as long as the boat was soaked up. If the bottom ever dried out, it would shrink some. Then some of the sealer would come loose. My grandfathers boats with boards crosswise were never sealed, never tarred. And if they dried out they could be soaked up again and work perfectly well. I remember being in one of those johnboats of his in the summer when the bottom of the boat inside was scarcely moist. If there was water in the boat, you carried most of it on your feet when wading.

Techniques of Building Johnboats

This old johnboat found on the lower Eleven Point River was typical of the boats of that region. it had no seats and wooden ribs.

Techniques of Building Johnboats

Of course in years back, boats seldom left the river. They were customarily chained to a tree along the river so they were readily accessible. Though they weren't likely to dry out, they were subject to decay. Algae growing on the boat worsened the situation.

My father knew that and seldom left a boat in the river. Normally he would return boats to our home and keep bottoms sealed by keeping an inch of water in the bottom and placing burlap sacks, which he then kept wet, up in the ends of the boats. In the summer, the boats were kept in the shade. Every few days somebody had to check to be sure the sacks were still good and wet.

The johnboats used on the Current and White Rivers had lengthwise board bottoms, three long boards about 12 inches wide and usually sealed with something. Then when they were wet they sealed so tightly they never leaked but then they had to stay soaked up. If they dried out the sealing material would fall out in places and the boat might never be watertight again.

A riverman from the 1920's and 1930's was happy to get two or three years use out of a johnboat with the heavy use it was given. On larger streams, where rocks and shallow shoals weren't a problem, a boat lasted longer. My father aimed at getting four or five years out of his boats. To do that, he treated the bottoms with wood preservative and painted the boats each year. The boat we called Old Paint, a sentimental favorite of mine, lasted over 10 years.

Dad had one substantial advantage that Grandpa didn't have: Dad could get very good lumber. In 1920, Grandpa was happy to get any kind of material that was reasonably sound.

Early builders of johnboats were tempted to nail the bottom boards tightly together, rather than leave the required spaces between them. The result of nailing boards too close together was a bottom so tightly swollen that half the boards bucked up or down. It is absolutely necessary to leave the space between bottom boards. The boards swell tremendously and the john-

Techniques of Building Johnboats

boat can be soaked up tightly in only a few hours.

Bottom boards must be of very good material. The edges must be straight and smooth and the boards well-seasoned.

The same is true of the boards used in the sides of a john-boat. They must be straight, seasoned, and unchecked. A crack in a side board can ruin a boat. My dad has always claimed that the sides are mostly responsible for leaks in later years.

Putting the tapered bow between the sides of the johnboat was a tricky job until Grandpa began using what he called "forming braces." He nailed the boat sides to these temporary braces as one of the first steps in building the johnboat. Then the ends were drawn together by tightening a rope around each end.

After Grandpa nailed on the bottom and nailed the end pieces and center braces in place, he removed the ropes and then the temporary forming braces, which would be used again and again. Grandpa came up with a set of forming braces for 12-foot boats and a set each for 15-, 16-, 17-, and 19-foot boats. Each set varied a little in size and angles.

Another necessary part of a strong bottom in wooden john-boats are the keels, or "rudders" as my grandfather called them. The pair of 1-inch by 2-inch strips, running the length of the boat and nailed to the underside of the bottom about 15 inches apart, accomplished many things. These strips helped a boat run straight as it was paddled. They also gave added strength to the bottom and absorbed much of the abuse from rocky shoals.

But since there is an angle, or rake, in the bottom of the boat at each end, the rudders had to be bent. Grandpa accomplished this by sawing about halfway through the one-by-two's (on the side to be nailed against the bottom) at the spot where the bend was necessary. He made three cuts, each about 1/2 inch from the next and placed the incised side against the boat bottom. He boiled a big container of water, placed burlap sacks on each rudder where a bend was to be made and then poured on the

305

Techniques of Building Johnboats

steaming water a little at a time. In 10 to 15 minutes, the rudders could be bent at both ends without breaking, and then nailed down.

In years past, rivermen put live wells in their boats. These were bottomless boxes, usually one foot by two foot, sealed tightly with tar, then sealed to the boat's floor, which became the live well's bottom. Two holes were drilled in the floor, inside the box. These could be kept plugged most of the time. But when the plugs were removed, the well held five to six inches of water, an adequate place to keep fish, or (if the holes were covered with screen) small minnows used for bait. it was a real job to keep bait alive in a bucket on a hot summer day. But in a live well, with fresh water circulating in from the bottom, bait would stay alive for days. This was a tremendous aid for a trotline fisherman who was after flathead catfish, because he needed live bait.

A live well in the center of the boat had a lid, hinged with leather straps, and at times it served as a seat. When the live well was not in use, the holes in the bottom of it could be plugged and the well used as a storage compartment.

The early johnboats were fitted with board seats over a side-to-side brace. But my dad, when building his own boats in the 1950's, saw an opportunity to use space beneath seats as storage compartments. He made many of his boats with dry storage space beneath one or more seats.

It was early in the 1960's that Dad decided on using a plywood bottom for his johnboats, building a sealed craft that wouldn't have to be kept "soaked up." The coming of butyl rubber in large containers provided Dad with a suitable agent for tightly sealing a craft. But he had doubts about the longevity of a plywood bottom.

Experimenting with exterior plywood, Dad found he could expect about five years of service from a 3/8-inch plywood bottom. He could get more years from a half-inch bottom, but the boat was heavier. The best material was 3/8-inch marine ply-

Techniques of Building Johnboats

These are the distinctive Current River johnboats built by Ed Murray in the 1940's.

Techniques of Building Johnboats

wood. Its great strength took the blows of a rocky shoal, yet kept the weight of a boat reasonably light. We always used the exterior plywood because marine plywood is so expensive. So back then Dad was building a boat that had 50 or 60 dollars worth of material in it and required 12 to 15 hours of work.

It should be pointed out that the plywood Dad could buy in 1970 was far superior to that which is available today. While talking with Cecil Murray who now builds Current River john-boats I learned that he is having similar problems acquiring plywood which does not seep or leak. It could be that the only answer to the problem in the future is a heavier marine plywood, or perhaps going back to the old board bottoms which had to be kept soaked.

My grandfather, never built a plywood-bottom boat. He couldn't see putting that kind of expense into them. He also thought a fellow was getting lazy when he had to have a permanently sealed boat that required no soaking to keep it tight. It was very little trouble, as he saw it, to keep one soaked up. And anyone who worried about the boat being too heavy was a bit of a weakling, he figured. But when Dad decided he had considerably improved the johnboat by using a plywood bottom, almost everyone who bought boats from him preferred it.

A johnboat with a plywood bottom can last many years if you store it properly when it's not in use. You may get 10 or 15 years of service from a johnboat if you store it in a dry basement, garage, or shed. If you must keep the boat outside, turn it upside down and keep it covered with a tarpaulin. More damage is done to the boat by the heat of the sun than by rain, wind and snow. If the wood is exposed each day to the heat of the sun, the wood dries and shrinks so badly that the seams can begin to leak. Of course you should always store the boat on sawhorses or blocks off the ground and perfectly level to keep it from warping.

What wood makes the best johnboat? It's difficult to say. Our family has always used white or yellow pine because it is

Techniques of Building Johnboats

fairly light, strong, and resistant to cracking. Dad preferred white pine for the bottom boards. For ends, it's best to use good strong oak, though 2-inch-thick pine will work.

I'm not saying pine is the best material for a johnboat, but other lumber may be hard to get or too expensive. Some johnboat builders in years past used mahogany boards for the boat sides, but that material, though strong and not likely to crack, is very expensive today.

At one time, lumber from the tupelo (black gum) was used for the bottom boards. This was fairly good material because it was hard and had little grain. But it's very difficult to put a nail through.

Cypress is said to be the best possible wood for boat building. It doesn't soak up much water and seems to resist rotting indefinitely. But cypress is also somewhat soft and is ground away by dragging over rocky shoals.

Redwood seems to resist water but has the drawback of being quite expensive. If you use cypress, redwood or mahogany, you will perhaps have a longer-lasting boat, but the expense will be far greater than that of pine.

Whatever wood is used, the life of a boat can be extended with a wood preservative and annual paint jobs; this needs to be emphasized. While my dad always preferred resin treated nails, I think nowadays, with the power screw drivers and bronze deck screws which will not rust, screws can hold together a johnboat better than nails. But no matter which you use, be precise.

Screws or nails that are off-line can ruin a boat, especially when you're nailing the bottom boards on. Be sure you don't get nails crooked and have them break out of the side boards. That kind of mistake opens the wood to water and decay. When you must remove a nail, plug the hole with a match-stick-size splinter of pine that's coated with glue, tar or butyl rubber and driven into the hole with a hammer.

Much was written about Charlie Barnes the old White River

309

Techniques of Building Johnboats

boat builder. Charlie recalled that the very earliest White River gigging boats were only 20 feet in length and 2 feet wide. Therefore it took only two 12 inch boards for the bottom.

For the White, Barnes built longer johnboats than my grandfather made for the Piney and they were about three feet wide at the center. His boats were much different from my grandfather's johnboats. Charlie used three 20-foot boards, 12 inches wide, for a boat bottom. They ran lengthwise and in the later years were tongue-and-grooved and sealed and joined. There's uncertainty about what material was used to seal the boat, but one man who worked with Barnes remembers using thin rags between the tongue-and-groove joints. Wooden strips--1/2 by 2 1/2 inches--ran the full length of the boat to cover the floorboard joints from the outside (bottom). These served as rudders or keels.

The White River boats were reinforced on the inside by wrought-iron ribs made from old wagon tires. These ribs held the shape of the sides without any center seats and gave the boat considerable strength.

Charlie Barnes built about 300 boats, the last of them in the mid 1950's. The following photos were taken of a boat on display at School of the Ozarks College in the 1980's.

Techniques of Building Johnboats

Bottom opposite page: rudders were placed over the seams of the bottom boards.
Right: Metal ribs were made from old wagon wheel rims.

311

21
BUILDING YOUR OWN JOHNBOAT

The following chapter is taken directly from the book *"The Authentic American Johnboat"*, which was published in 1978 and has long been out-of-print. Therefore as you read this remember that I wrote it in 1977. However the instructions still are relevant to building a johnboat today except for the fact that plywood of that time was better sealed, stronger and superior to the same grade of plywood today. Should you decide to use a plywood bottom be sure you find a marine plywood which will do the job.

-- Larry Dablemont

Building Your Own Johnboat

How to Build Your Own Authentic 14-foot Wooden Johnboat

My dad, Farrel Dablemont, may be the last builder of wooden johnboats in the Ozarks. He learned to build the boats by helping and watching my grandfather in the 1930's. Dad and his brothers and father lived on the Big Piney river, where they rented boats and guided float fishermen from the 1930's well into the 1960's.

Dad has estimated he built nearly 200 johnboats on his own for float fishing resorts on the Gasconade, Big Piney and Bourbeuse rivers in Missouri and he sold his boats to commercial fishermen on the Osage and Missouri rivers. Now in his early 50's, he continues to build five or six johnboats each year.

Besides building the johnboats, Dad is an expert in handling them. He has the same dexterity that the old-time river guides were famous for.

On the following pages, he demonstrates in step-by-step photographs (accompanied by accurate plans) how to build an authentic wooden johnboat. The process is complete whether your aim is to build the version with the plywood bottom (which can be stored dry) or the older version with a slat bottom (which must be kept wet).

A Most Important Preliminary

The key ingredient in producing a well-formed johnboat is the temporary forming brace. You'll need two. You can use scrap lumber to build them (as was done with those in the the photo), but their dimensions must be accurate. The forming braces will be removed late in the building process.

Dad prefers a 15-degree angle in the sides of the forming

313

Building Your Own Johnboat

braces. For each forming brace, cut two 1" x 10" boards at a 15-degree angle as shown and nail them together solidly with two or more 1" x 4" or 1" x 6" cross strips. These forming braces must be very strong.

For this 14-foot boat, the bottom of the front brace should measure 32 inches across; the back brace should measure 34 inches across (See Drawings 1A and 1B, and Photo 1.)

Photo 1

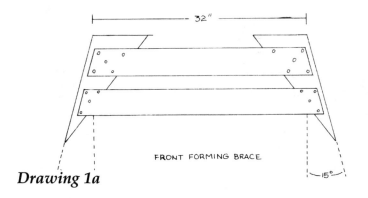

Drawing 1a

Building Your Own Johnboat

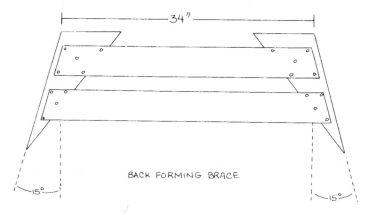

Drawing 1b

Building Your johnboat, Step by Step

First Stage: set up two sturdy five-foot-wide saw horses, eight feet apart and level each one perfectly, as in Photo 2. during the boat building, the saw horses must remain level.

Photo 2

IMPORTANT NOTE: The boat is built mostly upside down on the saw horses.

Building Your Own Johnboat

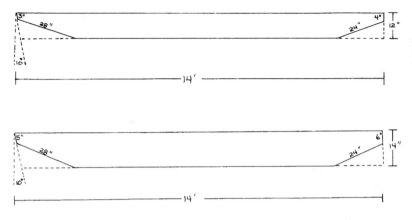

Drawing 2

Photo 3

Second Stage: Measure and cut side boards as in Drawing 2. The front of the board, which will be the bow, should be angled 10 degrees from the vertical. If you are using a 12-inch-wide board, the front of the board will be cut off at three inches from the top and the back will be cut off at four inches. But if you are using 14-inch boards (thereby eliminating the need to add a top strip later), the front will be cut off at five inches and the back at six inches (See Drawing 2 and Photos 3, 4, 5 and 6). Now you have produced two completed side boards (See Photo 7).

Photo 4

Building Your Own Johnboat

Photo 5

Photo 6

Photo 7

Third Stage: Nail 1" x 2" strips to the lower inside edge of each side board. Drawing 3 shows the pattern for the right side

PROPER ATTACHMENT OF 1x2 STRIPS TO SIDES

Drawing 3

Building Your Own Johnboat

board. The left side-board is a mirror image. The edge of the strip must extend beyond the side board's edge by about 1/8 inch as shown in Drawing 4 and Photo 8. This arrangement is essential for later

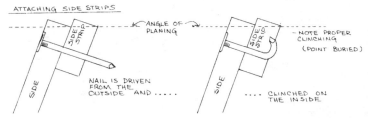

Drawing 4

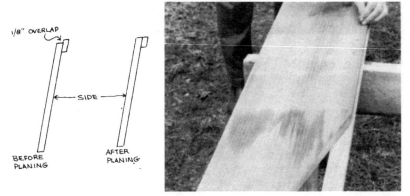

Photo 8

producing a flat surface (by planing) to meet the boat's bottom. Use No. 6 resin-treated box nail, one every four inches and staggered on the 1" x 2" side strips. Clinch (bend over) the nails on the inside and countersink the points with a dull punch (See Drawing 4 and Photos 9 an 10). Side boards with strips nailed to lower edge are shown in Photo 11. Note that strips end short of side-board ends, to make room for later insertion of boat's end pieces.

Building Your Own Johnboat

Photo 9

Photo 10

Photo 11

319

Building Your Own Johnboat

Fourth Stage: Attach the side boards to the forming braces. One brace is placed 48 inches from the front of the side boards and the other is placed 44 inches from the back of the side boards (See Photos 12, 13 and 14). The forming braces should

Photo 12

Photo 13

Photo 14

320

Building Your Own Johnboat

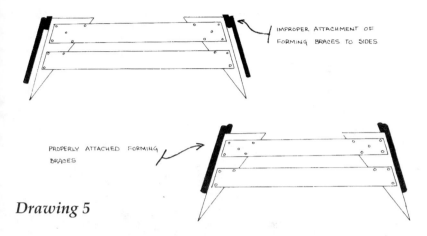

Drawing 5

butt against the 1" x 2" strips, so the side boards touch the forming braces (See Drawing 5). Fasten the side boards solidly to the forming braces with 2-inch screws, four screws for each brace. The screws and forming braces can be easily removed later, when it is time to put in permanent braces.

Fifth Stage: Now with the boat bottom up, use a rope and an adjustable knot to pull the side boards to within 23 inches of

Photo 15

Photo 16

321

Building Your Own Johnboat

each other at the front. Use the same procedure to pull the side boards within 25 inches of each other at the back (See Photos 15 and 16. Note nail placement to prevent rope from slipping off board). If the sides are not uniformly curved, turn the boat on edge and use your knee to bend the straighter side. Apply slow but steady pressure to make the side board curve properly (See Photo 17).

Photo 17

This problem seldom arises if the boards are matched and straight.

Building Your Own Johnboat

Sixth Stage: Now you're ready to cut and fit the end pieces. These should be two inches thick. Fitting them can be difficult because the edges must be not only properly angled from top to bottom but also beveled slightly from front to back to fit snugly between the side boards (see Drawing 6). **Drawing 6**

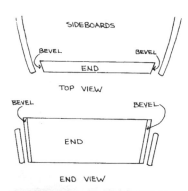

Precise measuring is the key (See Photos 18 and 19). Nail

Photo 18

Photo 19

each end piece between the side boards with No. 8 screw nails and use 5 or 6 nails in each side. The ends are point of much stress and the joints must hold tightly (See Photo 20).

Photo 20

323

Building Your Own Johnboat

Photo 21 shows the boat at this stage right-side up, ends and forming braces in.

Photo 21

Seventh Stage: Prepare the lower edges of the side boards to receive the boat's bottom. The curve of the boat makes the lower edges of the side boards angle inward. With a good plane, you can readily make both sides perfectly flat (See Photo

Photo 22

22 and Drawing 4). To check the accuracy of your planing, run

Photo 23

324

Building Your Own Johnboat

a flat board along the bottom (See Photo 23). Dips or humps will show up and more planing can make the lower edges of the side boards very flat. Also plane the bottom edge of both end pieces so the bottom will fit snugly there (See Photo 24.)

Photo 24

Eighth Stage: The rake (slope) of the boat in front and back creates an abrupt angle in the lower edge of the side boards. Before the bottom can be fastened in place, you must reduce the abruptness of the angles on both side boards, front and back, by planing off an 8-inch curve, about 1/2 inch deep (See Photo 25 and Drawing 7).

Photo 25

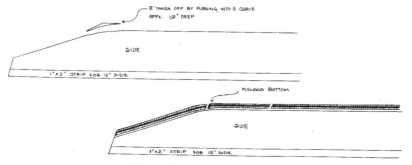

Drawing 7

325

Building Your Own Johnboat

Ninth Stage: If you have a 10-foot section of plywood, you need to make only two splices or joints in the bottom. If you have standard eight foot plywood, you'll need to make three joints (See Drawing 8, especially bevel details).

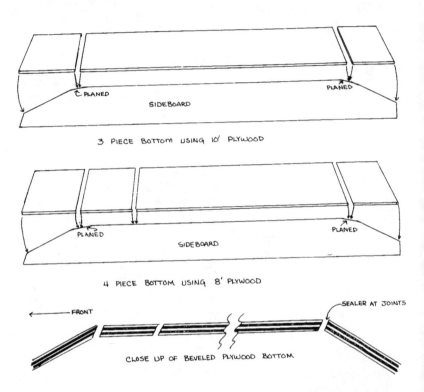

Drawing 8

The bottom pieces must be beveled and carefully fitted together. The slope of each bevel should point toward the back of the boat, to keep any small lip from catching on a rock or snag. The bevel is made by setting the power saw's blade at an angle. This angle may be varied slightly, but should be close to 45 degrees (See Photo 26).

Building Your Own Johnboat

Photo 26

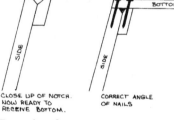

Drawing 9

Tenth Stage: When the plywood sections have been properly shaped to form the bottom of the boat but NOT fastened in place, put them aside temporarily and cut a notch the full length of each side between the side board and side-board strip, to form a small channel for the sealer compound (See Drawing 9 and Photo 27 and 28). Dad cuts the notch with a hammer and an old hunting knife, but you might prefer a chisel in place of the knife.

Photo 28

Photo 27

Building Your Own Johnboat

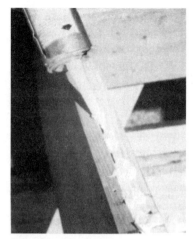

Photo 29

Photo 30

Eleventh Stage: Now you're ready to permanently fasten the bottom, section by section. Using the butyl rubber silicone sealer, fill each notch liberally and spread the sealer with a putty knife (See Photos 29 an 30). Now comes the most difficult and most important part of building your johnboat. The bottom sections must be nailed exactly in place, largest section first. The nails must angle precisely into the slanting side boards (See Drawing 9). Use No. 6 screw nails or flooring nails and space them two inches apart (See Photo 31). If a nail breaks out of the side board, your boat will leak slightly; the side board is also more apt to crack and split and the side will decay quicker.

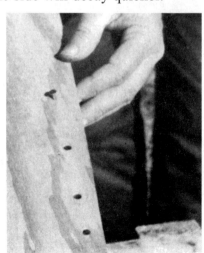

Photo 31

Building Your Own Johnboat

Photo 32

Photo 33

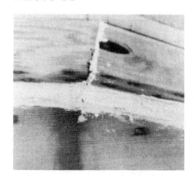

Photo 34

Twelfth Stage: When you finish nailing the main bottom section of plywood to the side boards, nail the same section to the adjacent side-board strips. Use No. 6 screw nails (flooring nails), place them two inches apart and stagger them from the other row of nails (See Photo 32 and Drawing 10).

Drawing 10

As you apply the other sections of the plywood bottom, liberally apply the sealer to the face of all joints and also seal the ends well (Photos 33, 34 and 35).

Photo 35

329

Building Your Own Johnboat

Thirteenth Stage: The bottom is now in place, but it's not firm and solid yet. The keels, or rudders, come next and they are a part of making the bottom stable (See Photo 36). Be sure they

Photo 36

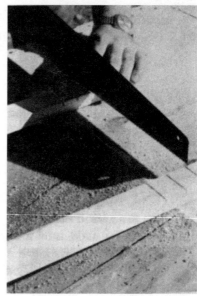
Photo 37

will be long enough to reach both ends after bending. At the points where the keels must bend, make three saw cuts 1/3 of the way through (see Photo 37). Then turn the cuts toward the boat bottom (See Drawing 11). Arrange these keels about 10 or 12 inches apart and be sure they

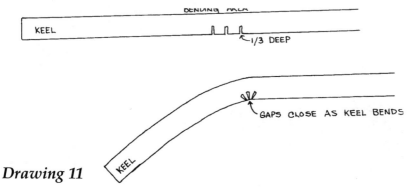
Drawing 11

330

Building Your Own Johnboat

Photo 38

are lined up perfectly straight (See Photo 38). They help the boat maintain its course. If one or both are crooked, the boat will tend to fade right or left as it floats.

Nail the keels in place first across only the flat part of the bottom with No. 4 box nails. They will come through the bottom just a little, so you'll need to clinch them tightly from the inside. When you do this, the nail point is countersunk (bent down) into the wood with a hammer and dull punch so it never catches on anything. Proper clinching also makes the keel-to-bottom bond very strong (See Drawing 12).

Building Your Own Johnboat

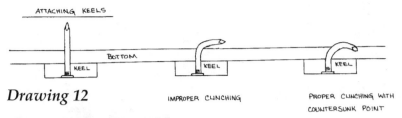

Drawing 12 IMPROPER CLINCHING   PROPER CLINCHING WITH COUNTERSUNK POINT

Photo 39

Photo 40

Fourteenth Stage: Before you can nail the rest of each keel in place, you must bend each to fit the rake of the bottom. The shallow saw cuts made at the two bending points of each keel help you to do this. But you must also wrap each keel in burlap or other heavy fabric at the bending points and pour on boiling water for 10 or 15 minutes to make the keel strips pliable (See Photo 39). Then remove the burlap, slowly bend the keels down, and nail them in place. Use No. 4 box nails to secure keels, one nail every four inches, staggered. Of course the keels at each end are nailed into the end pieces of the boat, bow and stern. When the nailing is finished, the keel adds strength to the bottom of the boat. Clinch nails as shown in Drawing 12. With keels completely nailed in place, boat looks as it does in photo 40.

Building Your Own Johnboat

Photo 41

If you should break or crack a keel while bending it, use a strip of pliable metal to cover 10 or 12 inches of the keel across the bending point. Use screws to hold the metal in place (See Photo 41). If you will use the boat in shallow rocky water where the bottom of the boat is constantly grinding against the substrate, it's a good idea to add such a reinforcing metal strip at all four bending points anyway.

Fifteenth Stage: When the keels are in place and the boat is still bottom up, use a saw, a plane and some wood files to trim the edges of the bottom to a perfect fit, exactly flush with the side boards.

Photo 42

Sixteenth Stage: Now turn the boat topside up, with the bottom resting on the saw horses (See Photo 42 and note that forming braces are still in place). If you have used 14-inch side boards, your boat is deep enough for most streams. But if you have used 12-inch side boards, you must add a 2-inch strip at the top of both sides. Don't try to nail these on in an ordinary way.

Building Your Own Johnboat

Nail one end of the 2-inch strip to the end piece at the bow. Then drill holes down through the strip and into the top of the side board (See Photo 43). The forming braces, which are still in place, help you to make the strip fit exactly along the side board.

Photo 43

Drill a hole about every four to six inches and drive a 3-inch finishing nail (No. 10) into each as you go (See Photo 44 and Drawing 13).

Photo 44

Building Your Own Johnboat

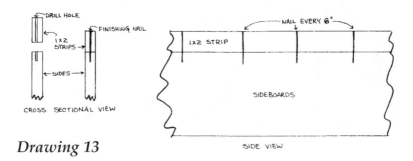

Drawing 13

Seventeenth Stage: When the strips have been added to the top of the side boards (see Photo 45), trim the side boards at bow and stern so they are flush with the end pieces. If you want

Photo 45

to use a small motor on your boat, you may want to reinforce the stern's end board with a pine board or a piece of plywood (See Photos 46 and 47).

335

Building Your Own Johnboat

Photo 46

Photo 47

Building Your Own Johnboat

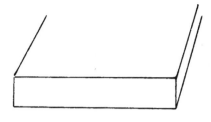

BEFORE PLANING

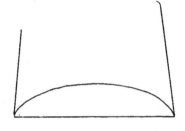

AFTER PLANING

Eighteenth Stage: Your johnboat has three joints between bottom sections if you used 8-foot plywood. Cut a pine strip, 1/2" x 2" or 1/2" x 3", to fit across each joint INSIDE the boat. Plane down the sharp edges of the upper side (See Drawing 14). The rounded strips are not apt to cause you to trip. Each strip runs the entire length of its joint (the width of the boat).

Drawing 14

Apply sealer liberally to the joint before installing each strip (See Photo 48). Fasten each strip with No. 4 nails, one nail

Photo 48

337

Building Your Own Johnboat

Photo 49

every four inches, staggered (See Photo 49). Then clinch those nails on the exterior, where they extend through the boat bottom.

Photo 50

Nineteenth Stage: Now you're about ready to cut and fit the seats. Before removing the forming braces, nail in the permanent braces on which the seats will rest. If there is to be no dry compartment under a seat, use a 1" x 4" permanent cross brace under the center of the seat (See Photo 50).

Photo 51

If there is to be a dry compartment under the seat, use two braces (1" x 8" or 1" x 10") and a Masonite or plywood bottom (See Drawing 15 and Photos 51 and 52). The seats are centered on these permanent braces and there can be some slight variation here.

The second seat from the back should be centered about six inches behind the rear tempo-

Building Your Own Johnboat

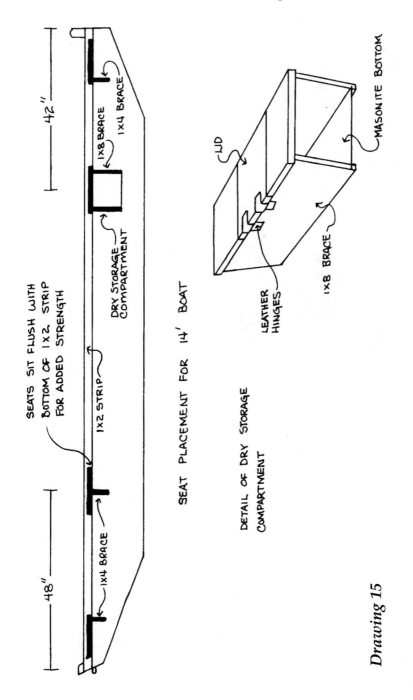

Drawing 15

Building Your Own Johnboat

rary forming brace. The second seat from the front should be six inches ahead of the front temporary forming brace. Be sure the permanent braces are nailed in so that the top of each brace aligns with the seam between the 12-inch side board and the 1" x 2" top strip. Use No. 8 resin-treated nails for seats and braces.

Photo 52

Twentieth Stage: When the permanent braces are solidly installed for the proper placement of seats, remove the forming braces. These same braces can be used on a future boat or boats.

Cut small wooden plugs to seal the screw holes in the side of the boat where you removed the forming braces. The butyl rubber sealer applied to a small wooden plug will seal these holes tightly.

Twenty-first Stage: Cut and fit seats (1" x 10" or 1" x 12" boards) to lie on top of the center braces. Nail the two center seats in (See Drawing 15). When this is done, the seat will be about one inch under the top of the side strip. The bottom of the seat will be flush with the seam between the 12-inch side board and the added 1" x 2" strip. That one-inch "lip" of wood above the seat keeps rods, reels and other gear from slipping off the seat into the river.

Building Your Own Johnboat

Twenty-second Stage: Now you cut and fit the end seats. They should also align at their bottom edge with the seam where the two-inch strip joins the 12-inch side board. End seats should be 14 to 18 inches wide, each nailed into the end of the boat and supported by a 1" x 4" brace. Be sure you put the desired eye bolt into the front end (see Photo 53) before nailing in the end seats (See Photo 54).

Photo 53

Photo 54

Building Your Own Johnboat

Photo 55

Twenty-third Stage: Trim and smooth end pieces (See Photo 55) and lightly plane off the sharp edges of the seats and sides to round them and prevent splintering.

Photo 56

Twenty-fourth Stage: The boat is now ready to paint. A good marine paint is highly resistant to water. If you don't want to use the higher-cost marine paint, use farm-implement paint or porch-and-deck paint. The best color is a drab green or dead grass (See Photo 65) and you can camouflage it if you like with a few sprays of brown and black paint from spray cans.

With any paint, mix 3/4 pints of linseed oil with 1/4 pint of paint for the primer coat. For the second coat (after the primer has dried), use the paint without adding linseed oil.

Building Your Own Johnboat

For Alternate Version With Slat Bottom

If you want to build the old-style johnboat that must be kept "soaked up," follow the procedure just described right through the seventh stage. Then continue as follows:

Starting at the center, cut and nail on crossways 1/2" x 6" or 1/2" x 8" boards (See Photo 57). Use No. 6 resin-treated nails

Photo 57

and drive one into the side board every two inches. Then drive another row of nails into the adjacent side-board strip, the same distance apart but staggered, NOT side by side with the nails in the other row.

Continue to add boards to the bottom, leaving space of 1/16" to

Building Your Own Johnboat

Photo 58

1/8" between boards (See Photo 58). If you are using 8-inch boards, make those spaces a little wider than if you were using 6-inch boards. The swelling of an 8-inch board is greater.

When you get to the rake angle, front and rear, plane off the corner along a straight line, as shown in Photo 59 and Drawing 16. Then one board sits on the 8-inch planed area. This cross

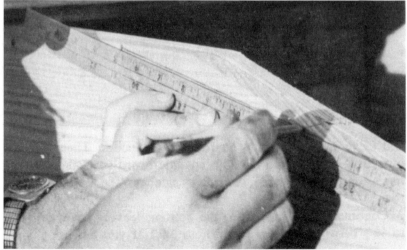

Photo 59

Building Your Own Johnboat

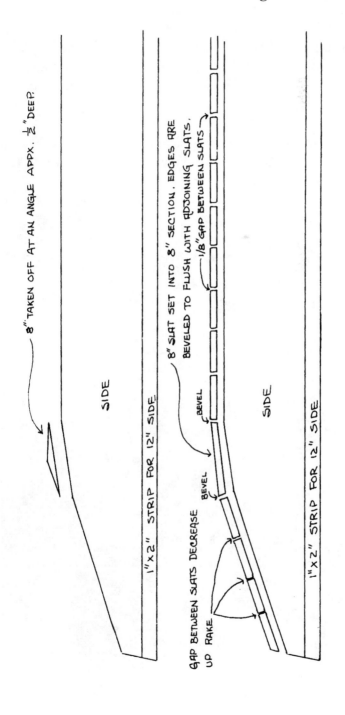

Drawing 16

Building Your Own Johnboat

board must have both edges beveled with a plane. It fits flush with the adjacent bottom boards. When the rake angle is reached, do not leave as much of a crack between boards from there to the end. Use NO SEALER between ANY of the joints. Cut 1" x 2" or 1" x 4" strips and nail them over the cracks above the rake angle in each end.

Then follow the procedure from the nineteenth stage to the end, as with the plywood-bottom johnboat. A bottom view of a finished slat-bottom johnboat is shown in Photo 60.

Photo 60

Building Your Own Johnboat

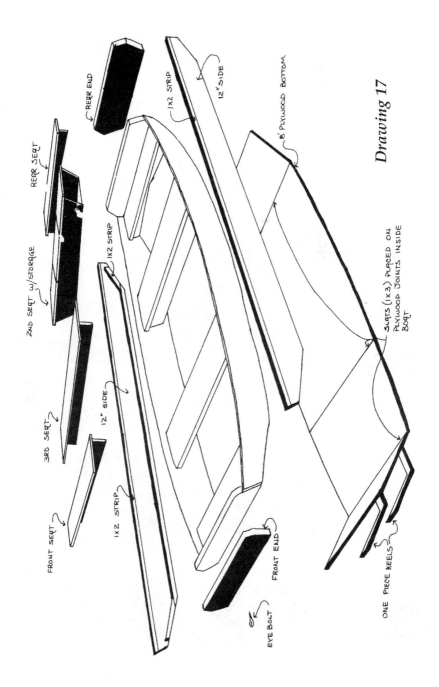

Drawing 17

Building Your Own Johnboat

The Over-all View

For a general idea of how the various parts of the johnboat fit together, study Drawing 17. At the center is shown a completed johnboat in the plywood-bottom version. Surrounding the completed boat are the various components as they would appear if the entire boat suddenly "exploded". Slight variations occur. No two johnboats are ever exactly the same. With the help of this drawing and the foregoing drawings and photos, you should be able to construct a workmanlike example of the authentic American johnboat as it evolved on the rivers of the Ozarks. A closeup of a completed johnboat appears in Photo 61. And Photos 62 and 63 show an overhead and a side view

Photo 61

Building Your Own Johnboat

Photo 62

of johnboats under way. The jacket of this book shows a fully loaded johnboat on an Ozark river.

Photo 63

349

22
THE LAST OF THE OZARK RIVER GUIDES

    A few years ago, my uncle and I began to take all-day interpretive float trips on the Niangua river, something still going on at the time of this books first printing. We would take 15 to 20 people per trip, six or eight boats. Some of the guests would paddle their own canoe or johnboat, but most wanted to go with guides, so I had to find several good river guides to go along. That's when I met Dale Williams, a grizzled old veteran river guide who was only 38 years old at the time. He was made to be a river guide.

    His experiences on the Niangua would fill a book, but Dale came from the rural Ozarks near West Plains and grew up fishing with his grandfather, who took him to Norfork Lake and all the rivers around them, the Current, Jacks Fork, Bryant Creek and the Eleven Point to name a few.

    Williams began guiding on the Norfork river as a boy, and came to the Niangua in his early twenties. Dale had a bunch of stories to tell, but one was really special. He would tell first about one of his most memorable trips, when he had a father and son and daughter fishing the river for trout in the fall, about five or six years back. Dale recalled how the thirteen-year-old

The Last of the Ozark River Guides

girl couldn't catch a fish, no matter what he tried. At the same time her father and brother were catching bunches of rainbow trout and her brother was really rubbing it in.

"About mid-afternoon I saw a big fish swimming up into the weeds," Dale said, "and I grabbed her rod, took the sinker off and put a big minnow on the hook. I threw it toward the weeds and gave it to her with the bail open, and watched the weeds moving as the fish came out and took the minnow. I told her to hang on, and she did!"

Williams said the fight lasted ten minutes or so, and with the drag set just right, a deep hole with no obstacles and a lot of luck, she eventually brought the big brown to the net, a 24-inch fish, about seven pounds or so.

"That little girl didn't want me to put it in the live-well in my boat," he laughed as he related the story to the group of floaters there on a river gravel bar not far from where it happened. "She was afraid it would get away, she wanted to just hold on to it all the way home."

Those people come back every year now, but Dale recalls, as his face grows somber and his eyes moist, the nine-year old that will never come back. She is alive today because he had a free day and was fishing the river one day in the summer, just behind a canoe in which she was riding with her father and aunt.

He heard the screams and quickly came upon a canoe upside down in swift water against a log jam, and everyone in the area trying to pull it free. The little girl was trapped inside. She was upside down, with a bent crossbar beneath which she had been sitting, trapping her against the floor.

Williams knew, from his years of experience, that the current was too strong and the canoe could not be pulled free. He dived beneath it to find her still struggling and even fighting him. He couldn't pull her free.

"I remember seeing long red hair and realizing that she was pinned beneath that bar. I tried several times to give her a

352

The Last of the Ozark River Guides

breath of air, and I think it may have worked a little, but it was hard to do with her struggling so hard," he said, with the group before him mesmerized with the story. "And so I pushed my feet against the root wad and pulled that crossbar with every ounce of strength I had. I guess the adrenaline had a lot to do with it, but it came loose, and I pulled her out. But by that time, she wasn't conscious."

Remembering back, Dale said he figures the little girl was underwater twelve to fifteen minutes. As luck would have it, one of the onlookers was an E.M.T. and the little girl, apparently lifeless, was immediately given C.P.R. and local rescue workers arrived with oxygen. Finally, a medevac helicopter arrived and they flew her to a Springfield hospital. For several days she lay in a coma, and Dale couldn't stop thinking about her. Finally he decided he had to go see her. He bought her a stuffed lion king toy. To give you an idea of when this happened, Disney's "Lion King' movie was very popular at the time.

Just about the time he walked in that day, the little girl came out of the coma. In a day the little girl was sitting up in bed, acting as if nothing had ever happened. She was on her way to a complete recovery.

There on the gravel bar, Dale Williams eyes grew moist as he recalls it, though he says the trauma of the event makes it somewhat hazy in his memory in places. Parts of it he remembers as if it were yesterday. He gives most of the credit to the people he handed her over to that day. He said he joined the local fire and rescue squad right after that, and figures that cold spring water that flows in the Niangua helped to ensure her survival. But there isn't any doubt about it, amongst all the things the little girl had going for her that day was a lean, tough, experienced river guide floating along right behind her, just trying to catch a fish or two on his day off.

It is always a pleasure to take those interpretive trips and stop on a gravel bar for a fish fry, and watch people drawn to

353

The Last of the Ozark River Guides

Dale Williams answers questions for a young floater.

Dale and my uncle as if they were magnetic. As I said, some people are born to be river guides, even in this day and time. I always felt I was too.

In my spare time as a boy, I was learning all I could about the river, and catching fish. There was a big eddy about two or three miles from our house called the Ginseng eddy and above it was the Sweet Potato eddy. In these two big holes lurked a smallmouth bass such as no one had ever seen the equal to. My intentions were to catch that lunker smallmouth, which I figured might have gone over the six pound mark.

It would have been easier to do that if I hadn't had to hold down a pretty important job in nearby Houston. When I was 11

The Last of the Ozark River Guides

or 12, Dad had bought the local pool hall. It was a country pool hall, a hangout for the hunters and fishermen of the area and for the old-timers who had known the river even before my dad was born, some of them had been float-fishing guides too.

During the day, my grandfather McNew ran the place. I arose at daylight six days a week, pedaled my bike into town to the pool hall on Main Street and helped my grandpa clean up before opening. That summer I sat wide-eyed and open-mouthed, listening to a collection of 60- and 70-year-old men recall the good old days, right there on the bench with three huge fish mounted on the wall and a row of spittoons beneath them.

I was close to Grandpa McNew. He was a sage of man, with the wisdom of countless aging men who have seen it all and could well advise us of a better course if younger men would only listen.

My other grandfather, Grandpa Dablemont, and my father taught me to fish and hunt. Grandpa Dablemont made me realize there was much to be learned that books couldn't teach. Grandpa McNew taught me there was much to be learned from everything including books. Not only that, he taught me how to shoot pool, how to snooker the other fellow, play the leave and put English on the ball.

For five or six years I worked in the old pool hall and learned to idolize that handful of old men who didn't mind telling stories to a kid. Many of them had built johnboats and guided fishermen on the river in their younger days. In the beginning, Grandpa just let me rack tables and collect money while he was there. And when he stepped out for lunch or for some other reason, I got to run the place. Eventually, I began to work there part of each weekday during the summers when school was out.

But come 3 o'clock, I was on my bicycle and gone. I'd stop by home for my shotgun or rod and reel. With one or the other tied across the handle bars, I'd head for the river to hunt squir-

The Last of the Ozark River Guides

rels or fish for that big smallmouth.

The old gravel road had some hills in it, but at the end of it was Myrtle Kelly's farm. Mrs. Kelly was a kindly lady who owned the prettiest place on the river. She was a widow, but in years gone by she and her husband had fished with Grandpa Dablemont all over the Ozarks. She had one of Grandpa's old johnboats fastened to a tree, chained and locked and all I had to do was ask her for the key. Sometimes she'd go along and we'd dig a can of night crawlers or set a minnow trap and still fish at the upper end of the Sweet 'tater eddy. Her nephew, Larry Whitehair, from Oklahoma spent some time with her and he and I fished together on occasion during the summer.

But much of the time I in the spring and fall, I fished alone, each evening until dusk, trying to hook that big one. Seems like once or twice a week I'd hook that big bass, but I'd never get to see him. Every time I'd hook a big turtle or catfish or log or rock it was that big bass until proven otherwise.

Then every morning at the pool hall I'd sit in the middle of the bench and tell Ol' Bill and Ol' Jim and Ol' Jess and Virgil and and Churchill and Grandpa McNew how close I'd come to haulin' that big smallmouth in by the gills. They'd all listen and glance at one another from time to time, winkin' and grinnin', which used to make me madder'n heck.

By the time I was 12, I'd learned to handle a johnboat reasonably well, though I lacked the strength to really be good with a paddle. I did my first paddling for my dad and grandpa that summer and fall. A couple of local fishermen who were good friends of my grandfather would come by and pick me up on Saturday afternoon and have me paddle for them while they fished.

I guided my first paying float fishermen within a year or so after that, before I was really strong enough to be good at it. My old friend Joe Richardson, from Houston, Mo. was my first client, as I recall. I paddled Joe through a shoal where there was a limb hanging out over the river which I had floated under

356

The Last of the Ozark River Guides

many times. I just ducked under it, and it was easy for me, I only weighed about 120 pounds and wasn't much more than five feet tall. Joe was a grown man and over six feet tall, and he couldn't get under that limb. He just caught ahold of it, and it swept him out of the boat into the cool river. Thankfully, it was June, and we got out on a gravel bar and he dried out quickly. Joe never said a discouraging word that day, though I'm sure he was thinking it. He was a good fisherman and caught fish every time he went, and he and I floated quite often. From that point on, he stayed dry, and I learned to be a better guide by pulling around the bad places.

When I was 13, I got my first guide's license so I could get paid legally and better for my service. My business was mostly people from the city who'd floated with my dad and uncles when they were younger.

Before my first trip as a licensed guide, my dad gave me some advice. "Just paddle the boat, son," he said. "Don't give advice on fishin'."

Early that morning, my client cast a small spinner toward the bank, in shallow water with a gravel bottom and not a rock or log within 50 yards.

"You won't catch anything there," I told him. "Too shallow, and not enough cover."

Just as I finished, a fat half-pound goggle-eye grabbed the lure. The fisherman hauled him in. I didn't say much the rest of the day.

Grandpa later told me about a wise old guide who practically never talked. One day he was particularly quiet and hadn't said a word all morning. Just before the lunch stop, his client hooked the old guide's hat on the back cast and flung it into the river. The old guide let loose with a long string of cuss words and the fisherman was a little relieved.

"Why is it," he asked, "that you haven't said a thing all morning until just now?"

"Wal," the old-timer said as he shifted his tobacco in his

The Last of the Ozark River Guides

cheek and retrieved his dripping hat, "up to now you was a-doin' all right."

I practiced with my boat paddle, and by the time I was 15 I was a competent guide. I started to get quite a bit of weekend business, even had some cards printed up.

I was the only guide on the Big Piney you could get for a dollar an hour. And though I never told anyone, I'd have paddled all day for nothing if they'd just listened without grinning when I told how close I had come to caching that smallmouth.

It wasn't a hard job, it was the best job I ever had. I guess I was born fifty years too late.

The guide's main job was to paddle the boat, maneuvering it into the best fishing positions and holding it in swift water where smallmouth lurked. He kept the fisherman the right distance from the bank and he retrieved lures that got hung up beneath the surface or in branches. He also had to know the best fishing lures and where the fish were in different seasons.

On overnight trips, the guide prepared the meals, collected firewood and cleaned the fish. Few of them complained about anything. Guiding was the work most of them were meant for. It was the most enjoyable thing they did. It brought together two different ways of life: the well-to-do city sportsman and the backwoods philosopher who found happiness in simple things.

The guide was a naturalist, an interpreter of the river and its life. There was no thrill like helping someone else enjoy the outdoors solely because of your ability. A guide took pride in that. And through my own experiences, I know that most guides enjoyed seeing a client catch a fish more than they themselves enjoyed catching one. That was the real test of competence. If you could take inexperienced fishermen and help them enjoy a successful trip, there was no question of your own fishing ability.

Float fishermen came from every walk of life and strong friendships grew between the guides and fishermen he worked

The Last of the Ozark River Guides

for. There were people that a guide hated to see leave and he might look forward to their return as much as to a visit from relatives and in some cases more, depending on the relatives. And in turn, sportsmen and their families sometimes planned their vacations around a visit to one area where their favorite guide would set aside all other work to cater to them. Quite often, wealthy sportsmen would leave elaborate and expensive homes in the city and bring a son to spend a week in a small cabin on a Midwestern river with an old river guide.

As times changed, the river guide became a rarity as did the johnboat that was his constant companion. Aluminum canoes and boats helped bring about the change, as sport fishermen began to acquire their own craft and float on their own.

Besides, the rivermen who loved the life of a guide became too old and their sons moved away to work in the cities where the lights were bright and money easier to come by.

Oh, there are still guides to be found, but they aren't the fellows in flannel shirts who eased a wooden johnboat along a quiet river with a sassafras paddle. As in most waters today, float-fishing streams have received considerable pressure. The fishing isn't the way it once was when big smallmouth lurked beneath every fallen log or submerged stump. The heyday of float fishing was the day of the wooden johnboat, the sassafras paddle and the leather-faced guide who wouldn't have traded places with a king.

23
THE DYING RIVERS

This is the chapter I do not want to write, and most people will not want to read. I have tried to start it many times, only to turn away and find something else to concentrate on. What I am going to say here is not going to please anyone.

Once upon a time, long before most of us remember, the Ozarks was a giant sponge. Heavy rain fell upon a canopy of trees, and seeped through a layer of dead leaves into a soft underlayer of rich, loess soil. A drop of rain, a gallon of rainfall, might have traveled slowly into the earth, into a water table, or into a small headwaters tributary or spring. That water might have taken a week to arrive at the mouth of an Ozark creek or river.

Today the Ozarks has been turned from a giant sponge to a giant brick...the forest shrinks, the leaf carpet is burned off annually, the hills are converted to pastureland, the small town suburbs expand to spread more concrete and pavement. The rainfall runs off in torrents, and may arrive at the mouth of that same creek or river in hours.

In the past ten years most all rivers in the Ozarks have risen to record levels on several occasions in the spring, and yet dur-

The Dying Rivers

ing the dry periods of the summer have fallen to the lowest level ever, with less water than anyone knew them to hold. If you don't believe it, ask some of the older rural people if they have not seen exactly what I have described. They'll all tell you about swimming in creek holes where there was four or five feet of clear water fifty years ago, which today may dry up completely in the summer, or have only a few inches of dirty stagnant water. My uncle, 80 years old as this is written, talks about the time in his youth when the shoals of the upper Big Piney River were three feet deep even during the dry months of the summer. Now some of those shoals flow only inches of water in July and August.

I can show you eddies of water on that river where I grew up, which were once ten or twelve feet deep, and harbored big bass and catfish....now those holes are filled with gravel and you can wade across them. On the upper Big Piney, and on it's tributary, the Little Piney, there were holes where you floated through deep green water and saw big rocks below you which were as big as the johnboats we floated in. Now those rocks are buried under gravel and sand, and the holes are just a few feet deep, and filled with scum. I've seen the same thing on the upper reaches of the Gasconade, Crooked Creek, the War Eagle, the Kings, the Niangua, Bryant Creek, and many more.

The Little Piney, between Houston and Mt. Grove, was a stream my dad and I floated often in wooden johnboats, never having to pull over a riffle. It had rock bass ten or twelve inches long, and smallmouth up to three pounds. On any given day in June, in the late fifties and early sixties, we would catch a limit of rock bass and eight or ten smallmouth above a pound. Now the Little Piney is a shallow creek, filled with gravel and unfloatable, with only a few suckers and green sunfish and pockets of slime and algae everywhere. We never saw that sickening muck in the water when I was young.

I remember seeing the first clumps of partially treated sewage floating out into the Big Piney out of Brushy Creek,

The Dying Rivers

which the city of Houston used for the emptying of its sewage treatment plants, in the early 1970's. You couldn't make five casts in the river without snaring a clump of the algae-coated gook. It was everywhere. I was floating with a couple of people from Wisconsin who had read what I had written about the Piney, and I couldn't wait to get them out of it, and away from it.

I could have cried that day, because I knew it was the beginning of the end for a clean river, and it was. Earlier, my uncle had seen the same thing happen to the upper river below Cabool.

Today, there is scum and algae in all the small headwaters of the Ozarks, something which didn't exist in my boyhood. It comes from the fertilizer and the waste which seeps into our streams from a thousand points along the watershed.

What I saw happening to the Piney was happening everywhere else. It was progress, more people, more opportunity to

The Dying Rivers

profit from the destruction of our resources. It has to do with some innate destructiveness in man which seemingly is unchangeable, part of his destiny as a creature on the earth. You can see it in the routine and daily behavior of this species, Homo Sapien. Man destroys himself with alcohol and drugs, tobacco, gambling, and overeating....with appetite and greed. You can see it around you every day. Almost every good thing God has given mankind has also been used by men in a destructive, damaging way.

I first began to see it on the river when I was very young, even before pollution from municipalities began. Hunting ducks on the Big Piney with my dad, there was a two or three mile stretch of river bottoms where hundreds of acres lay in pasture land, cleared many decades before I was ever born I am sure. I always wonder what those bottoms might have looked like in a time before the first farmers and ranchers began to change them.

You could imagine a little of it back then because there was perhaps a band of timber 60 or 80 feet wide, a protective fringe along the river between the pastureland and the water where tall sycamores and oaks and hickories and maples grew. There were always lots of squirrels and birds in that thin zone of woodland. I was about twelve or so when the landowner, with all those hundreds of acres of pasture, decided he needed more. He bulldozed that buffer strip of timber, pushed some of them up in piles to burn, and others off into the river. I guess even after that, he likely never had enough. Over the years the river began to carry away the exposed banks, and the pastureland was exposed to periods of high water. The eddies below there filled with the soil and gravel and silt which had so long been held by the trees.

That man likely lived his life with little more contribution to mankind than the scarring of the river which his greed created, and the money he put in his bank account because of it. His highest level of achievement was numbered in cattle, and acres

The Dying Rivers

of cleared land. His life passed, and so did the money he gained, but because he felt he didn't have enough, the river would never be the same again.

There have been many like him. On the middle part of the Piney, one landowner cut every sycamore he could reach, right on the very edge of the river, and sold the logs to a crate company, for almost nothing. The value they had, shading and holding the banks of the Piney, was surely greater than the few dollars each log brought. Most of them were hollow up fifty percent of the tree. More landowners began to clear the banks to sell the lumber, or to make more permanent pasture.

How could anyone have not known the trees held the banks in place? Or did they just not care? On almost every unprotected waterway in our region today, whether small creeks or navigable streams, you can see where the water, each time the stream floods, erodes a barren, exposed bank, a few inches or a few feet. The soil, silt and gravel goes into the river. Once, trees stood there, and root systems held the bank.

When I was young, there were only five or ten cows or steers where today there are several hundred. A few at a time, they increased, until there were thousands using the whole

365

The Dying Rivers

length of the river to water, thousands wearing deep paths in the banks, turning a solid river bottom into mud so deep you could sink down into it up to your knees. In the 1980's one of the fisheries biologists for the state Game and Fish Commission in Arkansas did an analysis of the War Eagle river, and he left out about four miles of river from the report. I asked him why, and he said that a very wealthy and politically powerful rancher had a cattle operation where he allowed his stock to use the stream in whatever way they would, and they crossed in several areas. He said that if he gave an accurate report of the river in that stretch and what the cattle had done to fish and aquatic life in that section, he would likely lose his job.

If, fifty years ago, we would have made an effort to fence cattle away from the river, and build large watering tanks along those fences, filled with water pumped from the river, we could have made a great deal of difference in the quality of our rivers. And still provided the needs of the cattle for ranchers it could have been done.

In the 1990's the Missouri Department of Conservation gave 225,000 dollars to a judge in western Missouri who owned

The Dying Rivers

631 acres of land on the Marmaton river, which is little more than a channelized muddy ditch, and can't be described much differently. They called it an "easement", but basically it was a political payoff to a man who was cronies with the right people, and often had MDC top-level employees and commissioners hunt on his land. He used it as his own private hunting club, often hosting sports figures and politicians.

That easement didn't even protect the trees along the river. An MDC spokesman said the only restrictions it implied pertained to buildings, and since it flooded often, that was never really an option. No public access was ever granted to the acreage. Some of the judge's family received large payments as well for land they held, and the MDC agreed to pay for all taxes on the family's land forever and ever. It reeked of greed and corruption, but the MDC said it was just an effort to protect that muddy ditch, the Marmaton.

That same thing could have been done on rivers like the Niangua and the Piney, and the Gasconade. Buffer strips of fifty or sixty feet, fences to keep the cattle away from the river, and watering tanks above the buffer strip, could have been made to work to protect the best of our streams.

And then there were the gravel dredgers. For many years, gravel companies just brought in equipment and began to take gravel from whatever stream they wanted. The results of gravel operations on Crooked Creek, in North Arkansas, filled deep holes and changed the course of the river in the 80's and '90s. For awhile, rules were set up so that certain regulations had to be followed by gravel companies, but seldom were they enforced. In the past few years I have watched a local gravel hauler on the Pomme de Terre river break all the rules and never answer to anyone. It has happened everywhere, but almost everyone agrees that the gravel is needed, and the river isn't all that important. The future looks bleak as far as controlling the gravel operations which fill the streams. No one wants to do anything which restricts this free enterprise.

The Dying Rivers

Our land ethic is the problem. We have always believed that a landowner has the right to do what he wants with his land, and if he is conducting a profitable enterprise, should not be interfered with, regardless of what damage he might do to the river. And yet, many, many landowners are trying to do what is best for the river. I have a neighbor who has many miles of riverfront, all protected by a buffer strip of trees. He owns hundreds of cattle and none have access to the river. He didn't do things right because it was the most inexpensive way to go...he just didn't want to cause harm to the river because his family used it too, to fish and to swim in. The trouble is, if one out of ten landowners cuts the trees and turns hundreds of cattle into the river, he does so much damage to the stream, the concern of the other nine doesn't save the river.

Today, one of the things which I worry about the most is the huge truckloads of sewer sludge from small municipalities being spread on pastures just above the creeks and rivers. One water department supervisor told me that in his area, which is the watershed of the Pomme de Terre river, the millions of gallons of sewage sludge spread over fields in the course of one year has doubled in only a few years, and it stands to reason that the way the community is increasing in population, it will double again in time, and then again. No one can say what that sludge puts into the river, and if anyone believes any accurate or thorough testing is being done on the water below the sludge-treated fields, you might also want to talk to some realtors about buying that big bridge in New York.

On the watersheds of many of our streams and rivers, this sludge spreading may someday be of such significance as to make it necessary to restrict human use of smaller streams, as far as fishing and swimming. In the region above the Pomme de Terre, the spreading of sludge was once done only in the late summer when there was little rain, but the spokesman I talked to said there is so much of it now that sludge is spread over a period of eight months. Most of the people who visit Pomme de Terre Lake, a few miles downstream, are from the Kansas City area, and bring their families to swim and play in the lake with absolutely no knowledge of the spreading of that sewage sludge or what it contains. but we cannot continually increase the quantity, and place it within a short distance of tributaries, on sloping land, and expect no problems to ever develop. This isn't just common fertilizer.

The Dying Rivers

I remember the spreading of sludge from Tyson chicken poultry processing plants poisoning the water of local wells in Green Forest, Arkansas in the 1980's, especially those less than 200 feet deep. Tyson's paid the well-owners a lot of money, suppressed the complaints by providing water, and continued spreading sludge on the watershed of the War Eagle and Kings River. You could not know what happened to the fishing in the upper reaches of those streams unless you could have known what it was before the giant poultry industry came on so strong in Northwest Arkansas.

The head of Tyson poultry products was a very good friend of Governor Bill Clinton, and he had given a tremendous amount of money to Clinton's political campaigns, so he had a free reign at polluting the waters in the northwest part of the state. Now the state of Oklahoma is threatening legal actions against Arkansas because waters flowing into Northeastern Oklahoma are so polluted. Similar pollution is found in the Elk and Spring rivers of Southwest Missouri, and appears to be coming to the northern tributaries of Bull Shoals lake as well. But while the mushrooming poultry operations are a concern to all of the Ozarks, it is the processing plants which have caused the greatest amount of pollution. To compound that problem, the population of that section of Arkansas has perhaps doubled through the influx of legal and illegal immigrants, which Tyson's had to hire because local people wouldn't work in the processing plants for the wages paid. That population boom has spelled disaster for those waterways. And yet, though I criticize what this industry is doing to our water, I eat fried chicken often. Even I am a part of the problem.

How can there be any answer, how can it be stopped as long as all of us are a part of it? How can we hope to change any-thing as long as we do all we can do to draw more and more tourists to the fragile Ozarks, where they will spend their money and help our economics. If we doubled the millions which come tomorrow, the money they bring would not be

The Dying Rivers

enough. We would want to double it again if possible, or triple it, even as the available lakes and rivers we use to attract them becomes dirty and foul.

How can anything change with populations ever increasing all over the world. The answers lie in numbers of people. As long as populations grow, there is no solution. And frankly, I don't think our populations will ever be controlled unless nature does it, and that is a horrible thought.

Our rivers bear the brunt of far too many people, and an unwillingness of anyone to talk about restricting the numbers. Where the canoe renters go, amassing great numbers of canoes to rent, there will be ever-increasing numbers of people using the rivers, and with those numbers, the problems they create. On any summer weekend on the Niangua, the Buffalo, the Elk, the Current, Eleven Point and Jacks Fork, there are long caravans of canoes, and on every shoal there are canoes backed up, waiting for their turn to go through a narrowed swift passage.

But most of them know nothing about the river other than going with the current, getting wet, getting there and getting out.

If the canoe renting business seemed a great idea 50 years ago, no one could have anticipated the drugs and alcohol which would some day become a part of it. On some week-ends law enforcement people stationed at points on the rivers make hundreds of arrests in just those two areas alone.

But you can find places to float the river undisturbed if you find places where canoe businesses do not flourish, or run shuttle services. And for that reason, they make it possible for me to get away from the crowds...they concentrate the masses in those areas they attend to. Most of them operate without the slightest regard for the carrying capacity of the river, and who would buy more canoes if they could put them all on the river at once. Who among them ever made enough money on any given day?

But where those throngs of people are found, the river loses

371

The Dying Rivers

most of it's appeal. On the Niangua below Bennett Springs State Park at the end of the summer, you can count hundreds of beer cans on the bottom of the stream in the clear water. Just recently, I saw a place a few miles below the Park where a private landowner had nailed up fifteen red and black signs on the trees along a two hundred foot gravel bar saying, "no camping,

no trespassing". In the middle of it he had a big sign which read...."Welcome Campers". He was soliciting paying campers who might use his new campground above the gravel bar in an adjacent field. All the Niangua meant to him was the opportunity to make money, and he meant to keep anyone off that gravel bar in order to do it.

Maybe it must be this way. Once when I was talking to my uncle about what a shame it was that we couldn't keep the rivers as we once knew them for future generations, he said something I hadn't thought about.

"Who says any future generation gives a darn about the

The Dying Rivers

river the way it was?" he asked. "Have you seen todays kids from the cities and the things they like? Just turn on the T.V.! Maybe what they want has nothing to do with the rivers we loved. They love something else."

He was right..... this is the era of rap music and television and video games and computers, and they are a part of that, not at all a part of the land.

I have thought about that. Nothing goes unchanged. The rivers which were deep, clean, and clear, had their place and time, and there is a time and a place for everything. Something will always remain, because the water has to flow downhill. Maybe if all you want is to go fast, get wet, get drunk and yell and holler a lot, the rivers will always be there for that, even if they do have some slime along the edges and you have to be careful not to get any of the water in your mouth. You can't see e.coli bacteria. And a hundred canoes an hour will leave no more tracks than one an hour.

Besides who really needs fish when you can bring a bucket of fried chicken? Who needs clean spring water if you have ice and beer?

But what most people do not know, is that the flow can stop. Water tables are dropping now by the year. When you get right down to it, most of todays generation doesn't know what a water table is, doesn't even know we had one.

Springs that always ran are now dry. Streams which once were floatable now have shallow dry shoals. Deep, deep wells are receding and polluted. The water carries what you cannot see. And more people do not know what 'e. coli' bacteria is than those who do.

Maybe the thing to do is not worry about what can't be changed, and to enjoy what we have today and not give any thought to tomorrow. But sometimes I wish I hadn't seen what our rivers were. Then it wouldn't hurt so much to have to watch them die.

Other books by Larry Dablemont

- **Ain't No Such Animal**
  ... and other stories from the Ozark Hills

- **Ridge Runner**
  ...from the Big Piney to the Battle of the Bulge

- **Dogs, Ducks, and Hat-Rack Bucks**
  ...short stories for the outdoorsman

- **Memories from a Misty Morning Marsh**
  ...a duck hunter's collection

- **The Greatest Wild Gobblers**
  ...lessons learned from old timers and old toms

- **The Front Bench Regulars**
  ...wit and wisdom from back home in the hills

For more information write to:

Lightnin' Ridge Books
Box 22
Bolivar • MO 65613

website: www.larrydablemont.com